Essays on Teaching Speech
in the High School

Published for the
Indiana University English Curriculum Study Center
EDWARD B. JENKINSON, *Director*

PREVIOUSLY PUBLISHED

On Teaching Literature:
Essays for Secondary School Teachers

Teaching Literature in Grades Seven Through Nine

Two Approaches to Teaching Syntax

On Teaching the Bible as Literature: A Guide to
Selected Biblical Narratives for Secondary Schools

What is Language? And Other Teaching Units
for Grades Seven Through Twelve

Teaching Literature in Grades Ten Through Twelve

Books for Teachers of English:
An Annotated Bibliography

Writing as a Process of Discovery: Some
Structured Theme Assignments for Grades Five Through Twelve

On Teaching Speech
in Elementary and Junior High Schools

FORTHCOMING VOLUMES

On Teaching the Old Testament as Literature

Essays on Teaching Speech in the High School

EDITED BY

J. JEFFERY AUER
Chairman and Professor of Speech and Theatre
Indiana University

and

EDWARD B. JENKINSON
Associate Professor of Education
Coordinator for School English Language Arts
Director, Indiana University English Curriculum Study Center

INDIANA UNIVERSITY PRESS
BLOOMINGTON LONDON

Published in Canada by Fitzhenry & Whiteside Limited, Don Mills, Ontario

Library of Congress catalog card number: 77–138413

ISBN: 0–253–32070–4

Manufactured in the United States of America

CONTENTS

Introduction   vii
by *Edward B. Jenkinson*

On Teaching in an Age of Dissent   3
PART I: Can We Hold Back the Humanistic Tidal
Waves with Better Communication?
by *Richard Gray*

On Teaching in an Age of Dissent   18
PART II: The Responsibilities of a Speaker in
an Age of Dissent
by *J. Jeffery Auer*

On Teaching Informative Speaking   33
by *Victor M. Powell*

On Teaching Persuasive Speaking   63
by *Robert G. Gunderson*

On Teaching Parliamentary Procedure   81
by *J. Calvin Callaghan*

On Teaching Discussion   98
by *Ernest G. Bormann*

On Teaching Argumentative Speaking
and Formal Debate   121

On Teaching Rhetorical Appreciation   154
   by *Richard Murphy*

On Teaching Speech Criticism   196
   by *Donald W. Zacharias*

On Teaching the Social Responsibilities of a Speaker   219
   by *Richard L. Johannesen*

INTRODUCTION

In a speech delivered during the 1968 Presidential campaign, J. Jeffery Auer, Chairman of the Department of Speech and Theatre at Indiana University, urged teachers "to bring dissent into the schoolroom, to encourage an open and mature confrontation of views on crucial issues, and to take a golden opportunity to try to train students in the art of being more effective and more responsible dissenters."

In that speech to teachers attending the Seventeenth Annual Conference for Junior and Senior High School Teachers of the English Language Arts at Indiana University, Professor Auer added:

> . . . we need to encourage our young dissenters to utilize their rhetorical growth and development—their grasp of rhetorical patterns and procedures—in oral and written discourse; and to use it within the context of social responsibility. The dilemma of a democratic society, and the basis of much of our traditional fear of dissent, is that we cannot bar the demagogue and the charlatan from the platform and, at the same time, keep it open for Quintilian's "good man skilled in rhetoric." Society can protect itself, as we know, by regulating the use of a wide range of lethal weapons, including automobiles and guns and even nuclear bombs. But the weapons of language, of speaking and writing, are life and death issues, and must, in a democracy, remain uninhibited and uncensored. The only restraint that need ultimately be placed upon lethal language is the restraint placed upon it by the dissenter himself. And we must take the responsibility for helping him, while he is in our classroom, to become not only an effective, but also an ethical communicator.

One year later at the same conference, Richard Gray, Chairman of the Department of Journalism at Indiana University, also spoke about the responsibilities of teachers in this age of dissent. After explaining some of the reasons why the young are dissenting, Professor Gray asked:

> What can we do to help the young? What can we do to provide some positive answers to their questions? I think we should quit playing democracy. We should quit preaching freedom of press and freedom of speech unless we really mean it. We should quit preaching, "Think independently; think critically," unless we really mean it . . . "Why not let them write about the real thing in the real world, the big issues that they are talking about—the spiritual issues? Why not let them debate the big issues? Why not make these issues meaningful class discussions?

Both professors had basically the same message for teachers of English: give students every opportunity to write and talk about the critical issues in society. That message is not new, and many teachers of English have been giving students such opportunities for years. But the talk in English class, though very important, has tended to be informal. Formal speaking, in many schools, has been confined to speech class. Professors Auer and Gray and the other contributors to this volume believe that students should have occasions to speak both formally and informally in English as well as speech class in order to learn how to become responsible communicators in an age filled all too often with irresponsible speakers and writers, obscene gestures, and irrational messages.

It seems appropriate to begin a volume on teaching speech with transcriptions of the Auer and Gray speeches. As delivered in 1968 and 1969, both speeches contained characteristics of "a lively conversational style" that Victor Powell champions in the first formal essay in this volume. According to Professor Powell, good oral style is personal, uses contractions, makes use of repetition, uses the rhetorical question, and requires the use of simple words.

Professor Powell, like all the contributors to this volume, is concerned with the listeners as well as the speakers. In his essay on persuasive speaking, Robert Gunderson considers the responsibility of the listeners:

Listeners should be alert critics, not amiable sponges. Units on evidence and reasoning should alert consumers of persuasion to the hazards of faulty analogy, evidence, and reasoning. Persuasive speeches should be followed by a meet-the-press type of confrontation. Persuaders should be cross-examined. The speech class is thus not a word-play land of adolescent show-and-tell, but a lively intellectual testing ground. The student persuader should be expected to find representative examples; select, organize, and phrase evidence and argument; and then be prepared to refute the strongest contrary position. In describing the job of the schools, President Nathan M. Pusey of Harvard has outlined objectives that are appropriate for teaching persuasion: "to educate free, independent, and vigorous minds, capable of analyzing events, of exercising judgment, of distinguishing facts from propaganda, and truth from half-truth and lies."

According to J. Calvin Callaghan, a unit on parliamentary procedure can help students develop "free, independent, and vigorous minds":

During this unit, the word which should be heard around the classroom more than any other is *why*. A teacher should ask it continually. Soon students will start predicting and pre-empting its challenge: then they will be truly ready to study this subject.

If I could, I should forbid any student to *memorize* any datum of parliamentary law. Its rules are not mastered by rote, though they can and should be *learned*. We should ask *why* in order to remember as well as to comprehend *what*. Sterile on a quiz is the imperative: List all motions which cannot be reconsidered! A more defensible examination question would be a situational one which permits—yea, compels—a student to reason an answer from premises he's supposed to know.

Learning how to participate in small-group discussion can be just as rewarding and exciting for the student as learning how to take part in large meetings with a knowledge of parliamentary procedure. According to Ernest G. Bormann:

Participating in and observing a group which has a task that its members perceive as relevant and important provides the student with an opportunity to apply the concepts of group discussion to the real world. Students who have worked together on an important project gain a greater appreciation of the complexities of group process and the relevance of the material to their daily lives. If the unit on discussion provides the students with a frame of analysis to apply to the new groups they join, then they can go on to apply this understanding to develop greater proficiency in one of the most important and potentially one of the most frustrating or gratifying of their daily experiences, that of working together with others in the context of a small group.

Richard Murphy underscores the importance of making the study of speech relevant:

> Whatever the teacher does, he should have some historical perspective for what he is doing. The intention, however, is not to limit the students' study to the past. Nor is the intention that teachers should lecture their students on matters covered here. One of the great hindrances to imaginative teaching is the teacher's proclivity to give to his students the materials he received in college or graduate school. The teacher should use this knowledge to make adaptations to his particular pupils. How much theory, how much practice can be determined only by the teacher. He should keep in mind, however, that knowing why one likes or dislikes something is a higher form of appreciation than liking or disliking or being indifferent to something by mere tropism. The teacher should keep in mind, too, the future life of the student. He may never again read an esoteric lyric under assignment, never again an obscure novel, but he will be constantly exposed to rhetorical appeals whether in political speeches, sermons, pamphlets and tracts, or letters to the editor of the newspaper. His life will be much richer if he can analyze these appeals and respond to them in a critical-appreciative manner, and sort the shoddy from the worthy.

Donald W. Zacharias notes that the teacher of English and speech must help the student become an intelligent consumer of oral discourse "who can analyze . . . appeals and respond to them in a critical-appreciative manner" as Professor Murphy calls for in his essay. Professor Zacharias writes:

> If you were to ask your students for their impressions of what they were supposed to be trained to do after they finished their first speech course, you would undoubtedly get a conglomeration of answers. Most of them, however, would fit into the category of improving their personal ability to communicate in public and private. These are reasonable and acceptable answers since speech

education has traditionally focused on improving personal skills in communication while neglecting the important task of showing students why a society values public speaking or what kind of speaking is of greatest value to the society. Recent events in the civil rights movement, peace movement, political conventions, and student activism have shown the importance of the spoken word, used in conjunction with rallies, television, placards, and threats of force, in advocating change. Teachers of English and speech on all levels must begin teaching their students how to be intelligent consumers of oral discourse and not merely hope that some day their best students will undertake the analysis of a speech in a graduate seminar.

If we teachers of English and speech do help our students become responsible speakers as well as intelligent consumers of oral discourse, perhaps we can realize a day when protesters allow all voices to be heard without shouting them down. Perhaps we will also realize a day when "the quality of public discourse will be improved and the scope of public debate expanded"—the goals of Richard Johannesen's essay:

> What, then, is a speaker's responsibility concerning freedom of speech? As a producer of public communication he must utilize his free speech rights with great wisdom; to abuse his free speech rights is to weaken them. Social consequences must be carefully weighed. As a consumer of public communication, he must protect the rights of free speech for all others, particularly those espousing controversial or minority viewpoints.
> If the students are stimulated to explore ethical problems in persuasion and crucial issues of free speech, hopefully the quality of public discourse will be improved and the scope of public debate expanded.

The essays in this volume do not constitute a course of study in speech nor an outline for effective units in English class. But the essays can be used effectively as the basis for designing sound courses of study or units in both speech and English in the high school.

When J. Jeffery Auer suggested that this volume be added to the English Curriculum Study Series, I asked him to outline it and to select and invite the contributors. Grateful acknowledgment is given to Professor Auer, also to Jan Blough, Julia Hamilton, and Lynn Sears, who typed the various drafts and proofread the galleys, and to the ever-patient editorial staff of the Indiana University Press.

This volume is a portion of the project of the Indiana University English Curriculum Study Center, which was supported through the Cooperative Research Program of the Office of Education, U.S. Department of Health, Education, and Welfare. The I.U. Center received additional financial support from the Cummins Engine Foundation, which awarded Indiana University a grant that provided funds for meetings and equipment that could not be financed by the grant from the U.S. Office of Education.

EDWARD B. JENKINSON

*Essays on Teaching Speech
in the High School*

On Teaching in an Age of Dissent

PART I

Can We Hold Back the Humanistic Tidal Waves with Better Communication?

RICHARD GRAY
Chairman and Professor of Journalism
Indiana University

Perhaps this anecdote describes the temper of the times. A little boy on the playground was bitten by a dog, and the principal, somewhat concerned, rushed him to the emergency room of the hospital. After the doctor examined the boy, he asked, "Was the dog foaming at the mouth?" "Yes, sir, he was." So the doctor ran some tests, and said, "Well, I'm sorry to have to tell you this, young man, but the dog was rabid and there's nothing I can do to help you. You're going to die." The boy asked for a pencil and paper and began jotting some things down. The doctor said, "Son, it's just not that imminent; you don't have to write out your

This is a transcript of a speech to teachers attending the Eighteenth Annual Conference for Junior and Senior High School Teachers of the English Language Arts on the Bloomington Campus of Indiana University, October 4, 1969.

3

will." The boy responded, "Will, hell! I'm making a list of teachers I want to bite."

I am afraid that attitude is all too true in some campuses across the country, but the students don't just bite. They begin to use more violent means of punishing and getting back at teachers. There are some indications that this kind of unrest is moving down and is becoming more and more common in the high schools. We have already seen reports of violence, demonstration, and boycotting in Milwaukee, in Chicago, in New York, and in cities on the West Coast. There seems to be a spreading of this kind of dissent. The old order seems to be upturned.

My task today is to speak about school communications in this age of dissent. What role can communications within the school play in helping solve some of the problems? I was asked to discuss some of the reasons for the dissent and what can be done about it. Some of the things I am going to talk about will seem very obvious, but if they are so obvious, why haven't we done something about them? I may bore you in some instances by going over the obvious, but let's take the obvious to its natural conclusion, or what I think is its natural conclusion.

I think that the first reason for dissent in the schools of this country is that our young people have lost roots. There has been a decline of the family in American life, and it seems to me that the school itself is partially responsible for this decline. It is now nearly impossible to have a traditional six o'clock dinner hour in the American home because of the various clubs, athletic programs, and school activities, including the school newspaper, that demand the time of young people. The young are taken out of the home at an earlier age, and the family becomes secondary to other considerations. The school is one of the most important of those considerations.

This loss of roots stems, in part, from the mobility of the American family. The executive is moved from city to city every two, three, or four years. Many large corporations make this a practice. If you want to move up in Weyerhauser Timber Company, for example, you must go from Portland, Maine, to San Francisco, California, to St. Paul, Minnesota, to Podunk Center, until you finally go to the home office in Tacoma to accept a vice-presidency. This is the case not only with Weyerhauser Timber; it is true with corporation after corporation after corporation. It is even true in universities. The market place is so good that professors move from one university to another in order to move up in the ranks. If a professor doesn't like the salary at Indiana University, or if he doesn't like his promotion or lack of promotion, he pulls his desk drawer open and takes out one of several offers and moves, upsetting his family in the process.

The disappearance of the American farm seems to be another factor in this rootless feeling. The ties to a community, to friends, to the earth gave a stability to young people in previous decades which they are now lacking.

TV has also played an extremely important role. TV has *not* interrupted homework, as some critics like to say it has. It seems to me that young people do *more* homework now. My children do more homework in elementary school than I did. Young people come to our classes as freshmen better prepared than ever before. But TV has cut into other areas, such as play time. The imaginative play time that young people formerly used to entertain themselves in our society, in fact in all societies, served an extremely important socializing role. This socializing is completely missed when one is passively seated in front of a TV set having little or no communication with peers or adults. A child, pestering his mother to be entertained, built lines of communication in former decades. Learning to play with playmates built communication with peers.

Students coming to college today seem to be very lonely young people. The counselors tell us that students are hard-pressed to name more than one or two intimate friends. They have lost ties in this regard, because, in some instances, they have spent six to eight hours a day before a TV set. They don't learn to play with adults or with one another.

That is why we hear so much about seeking meaningful relationships. Many times this gets translated into going to bed with someone on the college campus; that is the easy way to look at the phrase, *meaningful relationships*. I have been told that some young people go to bed with one another and never have a sexual relationship. This is *not* a particularly erotic generation. Sex becomes a poor substitute in many instances for deeper kinds of relationship. Young people are searching—searching for friendship and searching for love, but not sexual love. (Sometimes they get it all mixed up.) They are searching for relationships that will make them belong, make them important, make them feel at home, and give them some roots.

When they don't find such relationships, many times they withdraw. They withdraw into a world of drugs, they withdraw into a hippie world where they go into communal societies, or they escape into the mountains in Washington or up into British Columbia. Or they just withdraw into themselves, not speaking to parents or teachers or to anyone else. They withdraw into the TV set. They go into their rooms and play loud rock. In fact, with stereophonic sound and earsets, one can get turned on with rock music and can go completely into another world without the benefit of drugs. Watch young people. Many of them are doing that.

I used to withdraw during periods of stress in college, particularly when I was working on the Ph.D. If things got too rough, I went to a local movie house. I withdrew for two and a half hours into a world of fantasy, and I came out renewed. Now one doesn't have to go to the local movie house to withdraw, and the withdrawal lasts a lot longer than two and a half hours. It can go on and on—an escape world.

I think educators must begin to involve young people in meaningful relationships in schools; we must begin to make them a part of the school system, rather than just something that goes through it and comes out twelve or thirteen years later with a degree. It's not enough that students are the objects of education. They must become an intimate part of it. They should be serving on committees that help devise curriculum; they should be serving on committees that help devise codes of conduct and dress; they should be helping decide on the awarding of scholarships, on convocation programs, and, yes, on policy.

When young people are given opportunities to act responsibly and to be involved responsibly, I find that the vast majority respond in a very responsible, mature way. They begin to find some roots;

they begin to feel someone cares. They can say, "I'm important; I'm involved." That's the same sort of feeling young people used to get when they helped with the harvest on the farm, when young girls did work in the kitchen to help feed the harvest hands, and when young men milked the cows. They were an important part of the society; they knew that they were depended upon; they became adults at a much younger age.

We have extended and extended and extended the adolescent period as we have grown more and more affluent in American life. We now push students not only into college but also into master's degree programs and Ph.D. programs. They are always preparing for something in the future, instead of being involved right now, being needed right now, and being a part of something right now.

In a fascinating project at Lake Oswego High School in Oregon, the principal, the social science faculty, and the English faculty involved young people in education. They let students run their own school district. The students brought in voting machines and elected a school board. The school board appointed a superintendent. The superintendent took applications for faculty. These young people studied seriously for eight months and then put on an in-service training program for *their own teachers.* They talked to their own teachers; they talked to their fellow students; they visited other high schools; they brought in experts from colleges and from other high schools. They came up with some very meaningful suggestions for the improvement of curriculum and conduct in Lake Oswego High School, and I am happy to report that the adult school board took them so seriously that it has adopted many of the recommendations these young people made. These young people forgot about negative dissent and negative militancy, because a positive avenue was provided for outlet. Many of them told us, "Now I know why I've been in school for twelve years. Now I feel a part of something; now I feel important—important in life."

That is one method of communication—getting people involved and listening to what they have to say. Many times young people are not as militant as we think they are. All they want is to be heard. They want someone to listen to them and to think that they are important. Any teacher, no matter what area he is in, can play a role in that type of communication.

I think that the second problem that is bringing about dissent is the idealistic orientation of young people today. We are the victims of our own success in the schools. In the fifties and before, teachers preached to us that we should forget about panty raids, about our little grumblings about food in the dining hall on college campuses, and about the immature causes that we took up. You remember the gossip about fashions and boyfriends and athletics—the trivialities of life. Teachers kept saying, "Get serious. Think about the big issues; learn to think independently; learn to be a critical thinker." Now the students are doing just that, and we don't like it.

They are talking about war and they are talking about peace. Young people took the place of the Senate and the House of Representatives of the United States for a long period of time by being the only meaningful voice of dissent about Vietnam. That took place on campuses among young people, and it finally has become a popular cause—popular enough to make the President who had the largest popular vote in the history of the United States change his mind about running for reelection.

I would go so far as to say that today's young people are more spiritual than any group of young people I have known. They are not spiritual in the old pietistic ways that we grew up with. I am not saying they go to church more often or that they pay more attention in Sunday school classes. But they are finding spiritual meaning in the world around them. They are finding true spirituality in Paul Tillich's sense of the term. They are asking the big questions in life: What is the nature of man? What is the nature of God? What is the nature of the relationship of man to God and of man to man? They are always asking about the nature of justice. What is the nature of justice in Vietnam? What is the nature of justice in the ghetto? What is the nature of justice in the racial situation?

They are asking big, important, all-consuming questions. They are the first generation that is really the product of an urban society. Until the present generation, we have had our roots in rural America, even though we were gradually moving away from it.

That was our philosophical basis. We were primarily Jeffersonian in our outlook. Now we have a group of young people who do not have those ties. They are too far removed from rural America. This brings about some friction because they think in urban terms, and we tend to think, even now, in terms of rural morality, rural values, and rural concepts. We find it disturbing and puzzling that young people do not think that way. They have lived with war or the threat of war—the threat of complete annihilation at any moment —from the time of their birth to the present. So they have different concepts from ours.

What can we do to help the young? What can we do to provide some positive answers to their questions? I think we should quit playing democracy. We should quit preaching freedom of press and freedom of speech unless we really mean it. We should quit preaching, "Think independently; think critically," unless we really mean it. Let's stop playing student council with young people. As I travel across the country, I find less and less interest in student councils, and, in fact, many high schools have done away with them because they are so ineffective when young people are not interested. Young people do not want to play democracy; they want to play the real game.

We tell them to write about important things; yet some of us go on assigning such topics as "My Most Important Experience in Life" or "What I Did Last Summer" or "How to Build a Sailboat" or "My Most Embarrassing Moment." Why not let them write about the real things in the real world, the big issues that they are talking about—the spiritual issues? Why not let them debate the big issues? Why not make these issues meaningful class discussions? If we do discuss the real issues in our classes, it may prove embarrassing because the young are extremely frank; they are not embarrassed about the things that embarrass us. They do not have a lot of the hang-ups that we have from old rural America—the rural morality.

Why not let high school newspapers practice some of the freedom of the press that we preach about in our history books and in our social studies classes? Young people want to be heard on the important issues; they want to be involved in these issues; they want to speak out in realistic terms. But when we force them into our old modes, when we keep them from talking about the important issues, we soon get turned off, and they begin to tell us that school isn't very relevant. Many times it's not.

The third reason for unrest is the quest for excellence. I think this has brought about some real problems for us. Once again, we are the victims of our own success, and I think the high schools should receive the most applause. The high schools have improved tremendously in the United States in the last decade. The young people coming in as college freshmen today are so much better prepared than they were when I first started teaching a decade ago that there is absolutely no comparison. The criticism that came to the American high school because of Sputnik has had a great impact. We suddenly become aware of the knowledge explosion and of the fact that we had much more to put across in a much more complicated world. We began to realize that education is a crucial factor in world power. We looked at what the Soviet Union did in fifty short years after the Bolshevik Revolution in moving from ten percent literacy to seventy-five percent literacy. We saw what they did in technology and in science, outdoing us in missile thrusts because of that kind of education. I am not saying it is a better educational system than ours; I am saying that education suddenly became a crucial power factor in the world—a power factor for the success of nations and a power factor for the success of individuals. How much money are young people going to earn? What kind of status are they going to have in life? Are they going to Vietnam? A whole host of questions suddenly made quality education of prime importance, with emphasis on ideas, critical thinking, and analytical thinking. We are now doing a far superior job of preparing people in terms of the amount of knowledge and sophistication that they have.

Our young people are bright today, but it disturbs me that they cannot always communicate that brilliance. We have put so much stress on the content, on the analysis, on the ideas, that we have forgotten a very important function of education: to let people use knowledge to communicate knowledge—to let them speak to others about their ideas. Much of the cause of the problem is the responsibility of the college. We no longer insist on comprehensible essays and term papers. We get much more excited about the ideas than about the language conveying the ideas; consequently, we are producing a generation of individuals who cannot communicate.

If you do not believe me, talk to the captains of industry. They are very concerned that executives do not know how to write intelligent business letters and memos to their staffs. The President's Commission on Science is extremely concerned that our scientists can no longer communicate in meaningful terms with the average person in the United States or even with other scientists. We put so much stress in college on faculty publications and on certain means of promotion that we forget about teaching the basic elements of communication. So it is natural that high school teachers and elementary school teachers who get their training in this kind of a college program are going to go out and perpetuate the same kind of thing. It becomes a hopeless, endless circle in which many people never really learn to communicate effectively.

I think I can say this with a good deal of authority. When I was teaching at Northwestern University, I think we had some of the brightest students in journalism in the country—high, high college board scores in the six and seven hundreds, with several almost eight hundred. But many of those very bright people could not put three or four sentences together in a coherent paragraph. They did not know how to build transitions between paragraphs. They did not know about the logic of writing, about the organization of writing, about the effectiveness of writing. Many times they did not know about effectiveness in other areas of communication— speaking and the communication media that are before us.

I suggest that we go back to inserting some communication skills in our education program—integrating ideas with communication skills, not perpetuating the old system in which we taught students out of grammar books, having them do endless, pointless exercises. Let them write about the real issues and the critical issues, but let's give some attention to how effectively they are saying things.

A boy was asked, "What did you get on your paper?" He replied,

"I got two sp's, one synt, four gr's, and a punc. Then at the top there was a B– and a 'good idea but needs expanding.' " Now I ask you, what does that tell anyone? "A good idea but needs expanding." If the young man knew how to expand it, he would have done so. He wants to know how he should expand it. He wants to know what he left out. He wants the teacher to tell him what he can do to improve his writing. He doesn't want a "synt." He wants to know what's wrong with the syntax. Show him. If he knew, he would have used proper syntax in the first place. These are bright young people; they are not stupid. Instead of a "punc," they want to know how to punctuate. Put in the correct punctuation. We let them go to a dictionary for spelling, but some of them can't even find the word in the dictionary to find out how to spell it. Some are in pretty bad shape.

By the way, I think these problems are the products of the improved reading that we teach them. Young people do not proofread anything before they turn it in; they do not know how to proofread because they are speed readers. We have to teach them that they read in different ways for different functions, and that if they are proofreading, they should go back to the old way they were taught not to read: sounding out each syllable, picking a word apart syllable by syllable, making sure it's all there and not transposed, and so forth. But they don't do that because they've been taught to fssssshhh. . . . They think they can see on paper what they meant to say, and so they go right over the mistakes as they proofread.

Let's put more stress on communication skills; let's be better communicators ourselves. Let's demonstrate good communication in what we write. The college people can take this to heart more than anyone. I read more junk written in unintelligible jargon in sociological journals, in *Journalism Quarterly*, in English journals, and in psychology journals than I read anywhere else. It seems the more intelligent we are, the less effective we are in communicating. Maybe it's a cover-up for lack of intelligence—I've never quite been sure. But when other sociologists cannot understand a given sociologist, I begin to question what's going on in the communication process.

Let's demonstrate that there are new ways of communicating. I think high schools have done a much better job than colleges in this area. There are multi-media ways of communicating: slides, excerpts from old radio programs, music, five cameras going at once on five different screens. Go into the Disneyland exhibition on Lincoln. It's a marvelous communication experience. Go into the exhibition on "America the Beautiful" and take a trip across the United States with nine cameras coming at you, completely encircling you. You look ahead and see what the engineer sees as he goes across the country; you look out and see what the brakeman in the caboose sees; and you see what's going by on the sides of the train. Then you do the same thing on boats and on airplanes, and you get sick as the scenery tips back and forth. A total communication experience. I'm not suggesting that every English teacher can set up nine cameras to take the class on a trip through "Paradise Lost," but I am saying that we could be much more imaginative than standing up, as many college professors do, and using notes that are twenty years old. I think we can do much more to demonstrate communication skills to young people and to turn them on with psychedelic colors and with new approaches that they have become accustomed to from their exposure to television, wide screens, and stereophonic sound.

The *now generation* is another part of the problem of dissent. The now generation can be exemplified by the young man whose teacher asked him to identify Napoleon's army, and he said, "I think that's a new rock group that's appearing in town now." It seems to me that as bright as young people are, they don't have much of a sense of history. They don't seem to see where they fit in. They're only concerned with the here and the now. To some extent that's good; it reflects a change in theology in this country, if nothing else. We are less concerned theologically with the hereafter and more concerned with the here and now. Young people particularly are this way. They live on the edge of destruction; they see problems all around them—on television, in movies, and at home. They're much more aware of suffering from which we were protected because we didn't have the tremendous mass communication exposure that they have. They can see the suffering in

Vietnam, not just read about it. They can see it actually happen. They can see a man shot in a prison in Texas. This carries a different impact; it gives a different context for approaching things. It is a here and now generation.

This generation has no sense of the creativity that certain people have had in earlier periods of history. Let me cite an example. The reason we read so many four-letter words in the underground press and in essays these days is that we have not taught people proper diction and a proper way of expressing themselves. They fall back on four-letter words because they don't know how to express themselves in good English, in good syntax, and with good punctuation. My father was like that. He interspersed his language with four-letter words in order to catch time to think. A "damn" replaced an "uh, er" and so forth. And many times I think people use four-letter words not just for shock value; students are trying to put across a point and they become frustrated. They think that using four-letter words is the way to express themselves. It also gives them time to think.

Have we ever shown them that there have been many dissenters in the history of the United States who were extremely creative and who took other avenues of expressing dissent? Benjamin Franklin, for example, was one of the greatest dissenters in history. He helped write the first underground newspaper in this country when the Boston authorities took exception to what his brother was writing in the *New England Courant* in 1721. He started writing anonymous letters to the editor, which he signed Silas Dogood. He was only seventeen years old at the time, and he had some of the same complaints that young people have today. I have never read more devastating criticism of Harvard University than that written by Benjamin Franklin. He said Harvard was only concerned with turning out genteel young men to take their places as leaders of society. Listen to what he had to say about the stuffiness of the elders of the times, of their propensity for liking titles and status and so forth.

> In old times it was no disrespect for men and women to be called by their own names. Adam was never called Master Adam. We never read of Noah, Esq., Lot, Knight Baronet, nor the Right Hon-

orable Abraham, Vice-Count of Mesopotamia, Baron of Canaan. No, no, they were plain men, honest country geesers. They took care of their families and their flocks. Moses was a prophet and Aaron was a priest of the Lord, but we never read of the Right Reverend Moses nor the Reverend Father in God Aaron by Divine Providence, Lord Archbishop of Israel. We never saw a Madame Rebecca in the Bible, My Lady Rachel, nor Mary, though a Princess of the Blood after the death of Joseph called the Princess Dowager of Nazareth. No, plain Rebecca, plain Rachel, plain Mary, or, at best, the widow Mary and the like. It was no incivility then to mention their naked names as they were expressed.

We can learn a lot about creative expression of dissent from past dissenters that we can pass on to the young. "Unite or Die," Franklin's great slogan to unite the colonies against the French, is much more persuasive than "bullshit."

Why do the young lack creativity? They have the ideas. Why can't they express them? Why can't they communicate ideas in ways that don't offend people so much? If you can laugh at yourself, you can correct yourself.

Furthermore, Franklin taught us that if you want to bring about real change, you had better latch on to just enough of the establishment to give you support. You remember the Hellfire Club in Boston, which Franklin used to good advantage, or they used him to good advantage: I've never been sure which. A number of elitists who didn't like Cotton and Increase Mather's way of doing things formed an alliance with Franklin in his journal of dissent. But today's young people cut themselves off completely from anything that smells of the establishment. Even young, sympathetic teachers, who are only a few years older, get cut off. There are some lessons to be learned. If you want to be effective, you had better go along with the establishment far enough so that the power structure is going to be able to adapt some of what you're suggesting. The power structure is not apt to pay attention to an underground newspaper that shows a nude, hairy man—with hairy brain, I guess, too—posed, with his rear end prominently exposed, over a bust of a prominent educator. This turns off the establishment. There's nothing funny about it, and it's heavy handed. It's crude. It doesn't compare with Benjamin Franklin's creative and effective digs. I think that we can communicate to the young a sense of history, a sense of proportion about things.

A final reason for unrest is the growth of the megalopolis and the associated increase in consolidated schools that tend to do away with the importance of the individual. We bring thirty to forty thousand people together in massive universities where individuals become lost in the bureaucracies of so many vice-presidents and chancellors that one cannot keep them all straight. Students become bits of data for a computer—and then the computer goes wrong.

So the individual begins to feel unimportant. He searches once again for meaningful relationships, but he often finds animosity. Instead of people who care or who show their concern, there are older people who argue, "You can't do that because, because, because, because, because . . . ." If we will take the time to care enough and love enough to listen to young people and to encourage them to talk to us and to their peers, they will begin to come to some of their own solutions—they will tell one another why they can or cannot do this or that. Showing love and concern is the best way that I know of to communicate.

Do I seem unduly critical of the educational establishment? I am part of it; I love it; but once in a while I need to prick its bubble. I do it out of love. We have many problems facing us in education. Can we not learn to solve them? I am reminded of the story about Destiny coming down to a remote South Sea island, warning the people of that island that a great tidal wave would be coming, and asking three representative men what each would do. The first was a hedonist. He said, "I will eat, drink, make merry all night with wine, women, and song, because surely the end will come tomorrow. We will be flooded and I should get as much pleasure out of life as possible before then." The second was a mystic, who said, "I'll gather my friends and my family together, and we'll go to the highest mountains to the sacred groves and pray to the gods for deliverance." The third man loved wisdom. He said, "I will search the island for the very wisest man I can find, and we will sit down together and study how to live under water."

We have learned how to live under water; we go to the depths of the sea as well as to the heights of the heavens. We have had experiments in which mice have been allowed to breathe in highly oxygenated liquid; they can stay submerged for two or three hours and then come out to live perfectly normal lives with perfectly normal reproduction processes. If we can learn to overcome the physical tidal waves that threaten to inundate us, can we not also learn to overcome the psychological, the sociological, and the human tidal waves that threaten to inundate us? I think we can, and that is the challenge I leave with you—to do it through better communication.

On Teaching in an Age of Dissent

PART II

The Responsibilities of a Speaker in an Age of Dissent

J. JEFFERY AUER
Chairman and Professor of Speech and Theatre
Indiana University

Obviously, one cannot talk about the responsibilities of speakers and, more significantly, the responsibilities of teachers of speakers in a campaign year, without considering the current campaign. I would like to suggest to you that we are all rhetoricians; that we are all concerned with the art of public discourse; and as such persons, perhaps not as voters, but as rhetoricians, that we surely must be making some observations about what is going on. We must be interested in both the substance and the style of this campaign and of any campaign.

Our problem, obviously, is not one of the quantity of speeches in a campaign; it's one of quality. It's not one of volubility of our

This is a transcript of a speech to teachers attending the Seventeenth Annual Conference for Junior and Senior High School Teachers of the English Language Arts on the Bloomington Campus of Indiana University, October 12, 1968.

candidates and our speakers but one of responsibility. And as teachers of written and oral discourse, as teachers of the language arts, it seems to me that we ought to pay some attention to the kind of speechmaking that goes on (in and out of campaign years) in order that we may contribute something to raising the level of public discourse. I think we are better equipped to handle this responsibility than probably we have ever been.

We now have better trained teachers in the language arts, better learning resources, and better teaching than ever before in this century. I thing it's fair to generalize that what we do best is teach the technical skills of writing and of speaking. We do very well in encouraging our young people to write nice, neat—though often sterile—essays, and to make speeches on nice, neat, and sometimes sterile topics. But we do it well. What we do least well (and sometimes we do not do it at all, it seems to me) is to relate communication in the classroom with communication in society.

This is tremendously important because by failing to make this relationship, we endorse a double standard. In the classroom we insist upon this nice, neat, packaged approach to communication, and yet we know that in the outside world communication sometimes degenerates to nothing more than name-calling demagoguery. It's confused; it's reckless; and it's often irresponsible.

Mark Shedd, superintendent of schools in Philadelphia, recently said, "It is the passion and power of humanity that we seek to explore and expand. If we divorce school subjects from the guts and hopes of human beings, we can expect students to find them (those subjects) gutless and hopeless. I intend to encourage attempts to make our schools relevant to the concerns of students and to support teachers who are able to examine in a mature way the gut issues of our day: war, sex, race, drugs, and poverty."

We must recognize that students are ready, and indeed have been ready for longer than we think, for this kind of concern about the gut issues. Our best students are eager to find social relevance in the school work that they do at the high school level, in junior high school, and in college.

The *NEA Journal* has been doing, it seems to me, an excellent job from time to time within the last twelve or thirteen months of running interpretative pieces and commentaries about the nature of youth today in order to make clear to the readers that these young men and women are quite different from the young men and women we were. They're cool; they're irreverent; they have a deep-running notion that there isn't very much that is God-given or American-Constitution-given that isn't appropriate to be challenged or questioned. They no longer are giving automatic allegiance or taking things for granted. There is an emphasis on individualism, on self-determination, on self-realization.

In addition to an acute awareness of what society's hang-ups are, there is a sense of involvement in finding ways to resolve these hang-ups. There has been during this century a kind of tidal wave pattern of student behavior. We have had waves of awareness and involvement, and then we have followed these with troughs of apathy and indifference. We saw this manifested during the post-World-War-I period of prosperous apathy. But during the Depression period, there was great concern with public issues in the colleges and high schools of this country.

One of my dear friends, John Black, a regent's professor at Ohio State University, once said, "You know in this day when debate isn't as popular as it used to be, there's nothing wrong with debate that a good depression wouldn't cure. Because every time we've had a depression, we've had real hardship and real problems, and we've gotten involvement and commitment."

In the post-World-War-II period, there was another era of student disengagement and withdrawal from community. And now, of course, we're all tremendously aware that in the past decade there has been a resurgence of concern with causes; there has been a kind of commitment that we've not seen previously on the part of young people.

We need not, I suppose, talk about how this came about, although it's perfectly obvious that the influence of certain men like Adlai Stevenson and the two Kennedys, and the influence of certain opportunities like the Peace Corps and Vista and so on, have encouraged and given outlets to these young people for the kind of commitment that they have. They have become involved in civil rights; they have become involved with issues of war and peace;

and they have become involved with something called "demonstration."

As teachers in the high schools and in the colleges, we have no choice but to attend closely and carefully and seriously to these manifestations of student awareness, student concern, and student involvement. Students will not be laughed off, and surely they will not be hushed up. We need to try to understand those that we can, and those that we can't understand, we must tolerate. This means, I think, that first of all we must find out what young people are thinking. We must talk with them; we must look at the kinds of evidence that we can find of what they are thinking. And the most likely kind of solid evidence is communication with the young people themselves, which, in our own scholarly way, we are unlikely to engage in. We are much more apt to turn to a learned journal and read an article about what young people are thinking than we are to get out and talk to young people.

I should like to suggest that these young people have been shaped by some special influences that have been exceedingly significant—the influences of the television, the black revolution, drugs, and the involvement in Vietnam. They have seen, in a sense, a decay of the significance of the usual symbols of status in our society. They have abandoned the myth of the inevitability of social reform, with which some of us grew up. And they have the feeling now that nothing short, in many cases, of revolutionary determinism will solve the problems of society, and they fear that we are engaged in a kind of a technological development of building inhuman bureaucracy. We must decide whether or not these things are as significant as is alleged. We must look at them carefully. We must recognize that these are young men and women who do not want to be folded, mutilated, or spindled.

About a year ago there was a poem in *The Indiana Daily Student* called "My IU Primer," and I'd like to quote a couple of lines from this because I think it portrays, in an interesting way, the feelings of most of these young people.

> See the girl.
> See the girl giggle.
> Why does the girl giggle?

The girl is giggling because of her numbers.
309-52-5929 is the girl's number.
254 is also the girl's number,
And so is 337-9240.
And so is 35-25-35.
(That number is extra-curricular.)
The girl is giggling because she remembers all her numbers,
But now she's forgotten her name.
Smile, little girl.
Maybe you owe someone money,
And they will remember your name.

I have a feeling that beyond this attempt to understand what is at the root of the rootless feeling of many of our students, we must attempt to penetrate somehow the jargon that says, "find your own thing and do it," and we must recognize that marching or singing or demonstrating or making placards or circulating petitions may be the only things that make sense to some of these young people in terms of their objectives and their desires to communicate with the rest of us. If you want to know what the "in" group is doing, it's doing all of these things. The "in" group is having a teach-in or a sit-in or—as it's now known on the Indiana campus for the last two days anyway—a mill-in.

In my days we were also doing our thing, although perhaps in a less flamboyant manner. When I was a sophomore in college in 1932, in the heart of conservative Indiana at a very conservative college, I was making speeches during the campaign. And the title of the speech was "A Plague on Both Your Houses." I thought it was a pretty good phrase, but I discovered later that somebody else had used it. We were doing our thing, and we would be embarrassed if we had not been at that time, as I think we would be embarrassed for our young people if they were not in this day.

To sum up, I think these young people are engaging in what they believe to be dissent. They find a kinship with Thoreau and Thomas Jefferson, and perhaps with Robert LaFollette and Norman Thomas. This is a kind of noble lineage; this is the great American tradition; this is the essential element of a democracy as you and I know it.

Unhappily, much of today's dissent is not in that tradition. Many of our dissenters are great hands at being protesters, but not great hands at being listeners. Lyndon B. Johnson observed wisely that freedom of speech is always a two-way street—that we must not only guard every man's right to speak, but we must also defend every man's right to answer. Many of our dissenters today would not subscribe to that. They feel no obligation to contribute constructively to a national dialogue. They're long on activity and short on creativity.

My main concern here is the responsibility of the dissenter, and, more than that, it is with the teacher of the dissenter—with the kind of function that you and I may have in this total program.

I would like to outline two propositions. First, teachers of language arts have a special need to understand what dissent really is and then to help our students understand it. And second, teachers of the English language arts need somehow to capitalize upon the current passion for dissent and to help our students make this into a positive force.

I always find it easiest on occasions like this to discuss what dissent is by indicating what it is not. First, I would like to submit to you that dissent in its best sense is not mere disagreement for its own sake. Nor need dissent be disagreeable. If the dissenter makes a deliberate departure from an established doctrine, which is what dissent is all about, he ought to feel obliged, in my view, to make that dissent positive and constructive. There is no reason why, for example, the current policy of Vietnam should be immune from criticism. But, it seems to me, dissent is about as substantial as an empty gunnysack if we do not, in criticizing the Vietnam policy, offer some constructive proposal for an alternative form of behavior.

One of the maladies of our contemporary society is that we are against so much and for so little. If you ask people what they believe in, there are many who cannot tell you. Instead, they'll let you know what they're against. They are against Republicans, or they are against Democrats, or they are against fluoridation or landlords or do-gooders or union members or what not. But they do not affirm; they are negative. I submit to you that dissent goes beyond simple disagreement. One can, of course, say, "I'm a dissenter because I don't have to believe in anything, and I want to be an anarchist." This is a privileged position in our society because you and I will defend that individual just as much as we will defend each other. But it is not a very fruitful avenue to follow; it is not going to be productive in the long run for the individual.

In the second place, dissent is not an exercise in careless thinking or irresponsible writing or reckless speaking. In a democratic society, those who dissent have traditionally shared a common obligation to search for the relevant data and to try to make reasonable inferences from them. I think this ought to be a special obligation on our part to point this out and to assist students in finding the data and in making the inferences, hoping that they come to a reasonable conclusion. Surely we all need to recall Viscount Morley's definition of an educated man: a man or woman who knows what is evidence; who knows when a thing is proved; and who knows when it is not proved. I think both we and our students need to apply the techniques of analysis, of reasoning, and of critical thinking to the process of dissent, just as we apply some of the same techniques to the support of the Establishment. Without these qualities, dissent is unworthy.

Three years ago at a meeting of the National Student Association, Hubert Humphrey made some small headlines by saying to the students that the right to be heard does not automatically include the right to be taken seriously. The right to be taken seriously depends upon the substance and the quality of what is being said.

Third, I should like to say with considerable emphasis that dissent should not be a cover for treason or subversion any more than it should be a camouflage for stupidity and brutality. In our society we ought to expect (even if we do not always get) honesty, not sophistry—straight-forwardness, not subterfuge. Those who are criticized (and I speak primarily here of public officials) ought to be willing to debate their critics, not just denounce them. By the same token, I think the dissenters, like Senator Fulbright, Dr. Spock, or Senator McCarthy, must not denounce any effort to explain or defend the policies they attack simply by saying, "You're trying to stifle dissent." It works both ways.

I hope you're listening critically to what I'm saying at this point because not all advice on this matter is to be trusted. I have an example of that kind of advice. I will make no value judgment at all about this. I have deliberately selected a statement that dates back to September 30, 1967 so that the man whom I wish to quote will not be considered a presidential candidate. I quote, without comment, from *The New York Times* of September 30, 1967. "After telling a news conference at Virginia Polytechnic Institute that he would continue to welcome the support of the Ku Klux Klan, Mr. [George] Wallace said, 'I am for the right of dissent, but if I were president, the first thing I would do is to have my attorney general grab some of these bearded professors, take them before a grand jury and charge them with treason, and put them in a penitentiary where they belong.' " That is advice about dissent.

I wish to emphasize that when I say it's not fair to say a dissenter is a revolutionary, there are some dissenters, of course, who are revolutionaries. Some dissenters understandably hate the system; they do not seek merely to reform it, they would like to destroy it. But we must be careful not to blanket all dissenters under one category.

Fourth, dissent is not the copyrighted privilege of the young, or the alienated, or the depressed. One of the Hippie buttons that you can buy in the bookstore to pin on your Hippie lapel, if you have one, says, "Don't trust anyone over thirty." Now I have my special reasons, twenty-five special reasons, for resenting that. But I am also, I hope, honest enough to say that there is some justification for that slogan. Sometimes the people over thirty have difficulty communicating with those under thirty. Some of you may have read the story of Charles McHarry in *The Saturday Review* recently about the two men who were riding home on the commuter train together, and one of them said, "Is your son one of those alienated youths?" The other one said, "I don't know. We don't talk to each other."

In the October, 1967, *Harper's* magazine there was a splendid section devoted to this whole problem. Miss Rita Dershowitz responded to Walter Lippmann in a debate in print on this general question. Walter Lippmann suggested that there might be some wisdom in the minds of those who are on the far side of the generation gap. Miss Dershowitz replied: "That wisdom, if it really exists, simply isn't relevant to my life and to the conditions in which I live. An older generation's claim to insight, as a result of greater experience, is spurious, because my experiences are qualitatively different from those of my parents and, perhaps, even different from anything that has gone before."

As one of those who has gone long before Miss Dershowitz, I refute her not, but I do dissent mildly. I remind her and you, and I might remind our students, that it would be hard to find more free, more vigorous dissenters in all of history than Walter Lippmann, who is now seventy-nine; Justice Hugo Black, who is eighty-two; and Norman Thomas, eighty-four. Each of these people became eligible for Social Security something like two decades ago. Dissent is not the copyrighted privilege of the young.

Finally, I should like to suggest that dissent is not mere monologue or unilateral demonstration. In the American tradition of public debate, which is in turn drawn from the old British tradition of parliamentary debate, dissent is one-half of a dialogue. This dialogue serves democracy best when differing opinions are presented by earnest advocates to the same audience and under the same circumstances. Thus there is not merely an expression of opinion, but a direct and public confrontation of opposing views. The necessity of listening to the opposition is what makes the right to speak freely important.

In connection with the right to speak freely, I think that we cannot avoid making some comment on the behavior that took place in Washington last week when, by deliberate action, there was a prolongation of debate in the Senate in order to make it impossible to have the candidates for the presidency debate on television. James Reston's commentary on the values of direct confrontation and debate appeared in yesterday's *New York Times*, and it is worth quoting:

> The main objective in this election is to get a man of character and integrity. Nobody in the race has the answers to the problems of peace abroad and to civil order at home: therefore, we have to rely on faith and trust in the man in the White House. Nixon and Humphrey have different political arguments and different policies,

tendencies on questions of arms control and welfare, but in the end, the main problem is personal and the issue before the voter is how to judge the character of the three men in this race. That's what the battle in Congress over the television debate was all about. The point of changing the Federal Communications Act to permit debates among the candidates was to allow the voters to see them together and to judge how they reacted under pressure. It is, admittedly, a brutal test, but so is the presidency. And the test of a television debate is undoubtedly better than most of the tests we now have.

Reston's essay is a comment on the significance of what we are actually talking about here today. It is obviously not easy to set limits on dissent, especially when it takes the form of demonstrations by people in all walks of society; especially when it takes the form that it took in Chicago and that it has taken on many university campuses; especially when it takes the form that it has taken in the ghetto areas of some of our major cities; and especially when it takes the form that it has taken among perfectly respectable people who believe that the art of responding to a campaign speech is to try to drown out the speaker. We have come to a sorry state when a national candidate for office has to buy television time because that is the only way of getting twenty-nine uninterrupted minutes to address the public. The drowning out of a speaker introduces an entirely new concept of rhetoric. It might be called "the rhetoric of the act"—waving the placard; or "the rhetoric of nonverbal behavior" or "the rhetoric of the prolonged boo"—unarticulated and unphonated, just the long sound. It also introduces a whole new concept of what is civil and what is uncivil in the area of civil rights. This rhetoric questions whether or not individuals have the right to speak without interruption and whether they have the right to invite, under formal kinds of circumstances, a confrontation of opinion.

I suggest to you that these developments make it exceedingly difficult to define the precise limits of dissent; I don't think anyone can do this. We do not solve the problem simply by uttering pious platitudes such as, "Discussions can change minds and demonstrations can only crack heads." This isn't going to get us very far. And we do not help the problem when we ourselves, as teachers in public schools and colleges and universities and as advisors to students, advocate unreasonable forms of dissent. There is a long Supreme Court history of the defense of the right of peaceful picketing and of the defense of demonstrations that involve marching and so on; but there is insistence that those rights do not extend to the point of provoking violence—that is not reasonable dissent.

It is a little difficult, I thing, to find a good positive statement on what the issues are here; but a volume entitled *Concerning Dissent and Civil Disobedience,* by Abe Fortas, former Justice of the Supreme Court, is an excellent statement—thoughtful, reflective, and honest. This volume is well worth considering if you are interested in defining the limits of proper legal dissent and the kinds of behavior that we ought to engage in when we confront dissent of which we do not approve, but which, in a democratic society, ought to be permitted. For example, although we may not like the burning of draft cards, an individual who wants to burn a draft card and who is willing to pay the penalty and take the risk is behaving exactly the same way that you and I are behaving when we go sixty-seven miles an hour in a sixty-five mile zone; we are knowingly violating the law, but we are willing to take the risk of being caught.

I also want to emphasize that this problem of dissent is not made a bit easier by encouraging the mass media to exaggerate the proportion and the nature of dissenting behavior. I have seen television cameramen from national networks encourage students to wave and to behave vigorously as though they were angry and stirred up. I have collected other such information at various times. There is a delightful little piece from Claremont, California, about NBC filming a debate between two students—a hawk and a dove. The television cameramen came equipped with signs for the students to wave because the cameramen were afraid the students might not have made their own placards. I do think that we have a problem with this kind of image-making contribution of the mass media; we sometimes get exaggeration and distortion that we ought not be subjected to.

Dissent, then, is not mere disagreement for its own sake; it does not excuse careless thinking or irresponsible speaking or writing;

it is not a cover for treason or subversion; it is not the sole privilege of the young; and it is not mere monologue.

I suggest that we face the problem in our own classrooms by asking what we can do to help our students perfect the fine art of dissent. How can we capitalize upon the happy death of apathy among students? How can we capitalize upon their passion for dissent? The answer, I submit, is to bring dissent into the school-room, to encourage an open and mature confrontation of views on crucial issues, and to take a golden opportunity to try to train students in the art of being more effective and more responsible dissenters.

At a meeting of the American Council of Education, Kingman Brewster, President of Yale University, talked about the tragedy of today's highly motivated, impatient young activists who run a serious risk of disqualifying themselves from true usefulness by being too impatient to arm themselves with the intellectual equipment required for the solutions of the problems of war, poverty, and dignity. This is the nub of the matter. Those of us who teach various aspects of the English language must use our strategic position to help arm our students with the proper intellectual equipment so that they will qualify themselves for true usefulness through public discussion and dissent in attacking the real ills of our society. Nowhere else in the school curriculum can this be done so effectively as in the English class and the speech class, by working through essays, speeches, letters, themes, and debates.

We are all rhetoricians. We are all concerned with the art of written and oral discourse—that long, continuing tradition that began with Aristotle. Let us remind ourselves that this tradition has a set of canons. First of all, it is concerned with the canon of invention—discovery, analysis, selection, and synthesis of ideas. Second, it is concerned with disposition—the organization and arrangement of these ideas into patterns persuasive and useful in written and oral discourse. Third, it is concerned with style—the language in which we clothe our themes and our speeches. And, finally, it is concerned with delivery, with such problems of presentation as penmanship, spelling, and pronunciation.

These four canons are the pegs on which you and I hang our

teaching of writing and speaking. Our textbooks, our resource materials, and our own emphases contribute to a pretty good job of teaching style and delivery. But we spend the least time with the canon of invention. Here we are likely to be the least effective in our teaching, and here we have the least useful resource material. And it is here, I think, in the discovery of evidence, the analysis of evidence, the evaluation of argument, and the synthesis of these into persuasive, logical, and sensible conclusions, that we ought to be most concerned if we care about this possibility of the freedom of dissent being exercised responsibly in our society.

In conclusion, may I make four concrete suggestions? First of all, I believe that rhetorical invention, whether for writing or for speaking, begins with subject matter. This is where we begin our lessons, then, on the art of dissent; we open our class discussions, our reading, and our writing exercises to what Superintendent Shedd calls the "gut issues" of our society. This must not be simply a permissive attitude on our part; it must be one of positive encouragement. The student needs to feel that he is being invited, not to a *tour de force* of sensationalism, but to a hardheaded forum where tough-minded people can deal seriously with the real issues of our society.

Second, the foundation of rhetorical invention is information. In teaching English and speech, we must deal with the techniques for searching out and gathering relevant data and information. We must teach students to ask these questions: What is evidence? How do you assess the different kinds of evidence? How do you know when to rely upon an alleged fact? When can you utilize opinions? How do you recognize a good authority when you meet one?

As applied to real problems brought into the classroom from the real world, those are the kinds of questions we ought to be raising, and this is the kind of guidance our students ought to be given if we are to make them responsible dissenters.

In the third place, if the foundation of rhetorical invention is evidence, then its structure is argument. I think we must expand our traditional repertoire of narration, exposition, and description to include, and to emphasize, argumentation, if we are going to be socially relevant. We cannot help our students to become responsible and substantial dissenters if they are not given a feeling of security in knowing how to draw inferences, how to evaluate arguments, and how to use the total reasoning process. Our aim ought to be to help students to speak and write confidently, by first helping them to understand the art of reasoning, including the traditional patterns of induction and deduction, and so on.

Finally, we need to encourage our young dissenters to utilize their rhetorical growth and development—their grasp of rhetorical patterns and procedures—in oral and written discourse, and to use it within the context of social responsibility. The dilemma of a democratic society, and the basis of much of our traditional fear of dissent, is that we cannot bar the demagogue and the charlatan from the platform and, at the same time, keep it open for Quintilian's "good man skilled in rhetoric." Society can protect itself, as we know, by regulating the use of a wide range of lethal weapons, including automobiles and guns and even nuclear bombs. But the weapons of language, of speaking and writing, are life and death issues, and must, in a democracy, remain uninhibited and uncensored. The only restraint that need ultimately be placed upon lethal language is the restraint placed upon it by the dissenter himself. And we must take the responsibility for helping him, while he is in our classroom, to become not only an effective, but also an ethical communicator.

I will only mention a few examples of this facet of our task; you are as aware of them as I. We must consider: the obligation to find the facts before jumping to conclusions; the priority of an opponent's arguments over his character and his personality; the morality (or the immorality) and the legality of certain kinds of words and arguments that we might use; the confusion of probability with certainty; and the obligation that is always upon us to debate rather than to denounce.

These tasks, if undertaken by each of us in our classroom and if well performed, may well be our greatest contribution to society. As educators we are in a position to be exceptionally fearless and forthright. Because we live in a world of ideas and of inquiry, we naturally come to a state of healthy skepticism about what we see around us. We are not afraid, therefore, of dissenters so long as they are responsible thinkers. We know, as John Dewey once said, that "every thinker puts some portion of an apparently stable world in peril." But we also know that without thinkers and without honest public dissent and debate we are in even greater peril.

I do not deny for a moment the need for sending into society students who are well versed in history, in mathematics, in literature, and in science. But I am bold enough to say that the central concern of education at all levels must be to turn out students who are well-trained rhetorically—who are both responsible and effective writers and speakers—and who can, in the long run, compete successfully in the marketplace of ideas with those intellectual dropouts who abuse the right of dissent, who refuse the obligation to debate, and who pervert the democratic process. This process, and its best products, are precious enough, in a world of social and political discontent, to command our total commitment.

On Teaching Informative Speaking

VICTOR M. POWELL
Chairman and Professor of Speech
Wabash College

When we consider informative speaking, our first task is set for us
by those who believe that "informative speaking" cannot be justified as a separate and distinct assignment. I remember a colleague's
saying, "There is no such thing as a purely informative speech.
Why, even if a man asked you the way to the Post Office, you must,
by the manner of your reply, persuade him that you know the way
to the Post Office and are a reliable source of information or he will
not follow your instructions." This is an extreme view, but let us
concede the kernel of truth. There may indeed be an element of
persuasion even in delivering the most commonplace instructions,
but surely there is a significant difference in degree that becomes
a difference in kind. At the very least, we can make a useful distinction between the rhetorical task of explaining how Medicare is
financed under present legislation and the rhetorical task of persuading an audience that this method is good or bad.

In establishing informative speaking as a separate category, we
have authority with us. If we turn to *Webster's Third New International Dictionary*, we find under *exposition* the following definition: "discourse or an example of it designed to convey information
or explain what is difficult to understand; *esp:* a statement embody-

ing an analysis of the subject matter and the use of familiar illustrations or analogies." Here is a definition well suited to the teacher
of speech, and we can be especially grateful for the inclusion of
that last phrase, "and the use of familiar illustrations or analogies,"
for they are essential to the job of informing.

Let us close the case by calling an old and distinguished authority to our side. Writing in 1909, Charles Sears Baldwin carefully
distinguished between persuasion and exposition. He called persuasion the method of winning assent, and exposition the method
of lucid explanation. Of exposition he said, ". . . specifically, then,
exposition means the succinct and orderly setting forth of some
piece of knowledge. . . . It means a luminous report of conditions
in track athletics, debating, local or national or foreign politics,
rapid transit, contemporary stage; a concise explanation of Greek
tragedy, the turbine wheel, the Roman Legion, the feudal
system. . . ."

If, then, we have established informative, or expository, speaking as a distinct category, we may next need to ask the question,
for ourselves as well as for our students, "Why bother with it?" If
there is one thing that seems securely established in our theories of
learning, it is that learning is related to motivation. Our teaching
effectiveness should be increased if both we and our students are
convinced that an understanding of exposition can contribute to
our effectiveness as speakers. In motivating an interest in informative speaking, I want to rest my case on at least two grounds: first,
that exposition is basic to most other kinds or purposes of speech;
second, that the speech to inform is an important speech on its own
merits. Let's look at each of these propositions in more detail.

Information is basic to most other kinds or purposes of speech.
Information is vital to all forms of responsible persuasion, and
when persuasion has been indifferent to its informing function, it
has fallen on evil days. We can begin with the famous passage in
the *Gorgias* where Socrates separates the art of imparting knowledge from the art of imparting belief. He says, "Shall we then assume two kinds of persuasion, the one producing belief without
certainty, the other knowledge?" This distinction was destined for
a long and unfortunate history. Three hundred years later Cicero

referred to it in *De Oratore* when he refers to Socrates having "separated in his discussion the ability of thinking wisely; and speaking gracefully, though they are naturally united." And in our own day, Irving Lee wrote in the preface to his *Language Habits In Human Affairs*, "The sharp separation of the art of gaining assent from the art of making accurate statements is, perhaps, one of the most widely accepted legacies of the Platonic Dialogue."

I think we can agree, and the evidence is impressive, that sound, tested information is fundamental to responsible persuasion in a free society. Edward Barrett's book, *Truth Is Our Weapon*, is an interesting and detailed documentation of the proposition that our international persuasion is most effective when it relies upon accurate and lucid information. If a student undertakes to persuade us that a proposed piece of legislation, whether it provides for control of gun sales or for stricter regulation of teenage drivers, is good or bad, we surely must ask that he be able to tell us with clarity and precision what that legislation provides. Charles Sears Baldwin sums up this point when he says, "Argument cannot go on without exposition, but exposition can go on without argument."

My first reason, then, for giving importance to a study of informative speaking is that it is a fundamental building block for other kinds of speeches. But preeminently I would state the case for studying informative speaking on its own merits.

First, we can stress to our students the prevalence of informative occasions in this society. And we may need to stress it, for persuasion gets most of the attention of those who study communication. Persuasion is more dramatic, and the folklore of American Public Address is rich with dramatic incidents: Patrick Henry crying, "Liberty or Death," James Otis declaiming against "Taxation without Representation," and William Jennings Bryan winning a presidential nomination with a single dramatic speech. In our own extracurricular affairs, we sponsor few contests in informative speaking. But much of the work of the world depends upon the communication of information. The classroom lecturer, the shop foreman, the swimming instructor, the first-aid teacher—all must know how to give information.

But I think there is still another ground, and a vital one, for

motivating interest in the informative speech. The more complex
and specialized our society, the more important it becomes that
we should be able to talk across our specialities—to tell others what
we are doing and why it is significant for them. This idea can be
brought alive for the student through classroom discussion and
through a wealth of illustration and example available to us on
every hand. No group in our society is more conscious of this problem than are the scientists, and their testimony may help to reach
the student interested in science. Robert Oppenheimer, the late
distinguished physicist, both spoke and wrote about this concern.
In a speech reported in *Vital Speeches* for February 1, 1955, he
said: "The specialization of science is an inevitable accompaniment
of progress; yet it is cruelly wasteful, since so much that is beautiful and enlightening is cut off from most of the world. Thus it is
proper to the role of the scientist that he not merely find new truth
and communicate it to his fellows, but that he teach, that he try to
bring the most honest and intelligible account of new knowledge
to all who will try to learn." Another example comes from Dr. T. J.
Stare, writing in *Harper's* magazine for October, 1964. He tells of
an experience when he and two other distinguished doctors were
defeated by a popular radio personality in a struggle for water
flouridation: "This was a disheartening experience. I don't think
it proves that scientists must embrace the huckster's arts. *It does,
however, suggest that we must sharpen our skills in making scientific information comprehensible and acceptable to the average
citizen.*" (The italics are mine.)

Nor are our examples, or the need, limited to the areas of science.
A. Whitney Griswold, a president of Yale University, saw a similar
problem facing the legal profession, and of it he said, "The American people do not sufficiently understand the rule of law because
it has never been properly explained to them." And Walter Lippmann has regularly urged the importance of government leaders
being able *to explain* the problems of foreign policy and to keep
citizens informed of what is being done. Of course we also have
ancient testimony. When Aristotle lists the uses of rhetoric, he puts
second its usefulness in instructing when "scientific" instruction is
of no avail.

I have, of course, been alluding to *popularizing*. Unfortunately, in some parts of the world, and particularly in the academic world, *popularizing* is a dirty word. It must not be. Especially the free society depends upon the popularizing of information. If we believe that only an informed electorate can make this free society work, then there must obviously be those who are able and willing to inform it. Unfortunately, popularization has too often been associated with misrepresenting and with distorting. It need not be, and this is where part of the speech teacher's work will rest in teaching informative speaking.

A technique I think indispensable to effective teaching is the habit of regular and systematic clipping. When you read, read with a pen or pencil at hand. Suppose, for instance, you are reading *Life* magazine, and in a story about Norman Thomas you find an illustration of how he handled hostile audiences. Mark the paragraph, and across the face of the magazine write, "clip page __." Then before the magazine is discarded you clip that item and file it. This can work equally well with daily newspapers. A convenient way to organize the file for these clippings is to make a folder for each of the chapters of the textbook you use. This kind of material can bring life and immediacy and motivation to the classroom. No matter how fresh an item may look to an author as he writes a text, three, four, or even five years later those same examples and illustrations will look like ancient history to the high school sophomore. Then the teacher's file is indispensable.

Aristotle's observation that the end and object of a speech is its audience gives us entry to our next concern, the informative speaker's obligation to analyze his audience. Too often a discussion of audience analysis is reserved for a discussion of persuasion; but in at least three ways, audience analysis is important to the one who speaks to inform. It may help the student to find a subject; it may tell him whether his proposed audience is receptive to information on the chosen subject; and it will help him to determine at what level he should speak. Let's look at each of these in turn.

Perhaps the most familiar cry a speech teacher hears is: "But I don't know what to talk about." An audience analysis may serve the purpose of finding topics. It is probably best to begin with an analysis of the speech class, the audience the students will be talking to. Start with a blackboard list of the obvious things: age, distribution of the sexes, locale, level of education, and perhaps similarities of social and economic background. Then raise questions about the kinds of interests that this audience might share. (It can also be instructive to take for analysis an audience the students do not know; for instance, an audience of boy scouts in some distant city, or a downtown businessmen's service club.) One of the gains that should come from such an analysis is a realization that good topics come not only from the interest of the speaker but also from a careful consideration of the expected audience.

Our second purpose for the informative speaker's audience analysis is to determine if the audience will be receptive to information on his chosen subject. This may need some explanation. The purposes of speech have often been defined in terms of the *speaker's* purpose; that is, if the speaker determines that his purpose is to convey information, then it is an informative speech. Likewise, if the speaker determines that his purpose is to persuade his audience, then the speech is considered a persuasive speech. But it is possible that the audience's attitude toward the speaker's subject will frustrate his intention. Thomas Olbricht, in his book *Informative Speaking*, points out that although the speaker may think of his purpose as simply conveying information on his subject, if the audience has strong attitudes for or against this subject, they may see his information as obvious persuasion. I had, by coincidence, both a Greek and a Turkish student in the same beginning speech class when relations between Greece and Turkey had reached a crisis over the Cyprus problem. When we came to the final speech round, an assigned speech of information, the Greek student asked if he could give an informative speech on the Cyprus situation. He assured me that he could treat the subject as pure information. To show him his difficulty, I asked if he would be willing to let the Turkish student be the judge of whether his speech was information or persuasion. He thought for a moment, and then replied that he would look for another subject. It is obvious that Cyprus is, and was, a question that could be treated informatively. But it is also obvious that neither student could have accepted a speech from the other one as purely informative. It is important for our students to understand that the attitude of an audience toward a subject can finally determine whether the speech will be informative or persuasive.

Finally, the audience analysis should help the speaker determine at what level he should speak. The informative speaker is regularly beset by two dangers: he may underestimate his audience's knowledge of the subject and bore them by telling what they already know. On the other hand, he may overestimate the audience's familiarity with his subject and fail to inform because the audience had too little background to understand him. It is not easy, and indeed it may be impossible, to determine with precision the level of knowledge for a particular audience. Nevertheless, if we can make our students aware of the problem, if we can train them to always raise the question, "What does my audience know about my subject?" we may help them to avoid the most obvious mistakes.

One does not have to be in the classroom long, nor for that matter in general audiences long, to know that obvious mistakes are made. I think of the young man who made a speech to other young men on the subject of pool. The speech consisted of a detailed exposition of the size, shape, and general appearance of a pool table, not neglecting to mention its pockets, and similarly obvious observations about pool cues and balls. Sometimes this kind of speech is produced by sheer laziness, but we must at least admit the possibility that it is the result of ignorance. On the other hand, I remember the expert on Byzantine history who lectured for three evenings to an audience well above average in intelligence, but not in knowledge of his subject, and left his audience as ignorant of his subject when he was through as they were when he began. At the conclusion of the lectures one listener remarked, "Well, he certainly made no concessions to his audience." We must see that our students understand that in the context we are dealing with here, to make no concessions to an audience is to waste the time of both speaker and listener.

I do not want to leave this admittedly brief discussion of audience analysis without stating my conviction that audience analysis is central to speech preparation. A speaker prepares a speech for a particular audience at a particular time and place. As he prepares his speech, that audience should be forever in the front of his mind. It guides each step of preparation, determining in large part the organization, the choice of supporting materials, and the language used.

Three words state the essentials of a speech to inform: *clarity*, *accuracy*, and *interest*. The aim of the speaker is to gain understanding and, usually, retention. In his textbook, *Speech: Dynamic Communication*, Milton Dickens suggests three test questions for judging the success of an informative speech: How much information was new to the audience? How much information did they understand? How much information will they remember?

If these are the objectives of the informative speaker, we might try to state as succinctly the barriers that stand in his way. Borrowing from communication research, we might state the barriers simply as *frustration, fatigue*, and *low motivation*. By frustration we mean that the speaker has presented information that goes beyond the ability of his audience to understand. This takes us back to the fundamental importance of audience analysis and to the speaker's problem of speaking neither above nor below the level of his audience. By fatigue we mean simply that the amount of information is too much for the attention span of the audience. The third barrier is perhaps too well known to every teacher to need much explication. Low motivation exists when the information is uninteresting, or presented without effort to reinforce the attention of the listener. The informative speaker is under the same necessity to command the attention and interest of his audience as is the man who would persuade. Until interest is created, no information is absorbed. We pay attention to information when it is made pertinent to our own lives—our interests and our needs.

Recently I heard a student who undertook to inform his audience about European integration. The central idea for his speech read, "An understanding of European integration gives an insight into the politics of Europe today." The first sentence of his introduction read, "As a student of political science, with a great deal of interest in Europe, I'd like to tell you a bit about European integration."

The speech that followed was a dull recitation of facts, with no discernible concern for the interests of the audience. The student had made the fatal mistake of assuming that what interested him would interest his audience.

Our task as teachers of informative speaking is to make our students aware of the essential requirements of exposition, of the barriers that stand in their way, and of the devices available to them to surmount the barriers and accomplish their aim. Our task is to lead our students to see that clear organization, interesting and pertinent forms of support, and a lucid oral style are the keys to successful exposition.

In the quarterly, *Improving College and University Teaching*, for the summer of 1965, under the title "Secret of Master Lecturers," R. J. David reported a study that bears directly on our interests here. David went to the campus of Ohio State University and there obtained the names of three teachers who had the reputation for being superior lecturers. The teachers were an economist, an industrial engineer, and an anthropologist. David visited their classrooms to see if he could find what they had in common that could account for their reputations as superior lecturers. When he had listened to all three men, he attributed their success to two traits common to all of them: first, a simple lecture plan; second, an abundant use of illustrations. Each of these lecturers knew precisely what he could do in a fifty-minute period, and he did not try to do more. Each knew that information needs to be put in concrete, meaningful terms, and so each used pertinent and interesting illustrations to support his ideas.

The balance of this chapter will be concerned with three fundamentally important ideas and with methods for teaching them. We will be concerned with the clarity of organization, with the use of appropriate and interesting forms of support, and with developing a clear oral style.

We begin our consideration of organization by examining the first attribute of David's superior lecturers, the simple lecture plan. The speaker must know what he can get done in fifty minutes, or five minutes. This means we must begin by teaching the student to limit his subject. Recently a high school teacher told me of the student who announced he wanted to talk on football. The teacher asked the class how many were interested in hearing a speech on football. Very few hands went up. Then the teacher asked, "How many would like to hear a speech on the play that won last Saturday's game?" Now the response was enthusiastic. With such an illustration, the teacher could make his point that not only was the first subject too broad to be treated intelligently in five minutes but it was also too broad and vague to demand attention.

Subjects that are too broad must be dealt with as they come up in the classroom. But we can also take preventive measures. It can be instructive to lead the class through an analysis of a subject like "Recent Progress in Highway Traffic Safety." You will be well advised to have prepared such an exercise beforehand so you can give leadership to the discussion if the class is laggard. You might go from traffic safety to the components of improved driver training, improved highway construction, improved traffic laws, and improved automobile engineering. Each of these in turn can be subdivided; from improved automobile engineering, you might eventually arrive at a five-minute speech explaining some part of the federal requirements for automobile safety that are currently operative.

When a student has achieved a manageable subject and has gathered his materials for it (and we will say more about the materials later in this chapter), he needs to organize his material in a simple and easily followed plan. I know of no substitute for the outline in teaching organization. Further, I think in teaching outlining, the speech teacher can do a real service for his students. Recently two former students, both successful lawyers, told me that the most important thing they got from their speech class, and one of the most important things they got from their undergraduate training, was a mastery of outlining.

You will find at the conclusion of this chapter a sample outline that will serve to illustrate what I think the speech outline ought to be. You will note that the outline is done on a standard form that we call an analysis blank. This kind of standard form serves a purpose. For every speech the student makes, he must answer the four questions on the title page. They serve as regular reminders of some of the things we have talked about in this chapter. A place on the front page for the bibliography reminds him that he is expected to have done some research, and that the teacher wants to know about it. This also provides the opportunity to teach good bibliographical form. On the backside at the top of the page, the student must state, in the place provided, the central idea for the speech. The wide left-hand margin, labeled "technical plot," serves still another purpose. When the student makes his outline, he enters in the technical plot the forms of support he has used to make his speech clear, vivid, and interesting. Any teacher who would find this analysis blank useful is welcome to reproduce it and to modify it as he sees fit.

Most teachers are certainly familiar with the statement of the central idea as a fundamental of composition. I try to make it the keystone of the whole outline. The student sometimes confuses the central idea with the statement of purpose. To say "I want to tell the class about the famous architect Frank Lloyd Wright" may be the statement of a purpose. The central idea for such a speech might well be "Frank Lloyd Wright was a nonconformist in his architectural designs as well as in his personal life." From this central idea two mainheads immediately emerge to support it: Frank Lloyd Wright was a nonconformist in his professional work; Wright was equally a nonconformist in his personal life. Granted that examples are always neater than the messy realities that confront our students, this kind of an example may serve to demonstrate the relationship between a well-stated central idea and the mainheads of the speech.

When we discuss the relation of the mainheads to the central idea, we have a good place to start talking about the fundamental idea of subordination in outlining. The mainheads of the speech grow out of, support, and are subordinate to, the central idea. The form of an outline, the indentation, and the use of conventional symbols are all designed to display the relationships among the ideas of the speech. You will find the outline at the end of this chapter uses the following conventional outline symbols:

I.
  A.
    1.
      a.
        1.)
          a.)
          b.)
        2.)
      b.
    2.
  B.
II.

This particular set of symbols has the advantage of being widely used. But the particular system to show subordination is not as important as the idea that a standard system should be adopted and regularly used. Any good system will help to implant the idea of subordination, which is at the very heart of outlining.

The mainheads, those ideas symbolized by the roman numerals, need our particular attention. A speech that shows more than four mainheads should be suspected of being poorly analyzed or insufficiently limited. If poorly phrased, mainheads will obscure the movement of the ideas. Badly arranged, they defeat the purpose of the outline, which is to impose order on the composition.

We need to begin with the proposition that when the central idea is broken into its parts, that is, into mainheads, those mainheads should be few in number. Research and practical experience combine to support this important idea. Harry Emerson Fosdick remarked of a sermon he preached that had six points: "It came out like a broom, in a multitude of small straws." We know from experience that it is difficult to hold a long list of undifferentiated ideas in mind. We need hooks to hang them on—major ideas we can associate them with. In terms of communication theory, both frustration and fatigue are encouraged by a failure to find and limit the major ideas in a speech. In my own teaching, I try to underscore this idea by exercises done in class. As an example, I have found the following exercise useful:

Here is a list of specific items taken from a student speech on improvements in modern banking. Try to find no more than three major ideas or divisions under which these specific items can be grouped.

1. Drive-in facilities provide greater convenience.
2. After hiring, employees receive detailed on-the-job training.
3. Personalized checks are available from most banks.
4. Automated equipment speeds check handling.
5. Many banks have established small loan departments.
6. Prospective employees are carefully tested before they are hired.
7. Revolving credit plans offer customers a new service.

The class should need no more than five minutes for such an exercise. My own suggestion for organizing the speech follows. Central idea: A wide variety of improvements have made modern banking better banking.

I. Banks have improved their physical facilities.
   A. Automated equipment speeds check handling.
   B. Drive-in facilities provide greater convenience.
II. Banks have improved their personnel.
   A. Prospective employees are carefully tested before they are hired.
   B. After hiring, employees receive detailed on-the-job training.
III. Banks have improved the services they offer.
   A. Many banks have established small loan departments.
   B. Revolving credit plans offer customers a new service.
   C. Personalized checks are available from most banks.

This is not the only possible organization. Some students may argue for a two-mainhead speech:

I. Banks have improved customer services.
II. Banks have improved their personnel.

The argument for this organization is that the improved facilities exist simply to improve customer service. Material for exercises of this sort come to every teacher's desk. Filed away, they can be exceedingly useful in providing exercises for future classes. These in-class exercises not only illustrate the idea but they also involve the student actively in applying that idea.

So we move to another essential of outlining, the principle that the ideas expressed in the mainheads must be mutually exclusive. The material under mainhead I must be there because it could not reasonably be under any other mainhead of the speech. Again our speech on banking can illustrate the idea. One student suggested three mainheads for the banking speech:

  I. Banks have improved their personnel.
 II. Banks have improved credit plans.
III. Banks have improved customer conveniences.

Items 2 and 6, dealing with personnel, clearly will go under the first mainhead. Items 5 and 7, dealing with small loan departments and revolving credit plans, will presumably go under the second mainhead. When we come to the third mainhead, we have trouble. We can assume drive-in facilities and personalized checks, items 1 and 3, are customer conveniences, but surely revolving credit plans are meant to be a customer convenience and probably small loan departments could also fall under that category. Item 4, automated equipment for check handling, improves the efficiency of the bank, and if it makes the monthly statement more reliable, it may be a customer convenience—but it is not as obviously so as the other items we have put here.

When the mainheads are chosen and suitably phrased, the student must next ask himself, "How shall I arrange them? How are they related one to the other?" In Glen Mills's *Message Preparation, Analysis and Structure*, eleven patterns of arrangement are listed and discussed. It may be useful for the teacher to know these categories, but for the student beginning to master the idea of orderly composition, we need not make so many distinctions. Among the most obvious, useful, and easily understood patterns of arrangement are those of time, space, cause-effect, problem-solution, and related groups (classification). Little need be said to explain the basis of each of these patterns. We sometimes need to caution the student to be certain that when he assumes a cause-effect order, the alleged cause-effect relationship will bear up under analysis. A problem-solution order may most often be thought of as a persuasive pattern. But it is not exclusively so. I remember an excellent student speech of information using this organization. The first mainhead developed the problem of increasing the food supply to meet the needs of a rapidly expanding population. The second mainhead suggested the ways in which the resources of the ocean may be tapped to meet this problem.

The related group, sometimes called classification, is a much used pattern. Many of us first studied the federal government in high school civics under the classification of legislative, executive, and judicial branches. We have already discussed the necessity of seeing that the categories of classification are mutually exclusive, and we must add now that they must also, when put together, cover all of the subject.

The individual patterns of arrangement are not difficult to make clear to students. But it is often difficult to make them see the necessity of having one, and only one, pattern for a speech. Too often the speech starts out with the first two mainheads related in one order, while the third suddenly appears to be based on some different pattern. Here again I find the most effective means for inculcating this idea of adhering to a single consistent pattern of organization is to involve the students in the analysis of mainheads. I distribute to the class a mimeographed page with the mainheads from several speeches on it, and we discuss the faults of the arrangement. For example, here is a set of mainheads from such an exercise:

From a speech on the traditional fox hunt:
I. Close to the fox is a pack of hounds, heads to the ground, intent on only one thing, the fox.
II. Behind he hounds come the Master of the Hounds and his whippers and then the rest of the field.

  III. The men wear scarlet coats, black derbies or top hats, white riding pants, and black boots.

  IV. The hunters can be heard yelling such terms as "Are-hole," "They're drawing well," and "Tallyho" as they move through the hunt fields.

Mainheads I and II are related by time order; but when we come to mainhead III, the pattern has changed and III and IV are related in what is apparently some classification order. This speech could be consistently organized, using classification in the following manner:

> Central idea: the fox hunt is a colorful event closely governed by tradition.
>   I. Tradition prescribes the order of the hunt.
>   II. Tradition prescribes the acceptable dress.
>   III. Tradition prescribes the calls of the hunters.

I find it worthwhile to make a distinction for students between logical and rhetorical order. Logical order is apparent enough, and it is what we are usually talking about. Mainheads are arranged in a particular order because reason leads us to expect them in that order. If we use chronology, it is logical to begin at the beginning. If we use cause-effect, it is logical to start with the cause and move to the effect. But in classification order, strict logic often does not tell us which mainhead should come first and which last. For instance, in the speeches on the fox hunt and on banking, how would logic prescribe the order of those mainheads? Usually here we will be governed by rhetorical considerations; that is, what is most effective for the audience, or what is most important for the speaker in a particular speech? Much research has been done on the order of presentation and it suggests that the first and last positions in a presentation are both emphatic and likely to be remembered. This consideration can be important for information, just as it is for persuasion, and we might decide to put what we consider most important in the first and last positions with the least important point in the middle. Effectiveness with the audience governs arrangements, and even the logical order is justified on the basis that the audience will expect it and follow it most easily. When attention can be commanded by breaking the order that logic would suggest (for instance, beginning by painting the dramatic effect of erosion before discussing the causes), the audience-conscious speaker will not hesitate to do it.

Let me make one final point about mainheads. They should be carefully and precisely phrased. I am indebted to the late W. N. Brigance for a vivid characterization of the vague, imprecise mainhead. He used to call these "bucket" mainheads. Here is an example from a speech describing the requirements of a good baseball infield:

I. There are several requirements for a good shortstop.

Brigance called it a bucket mainhead because, as he said, "Change the last word and you could pour anything in the world into it." Cross out shortstop and write marriage, or high school, or fighter-bomber. To convert this kind of mainhead into one that is meaningful, you must say something specific; for instance:

I. A good shortstop must have quick reflexes and a good arm.

Now we have the idea, and we can expect the mainhead to be developed with specific material and illustrations from the careers of such men as Marty Marion, Phil Rizzuto, and Luis Aparicio. The bucket mainhead comes to us in many forms. "There are several reasons why this program will not work," "Much can be said both for and against this plan," and, "This condition is the result of many forces." In each case the speaker needs to refine his idea, state it specifically in the mainhead, and then develop it with specific supporting material.

We have paid detailed attention to clarity of organization in this discussion of informative speaking both because it contributes to clarity of exposition and because we assume informative speaking precedes persuasive speaking. It is here that the student is first challenged to put a mass of detail into an orderly progression.

When the student has achieved a clear and simple pattern of organization, we need to pay some attention to the important matter of transitions. A listener gains satisfaction from seeing an idea unfold, and clear transitions help the listener to see the order. I like to insist that transitions be included in the outline and be specifically labeled as transitions. In speeches of information, forecast and summary are especially helpful. Research confirms that spaced repetition is an effective device for implanting an idea. The old saw about telling an audience what you are going to tell them, telling them, and then telling them what you have told them is sound advice for exposition.

Let me say a final word about the outline we require from our students. You will notice that the outline at the end of this chapter is done in complete sentences. Most students and some teachers will protest this requirement. I suspect a student of objecting because the full-sentence outline is harder work than a key-word outline. But teachers have objected on the substantial ground that a required, full-sentence outline is likely to encourage memorization of the speech. I share the assumption of most of my colleagues that memorization is bad and that we do not want to encourage it. But while full-sentence outlines may increase the danger of memorization, they do not demand it, and the teacher can urge against it.

The full-sentence outline has two important advantages. In the first place, it improves the quality of preparation. It assures that every idea in the outline has been thought through at least once and fully expressed. In the catch-phrase outline, we are all subject to the temptation of writing down a word or two to symbolize a subject we intend to talk about and trusting to the inspiration of the moment to provide the details. Too often the moment comes without the inspiration. Then we are likely to be stumbling or vague and wordy as we try to recapture the fragmentary idea we had when we made the outline. My second defense for the full-sentence outline is that it provides a diagnostic device for the teacher. With a full-sentence outline in front of him, the teacher can see what the student intended to say and what he thought was an appropriate way of saying it. It is important that we teach our students the elements of a lively oral style, and one way to teach it is to insist that they write such a style into their speech outlines. If we discourage memorizing, we will not expect the student to say verbatim what he wrote into his outline, but the outline will be evidence that he does, or does not, understand what an oral style is.

A conscientious student will learn what the best method of speech preparation is for him, and the experienced teacher will recognize that not all minds work the same way. But while the student is learning for himself, the teacher has an obligation to make recommendations. My own recommendation is that the student write out a complete full-sentence outline; that when he has done this and has read the outline through once or twice to fix the ideas in mind, he then make for himself a fragmentary or key-word outline, and that he rehearse by speaking from the fragmentary outline. I would never let the student take the full-sentence outline to the platform with him, unless I wanted an exercise in reading a speech. If the student uses notes, let them be the fragmentary outline that will jog his memory and keep his ideas in order. This is the most effective method I know for developing in students an ability to speak extemporaneously.

We have mentioned the importance of teaching our students to use a good, clear, oral style. We come now to consider oral style in more detail. All language of course should be clear, but speaking makes special demands. The listener cannot "turn back the page" when he does not understand. Nor can he conveniently go to the dictionary for a definition when he needs it. Clarity of language must be the concern of every teacher, and it is particularly important to one who must speak to inform. I have stressed the idea of *oral style*. We have plenty of evidence, even from outside the field of speech, that oral style is in some respects peculiar. In *Newsweek* magazine of May 6, 1963, in the section devoted to books, a reporter wrote a symposium at Princeton University. He referred to one of the speakers at that symposium as a man "who has lived forty-nine years without apparently noticing any difference between the written and the spoken word." Raymond Moley, a columnist and a man long active in American public life, writing an essay for the book *Politics USA,* had occasion to comment on the difference between written and oral style. He wrote, "I have heard many leaders in business and politics labor with a script written by someone who had missed entirely the difference between the composition of a speech and that of an article. People employed by business concerns, trade associations, and political leaders write mostly for reading rather than speaking." Both of these men sense the significant difference between these two styles. A lively oral style will add to clarity, but students should master it for still another reason. Recently I saw the result of a survey of the speechmaking habits of businessmen. Of the businessmen who replied to this survey, ninety percent of them said that when they have to make speeches, they read from a manuscript. This is a fact we must recognize and deal with. A major problem of the manuscript speech can be eliminated if the writer of that speech has learned to write it for the ear, rather than the eye.

We should make our students aware of, and encourage them to use, these characteristics of a lively conversational style:

1. Good oral style is more personal. It makes generous use of the first and second person pronouns. You will find a citation in the bibliography to an old but famous speech of information, Thomas Huxley's lecture, "The Method of Scientific Investigation." In the fourth paragraph of that speech, Huxley uses *you* or *your* over thirty times, *I* five times, and *we* twice.

2. Oral style uses contractions. It is characteristic of conversation, and of the rhythm of talk, that we use contractions. What teenager would say to his fellow, "Let us go get a hamburger"? On occasions of great formality, or on rare occasion when we want emphasis, we may indeed use the full form. But in lively, informal conversation, we say *you'll, we'll, let's, I'd,* and so forth.

3. Good oral style makes use of repetition. It uses not only the spaced repetitions of forecast, summary, and restatement, but also repetition within the sentence. In "The Story Behind The Atomic Bomb," a speech you will find listed in the bibliography, Gustavson makes use of repetition within the

sentence. Speaking of one of the important milestones on the way to making the bomb, he says the scientists discovered, "the uranium particle actually falls apart, goes to pieces, breaks up roughly in half . . ."

4. Oral style uses the rhetorical question. Rhetorical questions, well used, can be helpful both as transitions and as devices to keep audience interest. In the speech referred to above, Gustavson used thirty-one rhetorical questions.

5. Good oral style requires the use of simple words. Eloquence, whether written or spoken, has always preferred the simple word. In his book on Kennedy, Theodore Sorensen tells that President Kennedy asked him to find the "secret" of Lincoln's Gettysburg Address. "My conclusion," said Sorensen, "was that Lincoln never used a two or three syllable word where a one syllable word would do. . . ." Sorensen adds that Kennedy applied the same principle to his own inaugural. The speaker should prefer *lives* to *resides, get* to *acquire,* and *let me* to *allow me.* And in the important connectives, he should prefer *but* to *however, so* to *consequently,* and *so* to *therefore.*

The speech teacher should be as concerned as his colleague in English to teach other attributes of good style, whether oral or written. Employ the active voice, avoid jargon, and use adjectives and adverbs sparingly—these are injunctions we can keep regularly before our students.

I have already made my case for the full-sentence outline as an important device in teaching style. Before I return an outline to the student, I circle in red everything I consider a violation of good style. Unnecessary use of the passive voice, failure to use contractions, the use of *however,* are among the things that will be marked. My second technique is simply the collection of examples and illustrations, good and bad, that we find on every hand. I use many for discussion in class. For instance, I like the illustration Frances Perkins gives in her book, *The Roosevelt I Knew.* Telling of Roosevelt's instinct for the common word, she writes of working on a speech for President Roosevelt in which she had written of the Social Security System. She summarized with the sentence, "We are going to construct a more inclusive society." Madam Perkins reports that when that sentence came back to her from Roosevelt's hand it read, "We are going to make a country in which no one is left out." We can help our students to understand the difference between those two sentences. These same illustrations and examples make excellent in-class exercises. I pass out sheets of them, and together we rewrite them. Here is one example:

> The following paragraph comes from a speech dealing with the economic development of Latin America. Rewrite the paragraph, retaining all the facts and the meaning, but putting it in good oral style. "Integration" in this speech means integrating ("meshing" or "coordinating") the economics of Latin America.
>
> It should be stressed that 91.4 million dollars was invested in the Latin American manufacturing sector in 1962, this being the third consecutive year in which that sector exerted the most powerful attraction for foreign capital. This gradual change that has been observable in the composition of investment, with growing emphasis on the manufacturing sector and progressive disinterest in the traditional investment fields—mining, petroleum, and public utilities—is an indication of the potential participation of foreign private capital in the Latin American development process, particularly in the march toward integration, the initial phase of which we are now witnessing.

Here is a possible re-write of the paragraph:

> Note that in 1962 outsiders invested over 91 million dollars in Latin American manufacturing. And 1962 was the third year in a row that manufacturing attracted the most foreign investment. We are seeing a gradual change in the makeup of investment in Latin America. Manufacturing is becoming more attractive while the traditional investment fields—mining, petroleum, and public utilities —are losing favor. This change indicates the bright future for foreign private capital in Latin America's economic growth, and particularly in its growth toward integration.

The best examples will come from our own classrooms, but they can be supplemented from reading speeches in *Vital Speeches* and reports of speeches in the daily and periodical press.

We come finally to consider the forms of support for informative speaking. We have set as our goals for the informative speech *clarity, interest,* and *accuracy.* We have said and will say little of accuracy. Its importance is obvious, for inaccurate information is worse than none at all. Accuracy will come from careful preparation, from an ethical concern that is in essence a sense of responsibility, and from mastering the characteristics of clarity.

We must speak of interest in more detail. Again we are in the business of making meaningful distinctions, rather than setting up hard and fast categories. Good organization and lucid style will contribute to interest, just as carefully chosen forms of support will certainly contribute to clarity. And some forms of support, for instance, the analogy and the use of visual aids, may be used primarily for their contribution to clarity. For convenience, we have here chosen to treat forms of support for their value in contributing to interest.

Until interest is held, no information is communicated. A pertinent study appeared in the *Speech Teacher* for September, 1965. Professor Robert K. Tiemens reports there a study designed to find the relationship between several elements of speechmaking (for instance, voice and action, organization and choice of subject and of materials) and the amount of information actually retained by the listener. Most significant for us was Professor Tiemens' finding that the correlations between the experimental subjects' ratings for best speaker and the amount of material retained from the speech was a modest .373. The correlation between the experimental subjects' rating of the most interesting speech and the retention test score was an impressive .693. This was an admittedly limited study, but certainly this finding suggests that the choice of subject and material was the most important factor in achieving high retention test scores.

There is not space, nor is there need, to treat in detail the common forms of support. The illustration, example, testimony, visual aids, the analogy, and statistical material are familiar classifications to every teacher. We need them and we need them in variety from our students. These are the specifics that put life and interest into abstractions. All are important to all kinds of speaking, but since our concern here is with the informative speech, I would say a particular word about the analogy and about statistics.

The analogy is of particular importance in communicating information. As someone once said, "You can't tell anyone anything he doesn't already know." This was one man's way of saying what the psychologists have demonstrated, that we cannot assimilate a totally new idea. We must associate new ideas, new information, with the information and ideas we already have if the new material is to be meaningful. The analogy relates new material to the familiar and is therefore a major support for the informative speaker. We have referred before to Gustavson's speech, "The Story Behind The Atomic Bomb." Gustavson is a master of the analogy. When he discusses the difficult matter of separating uranium 235 from uranium 238, he draws an analogy to the farmer's cream separator and to putting "kids" on a race track. When he wants to explain the abstract matter of determining atomic weights, he does it by drawing an analogy to weighing people in order to find an average.

The second matter of which we need to say a special word is the handling of statistics and figures. We live in an age when anything expressed statistically is accorded special veneration. We need to make our students aware of the old saying that while figures don't lie, liars can figure. I know of no more delightful way to give them some intelligent skepticism than through Darrell Huff's delightful little book, *How to Lie with Statistics.* I would add two more special injunctions about using figures and statistics. In the first place, if we get too many of them, they are an "indigestible" form of support. Because in this technological age they are easy to come by, students are likely to load their speeches with figures and statistics. They quickly overwhelm us. We also need to tell students to round off figures, when accuracy is not of first concern. Why tell an audience that "Ninety-one point four million dollars" was invested in Latin America, when they will more easily remember "well over ninety-one million"? Finally, students must learn to translate figures that fall outside the experience of the audience. If you tell a five-year-old child that a mile is 5,280 feet, you have told him nothing. If you tell him a mile is as far as from home to the grocery store, you may have given him a piece of useful information.

We are surrounded today by very large figures (the national debt is three hundred billion dollars) and by very small figures (machine tools work to tolerances of one ten-thousandth of an inch). The speaker must make these figures meaningful for his audience, and the means he chooses will determine the effect he conveys. For instance, man has had a recorded history on this earth of about six thousand years. So stated it may seem very long, but I once heard an historian put it this way: The age of the earth is variously estimated, but it is probably at least five billion years old. If we were to express these five billion years in terms of a twenty-four hour clock, mankind has been on earth but seventeen seconds, and he has had a recorded history for one-tenth of a second.

I have mentioned previously the use of the technical plot in an outline as a technique for teaching the use of forms of support. You will find it illustrated in the outline at the end of this chapter. Requiring the student to label every form of support in his speech will make him conscious of using forms of support and it will serve another purpose. If he finds in his technical plot facts and figures repeated again and again, or perhaps testimony used repeatedly, he should recognize that he needs to use a greater variety of support, for these two forms are the least likely to maintain interest over a period of time. A second technique is the old but indispensable use of illustration and example. The two informative speeches in the bibliography, the one by Huxley, the other by Gustavson, are the two best I have found. I think the most important single element of teaching these devices of composition is to confront our students with the very best that is done, to invite them to study these, and to study these with them. They will come to understand the techniques and skills of good speech composition and to apply them to their own work.

ANALYSIS BLANK AND OUTLINE

Name_____Course_____Recitation Hour_____

Speech Subject   Frank Lloyd Wright, Nonconformist. Date_____

ANALYSIS

1. What general knowledge has the audience of my subject?
   The audience probably knows Frank Lloyd Wright was an architect famous for designing unusual buildings. They may be aware of some of his work, for instance, the Imperial Hotel in Tokyo, but they are probably not informed in any detail about his work.
2. What is their attitude toward it?
   I would not expect any prejudice, for or against. I hope to arouse curiosity and interest.
3. What is my specific purpose in speaking to this audience?
   I want to inform the audience about Wright's originality in architecture and make them aware of his personal idiosyncrasies.
4. How do I plan to get this response?
   By a clear organization, using only two mainheads, and supporting them with interesting specific information.

BIBLIOGRAPHY

(Include personal background, conversation, observation, reading)

Meyer, E. L. "America's Greatest Architect." *Scholastic* (Feb. 12, 1938) XXXII:21+
Unsigned. "F. L. Wright's Upside-down Flower Column Construction." *Science News Letter* (Oct. 9, 1937) XXXII:227+
Unsigned. "Ideas for the Future." *Saturday Review of Literature* (Sept. 17, 1938) XVIII:14–15
Unsigned. *Time* (October 25, 1937) XXX:68
Unsigned. *Time* (January 17, 1938) XXXI:29–32

Central idea: Frank Lloyd Wright was a nonconformist in his architecture and in his personal life.

ANALYSIS BLANK AND OUTLINE—(Cont.)

TECHNICAL PLOT

OUTLINE

Introduction

You may have heard the saying, "Man takes a positive hand in creation whenever he puts a building upon the earth beneath sun." If this is so, then Frank Lloyd Wright could claim a significant part in creation, for in his lifetime he put 270 buildings on earth.

TRANSITION

(I want to tell you something about this unusual man and his work, for both made an impact on our time.)

Body

I. Frank Lloyd Wright's architectural work was amazingly different and surprisingly sound.

  A. Wright's designs did not follow the conventional patterns of architecture.

EXAMPLE

    1. If you were to see the David Wright house in Arizona you might not recognize it as a house.

EXAMPLE

    2. He made the Unitarian Church in Madison, Wisconsin, a study in triangles.

  B. Although his designs were unusual, they met every test for structural soundness.

ILLUSTRATION

    1. The ceiling of one of the main office areas at the Johnson's Wax plant in Racine, Wisconsin, is supported by unique pillars.

      a. If you were to look at these pillars, you'd swear they couldn't support the weight of the ceiling.

        1.) The pillars are only eight inches wide at the bottom.

        2.) They are topped by discs twenty feet wide.

VISUAL AID

        3.) You can see on this drawing how fragile they look.

ANALYSIS BLANK AND OUTLINE—(Cont.)

      b. When tested, these pillars proved to be of great strength.
         1.) Other architects had declared that such pillars could not support more than two tons.
         2.) Wright arranged a test to answer these criticisms and was able to pile sixty tons on a single pillar.

ILLUSTRATION   2. The Imperial Hotel in Tokyo was the most famous example of Wright's functional genius.
      a. He set out to design a hotel that would be both earthquake proof and fireproof.
         1.) Rather than give it a solid foundation, he rested it on a layer of mud.
         2.) He demanded a large expensive pool be built near the hotel.
      b. When the earthquake of 1923 hit Tokyo, the Imperial Hotel survived unharmed.

TRANSITION   (You can see that Wright was not bound by conventional standards in his architectural work, but that was not the limit of his unconventionality)

II. Wright also rejected conventional standards of behavior in his personal life.
    A. He liked to level public insults.

EXAMPLE   1. He called the city of Pittsburgh "a centralization of obsolescence."

EXAMPLE   2. In Boston he said, "What Boston needs is 500 first class funerals."

    B. Wright was careless with money.

EXAMPLE   1. The final cost of the Johnson Wax building was 80% higher than the original estimates.

ANALYSIS BLANK AND OUTLINE—(Cont.)

EXAMPLE   2. Wright underestimated the cost of
                                        the Imperial Hotel by three and a
                                        half million yen.
EXAMPLE   3. He lost his own home to a bank,
                                        but got it back later with the help of
                                        friends.

Conclusion

A nonconformist in his work and in his
personal life, Frank Lloyd Wright left a rich
heritage to America and for his work we are
all in his debt.

BIBLIOGRAPHY

Flesch, Rudolph. *The Art of Plain Talk*. New York: Harpers, 1946. (Paperbound edition—New York: Collier, 1962.) An exceedingly readable discussion of the elements of plain talk. It includes Flesch's "readability" formula. Especially useful for its many illustrations and examples. You don't have to accept the idea of writing or speaking by a formula to profit from this book.

Gowers, Sir Ernest. *Plain Words, Their ABC*. New York: Knopf, 1957. (Paperbound edition—*Complete Plain Words*. Baltimore: Penguin Books.) Another excellent, readable discussion of the elements of a plain, lucid style. It, too, has a wealth of illustration and example.

Gustavson, Reuben G. "The Story Behind the Atomic Bomb," in W. N. Brigance, *Speech, Its Techniques and Disciplines in a Free Society*. New York: Appleton-Century-Crofts, 1952, pp. 563–574. Also in *Vital Speeches*, Vol. 11, 762–67, October 1, 1945. Gustavson, a chemist, was speaking to the Executives Club of Chicago. Although the speech is old, its material is not dated. It is the best example I know of presenting scientific information for laymen. In the elements of oral style and the use of forms of support for clarity and interest, it is superb. Incidentally, it is an excellent example of sound information providing the base for persuasion, for I believe the speaker's ultimate goal here is persuasion. A careful study of this speech will reward both teacher and student interested in exposition.

Huff, Darrell, and Irving Geis. *How to Lie With Statistics*. New York: Norton, 1954. This book, available in both hardbound and paper editions, is a delightful discussion of the way statistics can be manipulated to deceive and mislead. You don't have to be a statistician to enjoy and profit from this book.

Huxley, Thomas Henry. "The Method of Scientific Investigation," in *The Speaker's Resource Book,* 2d ed. Carroll C. Arnold *et al.,* editors. Chicago: Scott, Foresman, 1966, pp. 264–269. This is one of the classics of expository speaking. Like the Gustavson speech, it displays the techniques of presenting abstract ideas to lay audiences. This edition includes an analysis by Walter Blair.

Mills, Glen E. *Message Preparation, Analysis and Structure.* Indianapolis: Bobbs-Merrill Company, 1966. This paperback is an excellent discussion of speech preparation, from choosing the subject through making the outline. In brief compass, it gives the teacher a substantial background for teaching speech preparation.

Olbricht, Thomas H. *Informative Speaking.* Glenview, Illinois: Scott, Foresman, 1968. This paperback is the only book I know that deals exclusively with informative speaking. It provides theory as well as useful illustration.

Rogge, Edward, and James C. Ching. *Advanced Public Speaking.* New York: Holt, Rinehart and Winston, 1966. A college textbook with four excellent chapters (3, 12, 13, and 14) dealing with exposition. Particularly useful for its citations to research studies and findings.

On Teaching Persuasive Speaking

ROBERT G. GUNDERSON
Professor of Speech and Theatre
Indiana University

In addressing a temperance rally at Springfield on Washington's Birthday, 1842, Abraham Lincoln recalled an aphorism from *Poor Richard's Almanac* to instruct his fellow townsmen on the principles of effective communication: "When the conduct of men is designed to be influenced, *persuasion,* kind, unassuming persuasion should ever be adopted. It is an old and true maxim, that a 'drop of honey catches more flies than a gallon of gall.' So with men," Lincoln concluded. 'If you would win a man to your cause, first convince him that you are his sincere friend. Therein is a drop of honey that catches his heart, which, say what he will, is the great high road to his reason. . . . " Although Lincoln completed less than one year of formal education, his observation reflects an astute awareness of motivational psychology and of the principles that govern behavior.

As a form of applied psychology, persuasion suffers from concepts and terminology contaminated by discarded assumptions and obsolete theories. Oversimplifications of the past now seem almost as naïve as the pronouncement of the eighteenth-century psychologist who declared that "the brain secretes thought as the liver secretes bile." Faculty psychologists once divided man's psyche into faculties of sense, passion, will, reason, and imagination. Reflecting these classifications, courses in English composition and speech once were divided into units on description (to stimulate the senses), exposition (to enlighten the reason), narration (to excite the imagination), argumentation (to convince the will), and persuasion (to arouse the passions). Although faculty psychology has long since been outmoded, some of the distinctions that it initiated still persist. In applying a psychology that assumed a duality of mind and body, for example, rhetoricians appropriately distinguished argumentation from persuasion. Argumentation exploited logic in appealing to the will in order to influence belief; persuasion exploited pathos to excite emotion in order to promote action. Contemporary rhetoricians now look upon argumentation and persuasion as part of an integrated process influencing behavior. At least for intelligent listeners, persuasion is not effective if it is illogical, and argumentation is not convincing if it fails to arouse emotion and produce response.

Definition of Persuasion

Persuasion is a linguistic trick or treat—oral bribery or blackmail; or, more formally, it is the art of influencing behavior by verbal motivational appeals. Some may argue that the words *oral* and *verbal* unnecessarily limit the concept of persuasion. Action, gesture, and costume (or lack thereof) are becoming increasingly popular as means of dramatizing dissent, and few would deny the intensity, and sometimes the effectiveness, of these nonverbal means of influencing behavior. Traditionally, however, the academic study of persuasion has been characterized by its concern for the manipulation of verbal symbols. The more overt the action or the gesture, the more persuasion degenerates into coercion or seduction.

Even when limited to verbal appeals, persuasion is but a step removed from an assault upon an individual's sovereignty. It takes a very agile rhetorician to identify an example of persuasion that does not threaten evil or promise reward. The teacher uses pass or fail; the preacher promises heaven or hell; the advertiser dramatizes social success or ostracism. The methods may be more sophisticated, but they are not substantially different from those of the animal trainer who uses the carrot or the stick. Mental coercion, even when masked in the engaging phrase of Edward L. Bernays, "the engineering of consent," is an assault upon personality.

Allied terms sometimes can hardly be distinguished; rhetoric, propaganda, and education have been used interchangeably with persuasion. Aristotle defined rhetoric as "the faculty of discovering in a particular case all the available means of persuasion." Others have described rhetoric as the strategy of oral and written discourse, or as applied logic. In Archbishop Richard Whatley's lexicon, logic was "the science and the art of reasoning." To George Campbell, it was "the art of fighting with words about words." Propaganda has inherited a sinister connotation, but Harold D. Lasswell's popular definition provides little, if any, differentiation from persuasion: "The manipulation of words or word substitutes to modify attitudes on controversial issues." What might be classified in one country as propaganda might pass as education in another. Both use oral and written symbols to influence behavior, though as A. F. Wilenden has said, education starts with a problem; propaganda with a solution.

If persuasion must influence behavior, some overt action must result, thus raising troublesome questions about attitude and opinion, evanescent concepts that constitute the will-o'-the-wisps of contemporary social psychology. Attitude has been defined as a readiness or predisposition to act, or more recently, as "a cluster of evaluative or approach-avoidance behavior."[1] Opinion has been defined as an expressed or verbalized attitude. If problems of definition and of measuring the effects of persuasive appeals still present formidable obstacles to students of communication, the reasons can be found in the complicated process of forming opinions. "Many of our deepest opinions," says Elmo Roper in an inspired analogy, "are probably formed somewhat as a coral reef grows: by so many billions of interactions between wave and land, between solution and solid, that no one constellation of facts can ever satisfactorily account for . . . [them]."

Theories of Persuasion

Conflicting theories not only make definition difficult but also contribute to conflicting interpretations of the persuasive process. Each school of psychology has its matching formula for persuasion. In applying the psychology of William James, James A. Winans concluded that persuasion was the process of capturing and maintaining "fair, favorable, or undivided attention to propositions."[2] Modern advertisers quite clearly have embraced this view of influencing behavior, for they attempt to saturate listeners or readers with their appeals, using a seemingly endless repetition in order to maintain undivided attention to their commercial propositions. In applying Pavlov's behavioristic principles, the Chinese Communists have used the concept of attention in their brainwashing, a process that maintains the subjects' undivided attention to prescribed dogma—excluding all other appeals.

Charles H. Woolbert[3] and, later, William Norwood Brigance[4] applied motivational psychology to persuasion. Although recognizing the important role of attention, Brigance emphasized desire not only as a means of capturing and maintaining attention but also as a means of determining action. His steps in the persuasive process provide the student with a clear, functional pattern for constructing a persuasive speech: Get attention; arouse desire; produce action. The behavioristic stress upon results is consistent with the realistic goals of contemporary persuaders in an acquisitive society.

Still more recent theories of persuasion have been applications of various tension-reduction theories of behavior: Theodore H. Newcomb's "strain for symmetry" theory, Leon Festinger's "cognitive dissonance" theory, and Charles Osgood and Percy Tannenbaum's "congruity" theory. Formulas for speechmaking that follow a need-solution pattern antedate these theories, but nevertheless may be considered as patterns based upon tension-reduction psychology. The formula using John Dewey's steps in the thinking process[5] provides a rational and ethical structure for a tension-reducing persuasive discourse: "(1) locating and defining the problem; (2) exploring the problem; (3) examining suggested solutions;

(4) choosing the best solution; and (5) securing acceptance of the selected solution." Another successful formula based upon tension-reduction theory is the "motivated sequence": (1) get attention; (2) establish a need; (3) demonstrate a way to satisfy the need; (4) visualize the results; and (5) secure action.[6] The most recent application of tension-reduction theory emphasizes the dynamic interaction of "persuader, persuadee, and the persuasive message" by listing the phases in the process in gerundial form: "Receiving, Focusing, Associating, and Resolving."[7]

The Persuasive Process

Although experimental psychologists may be abandoning the familiar terms *attention* and *motivation,* persuaders dare not ignore Winan's injunction to command "undivided attention," nor Brigance's to arouse a response. In the popular mind, attention is closely related to concentration, an attribute of the high school sophomore that enables him to study algebra to the tune of "Honky-Tonk Woman" or its contemporary equivalent. One's sensory apparatus must focus selectively upon specific stimuli among the many that assault him. Herein lies a challenge to contending persuaders. Principles of intensity, change, contrast, and novelty are ingeniously employed to engage the public eye and ear. Bizarre attire, obscene gesture, ancient Anglo-Saxon words, and unexpected behavior serve those who demand a hearing. Although shock techniques may be counterproductive, those who exploit them testify to the urgency of getting attention.

In a useful model emphasizing nonverbal communication, Gerald R. Miller presents a diagram that helps to clarify the relationships among verbal, physical, and vocal stimuli.[8] Miller's Receiver-Decoder, for example, might quite understandably focus attention upon the annoying physical and vocal stimuli of the dissident persuader and consequently ignore the substantive content of his message.

Teachers of English and speech will no doubt find it congenial to concentrate their teaching upon verbal means of maintaining attention. The "factors of interest" identified by A. E. Phillips[9] provide a useful listing for the student: the vital, the unusual, the uncertain, the similar, the antagonistic, the animate, and the concrete. Although Phillips' examples may be dated ("What shop window," he asks, "gathers the crowd? That with the moving top—the running engine, the climbing monkey."), teachers can assign students to translate his examples into the contemporary idiom. Each student can, for example, prepare an introduction using a different factor of interest. Or students can be challenged to identify additional factors that Phillips may have overlooked.

The strategy of maintaining attention is often dependent upon the right word, for as Mark Twain observed, "the difference between the right word and the almost right word is the difference between lightning and the lightning bug." Teachers often can demonstrate great success in enhancing verbal facility, but achieving a lucid style requires concentration upon simplicity and concrete detail. In praising a direct and unembellished style, Thoreau concluded that "the art of composition is as simple as the discharge of a bullet from a rifle. . . . "

Understanding the motivation—the needs, wants, and desires—of listeners is more complex than Thoreau's prescription for an effective style. "The passions are the only orators who always convince," observed La Rochefoucauld in his *Maxims*. "They have a kind of natural art with infallible rules; and the most untutored man with passion is more persuasive than the most eloquent without." Psychology textbooks once listed as many as one hundred passions or motives to which a persuader might appeal, ranging from self-preservation to aesthetic gratification, but current fashion is to dismiss such lists as simplistic. The persuader would do better to survey specific listener responses, just as advertisers survey the market practices of customers. Hoping to appeal to a sense of fairness and justice, Upton Sinclair, in *The Jungle*, described the long hours and intolerable working conditions in the meat-packing industry. His readers surprised him by becoming outraged, not at the exploitation of the workers, but at the unsanitary hazard to their own health. "I aimed at America's heart," he was reported to have said, "and I hit it in the stomach."

Verbal intimidation and appeals to fear have disadvantages that transcend inherent ethical considerations.[10] The disadvantage is particularly evident when the fear-arousing stimulus prompts "defensive avoidance," a reaction that leads listeners to conclude that "it won't happen to me." Positive goals and positive rewards are more consistent with modern pedagogy as well as with commendable ethics.

The successful persuader appeals to his listeners with their reasons and motivations. In developing this concept of *identification,* Kenneth Burke[11] asserts that "men have common sensations, concepts, images, ideas, [and] attitudes that make them *consubstantial.*" The persuader identifies his ways with those of his listeners. "True," Burke says, "the rhetorician may have to change an audience's opinion in one respect; but he can succeed only insofar as he yields to that audience's opinions in other respects." A somewhat similar concept, though one less adequately developed, "The Yes-Response Technique," is described by Harry A. Overstreet.[12] Overstreet suggests that speakers begin by establishing a common ground of agreement, introducing no possible element of conflict until the listener is in the habit of nodding his assent.

If motivation is designed to arouse, sustain, and direct action, the persuader must achieve some kind of overt response. Too often persuaders content themselves with vague, poorly defined statements of what response is expected from listeners. Sometimes they are advised merely "to think about the problem." Salesmen risk starvation when they fail to motivate the desired sale to customers, but speakers who fail are often unaware of the extent of their failure. Persuaders should seek a commitment of some sort, for once an individual publicly identifies himself with a proposition, he is more likely to adhere to it. Thus effective evangelists, politicians, and teachers—past and present—have insisted upon a public testimonial, a raised hand, a postcard to a congressman, or a signed pledge or petition.

Suggestion

Any discussion of persuasion should include an analysis of audience psychology and of the role of suggestion in influencing behavior. A speaker stimulates his listeners; they stimulate one another (social facilitation); and in turn they stimulate the speaker (circular response). As a result of this interaction, audiences achieve varying degrees of unity or polarization (an analogy to magnetism), that enhance the effectiveness of the speaker's suggestion. Persuaders from Demosthenes to Billy Graham have recognized these relationships and have exploited strategies to gain assent by means of suggestion, a term that eludes easy definition. Social psychologist Kimball Young described it as "a phase in anticipatory activity" that "short circuits logical analysis, inhibits critical restraint, and leads at once to the desired conclusion."

Consumers of persuasion should of course be made aware of these subtle ways of manipulating consent. Since suggestion works most effectively at the margins of attention, it can trick unwary intellectuals as well as the ignorant and uninformed. Even the most intelligent listener can be duped by suggestion that relies upon habitual behavior patterns—routine situations in which it is more comfortable to say *yes* than *no*. When, for example, the filling station attendant says, 'Fill 'er up?" the absentminded professor may unthinkingly nod assent even though he may not have enough cash in hand to pay for a full twenty-five gallon tank. But this kind of vulnerability is not limited to the absentminded. That great prototype of American statesmanship, Warren G. Harding, presumably could not say *no*. As his father confessed, "It's a good thing Warren wasn't born a girl; she'd been in trouble all the time."

Like its extreme manifestation, hypnotism, suggestion requires faith. Without confidence in the authority of the persuader, listeners often reject suggestion. Thus persuaders take special pains to increase their prestige or ethical appeal. Symbolic dress and conventional insignia provide means of dramatizing authority: robes and powdered wigs for judges; stars for generals, bars for lieutenants, stripes for sergeants; badges for boy scouts; academic regalia for professors; letter sweaters for athletic heroes. A raised platform, a speaking stand, a microphone—each gives the speaker an added element of authority. A laudatory introduction and introductory applause further increase his ethical appeal. In short, anything that increases faith in a speaker increases his ability to exploit suggestion. Additional conditions that facilitate suggestion can be listed:

Audience setting: (1) impressive surroundings; (2) unified crowd; (3) familiar ritual; (4) applauding, group singing, responsive reading, mass cheering; (5) tension, fear, excitement.

Speaker-audience relationship: (1) ignorant, uncritical listeners; (2) forceful, authoritative speaker; (3) polarization.

Speech: (1) repetition; (2) intensity of the message; (3) vivid, metaphorical phrasing.

Delivery: (1) forceful voice (intensity enhances suggestibility); (2) vigorous, well-motivated action and gestures; (3) authoritative manner; (4) proper timing.

Proof in Persuasion

Strategies of audience psychology, like suggestion, are of course shoddy substitutes for proof; but proof in persuasion should be presented in an impelling idiom: in fables, parables, analogies, and examples. "For," said Francis Bacon, "as hieroglyphics came before letters, so parables came before arguments. And even now if any one wish to let new light on any subject into men's minds, and that without offence or harshness, he must still go the same way and call in the aid of similitudes." The great persuaders—those who have changed the course of history—have indeed demonstrated genius at translating complicated concepts into clearly stated concrete examples. Christ spoke in parables; Lincoln used frontier stories.

FABLES

Significantly, among Lincoln's limited reading was Aesop's *Fables*, a collection of animal tales, each with a "moral" or generalization. Aesop, a Greek slave, told short fables to dramatize his ideas to Croesus, King of Lydia. A contemporary of Solon and of the seven wise men of Greece in the sixth century B.C., Aesop gained fame as a riddle-lover and rhetorician. Aristotle cites him in *The Rhetoric* for the story of the fox and the ticks, and many of his "morals" are implicit in our thinking—subtle premises of our Western heritage: "Appearances are deceptive" from "The Wolf in

Sheep's Clothing"; "Prepare for the days of necessity" from "The Ant and the Grasshopper"; "People often grudge others what they cannot enjoy themselves" from "The Dog in the Manger"; "Little friends may prove great friends" from "The Lion and the Mouse"; "The grapes are sour" from "The Fox and the Grapes"; "The boy who called 'Wolf, Wolf!' " from "The Shepherd's Boy."

The fable has a unique virtue in repressive societies. Disguised as an animal tale, it can project ideas that otherwise might be suppressed. Some of Aesop's less well known fables provide eloquent examples of folk protest: "Any excuse will serve a tyrant" from "The Wolf and the Lamb"; "Self-conceit may lead to self-destruction" from "The Frog and the Ox"; "You will only injure yourself if you take note of despicable enemies" from "The Bald Man and the Fly"; "It is easy to be brave from a safe distance" from "The Wolf and the Kid."

In his *Fables for Our Time,* James Thurber has demonstrated the contemporary effectiveness of this form of persuasive proof, and classroom persuaders can profit from exercises that attempt to bring Aesop up to date. Using the fable in persuasion can provide a link betwen speechmaking and literature, for as Aristotle said in *The Rhetoric,* facility in the use of fables "comes from literary training."

ANALOGY

Fables are a specialized form of analogy—a form of proof that can be compared to the algebraic ratio a is to b as c is to d. Lincoln's analogy before the presidential election of 1864, "Don't change horses in the middle of a stream," influenced voter behavior because in a predominantly rural society people apparently believed that the hazards of changing presidents in the middle of a war were comparable to the hazards of changing horses in mid-stream. When the admission of Missouri raised the question of the extension of slavery in 1819, Thomas Jefferson dramatized the alarming nature of the problem by comparing it to "a firebell in the night."

The persuasiveness and the validity of an analogy are dependent upon the similarity of the items compared. Jefferson's firebell projected the proper emotional tone, for example, but it was an understatement when tested against the reality of over six-hundred thousand killed in a civil war. Conventional hyperbole sometimes fails to communicate the horror of reality, as when an American observer of an atomic blast exclaimed, "That's dynamite!"

Henry Clay used analogy in 1816 after he voted to increase the pay of members of Congress from six dollars a day during sessions to fifteen hundred dollars a year. Many of his constituents were upset by this extravagance, and one old hunter declared his intention to vote against him. "My friend," said Clay, "have you a good rifle?" "Yes." "Did it ever flash?" "Yes, but only once." "What did you do . . . throw it away?" "No, I picked the flint, tried it again, and brought down the game." "Well," said Mr. Clay, "I have flashed only once—on this compensation bill—and are you going to throw me away?" "No," cried the Hunter. "No, Mr. Clay. I will pick the flint and try you again."

In urging college students to demand a significant role in educational decision-making, Jerry Farber used an extended analogy of "the student as nigger." "Students are niggers," he asserted. "When you get that straight, our schools begin to make sense." The persuasive effectiveness of Farber's proof is dependent upon whether the personal experiences of his listeners coincide with his examples, each of which enforces his basic analogy:

> At Cal State L.A., where I teach [English], the students have separate and unequal dining facilities. If I take them into the faculty dining room, my colleagues get uncomfortable, as though there were a bad smell. If I eat in the student cafeteria, I become known as the educational equivalent of a niggerlover. In at least one building there are even rest rooms which students may not use. At Cal State, also, there is an unwritten law barring student-faculty lovemaking. Fortunately, this anti-miscegenation law, like its Southern counter-part, is not 100 percent effective.
>
> Students at Cal State are politically disenfranchised. They are in an academic Lowndes County. . . . The students are, it is true, allowed to have a toy government of their own. It is a government run for the most part by Uncle Toms and concerned primarily with trivia. . . .

EXAMPLES AND STATISTICS

The personal experience of the persuader—or that of friends or prominent public figures—gives credibility to persuasion. A winner of a national oratorical contest chose a topic on which he could testify as an expert—hemophilia, a disease that later caused his death. Actor William Talman described his family against a backdrop of television pictures of his home. His one-minute persuasive appeal against smoking was voted "the highest rated public service announcement of 1968." "You know I didn't really mind losing those courtroom battles," said the district attorney on the "Perry Mason" series, "but I'm in a battle right now I don't want to lose at all because, if I lose it, it means losing my wife and those kids you just met. I've got lung cancer. So take some advice about smoking and losing from someone who's been doing both for years. If you haven't smoked—don't start. If you do smoke—quit. Don't be a loser."

When urged to use examples from their experience, students usually complain, "But nothing has happened to me!" Those who have presented this complaint have included a paratrooper who had bailed out over occupied France during World War II, a missionary's son who had lived on Easter Island in the Mid-Pacific, and a national scholarship winner with a hobby of astrophysics. Teachers should encourage students to talk on subjects that make a difference to them—those on which they feel strongly and about which they are qualified to give personal testimony and example. As consumers of education, television, automobiles, cosmetics, commercialized entertainment, syndicated news, and ready-to-wear fashions, they have more experience than they realize. As potential Ralph Naders, they can cite examples, survey friends, interview authorities, and explore statistical yearbooks.

Facts, figures, statistics, and testimony are the raw materials of persuasion, the *sine qua non* of responsible discourse. Contrary to popular stereotype, relevant facts are not boring. Vagueness, unintelligibility, and lack of relevance are the things that are boring. Statistics must be made meaningful by comparison. The exact number of bombs dropped upon Vietnam means less than a comparison of the number dropped in Vietnam between 1965 and 1970 and the number dropped in Europe between 1941 and 1945. There is a certain intrinsic interest in census figures of 1800 listing Philadelphia as the largest city in the United States with 70,000, New York second with 60,000, and Boston third with only 24,000. The information is enhanced by contrast. Every city in the United States was smaller in 1800 than Anderson or Muncie, Indiana, today. Boston was smaller than Columbus, Indiana, and not much larger than Hobart.

Organization—A One-Point Paradigm

In addition to the formulas for persuasion listed above (from Winans, Brigance, Ewbank and Auer, Monroe, and Scheidel), a one-point paradigm based upon Kenneth Burke's concept of "representative anecdote"[13] can simplify the problem of structuring a persuasive message: (1) an extended representative example (like Talman's); (2) statistics to show that the example is typical and valid (Talman was one of 64,400 to die of lung cancer during 1968; *World Almanac*, 1970); (3) an impelling final statement ("If you haven't smoked—don't start. If you do smoke—quit. Don't be a loser.").

In this one-point formula, the anecdote or narrative organizes the message, giving clarity and vigor. Although effective fables, analogies, and examples are hard to find, they are easy to remember both for the listener and for the speaker. By thus dramatizing his argument for an audience, the speaker helps to solve a persistent problem in his delivery—undue reliance upon notes or manuscript. For longer speeches, the persuader may build each of his points around a representative anecdote. In his "Acres of Diamonds," for example, Russell H. Conwell used seventeen extended examples, each supporting the rather hackneyed idea that success can be found in your own back yard.

A weakness of the one-point paradigm is inherent in its simplicity. Complicated topics will require a more complicated structure. The antismoking appeal, for example, relies on the assumption that listeners are already convinced of the cause-and-effect relationship between smoking and cancer. To demonstrate this relationship persuasively no doubt would require a different form of organization.

Since Aristotle, rhetoricians have speculated upon the effectiveness of climactic and anticlimactic order. Some have favored putting the strongest argument first; others have favored putting the strongest argument last. After generations of controversy and research, there is still no conclusive answer. Gary Cronkhite lucidly summarizes the contending evidence and concludes that *"the strongest arguments should be placed first or last* rather than in the middle of the message."[14] A weekend or two of tournament debating should convince even the most indifferent judge that high school persuaders often have acquired only the superficial manifestations of organizational structure. Principles of suspense and climax, of imagery and analogy, and of representative examples should be applied in an effort to transcend the tedium of insensitive "point one-two-three" thinking.

Persuasive Phrasing

Joseph Conrad may have exaggerated when he said that "he who wants to persuade should put his trust not in the right argument, but in the right word." The persuader must find both the motivated argument *and* the right word. Events presumably speak for themselves, but they speak in various tongues. Conflicting loyalties require verbal rationalization: "War of the Rebellion" or "War for Southern Independence"? "Slave State" or "People's Democracy"? "Law and order" or "police state"? Whether an event is described as a "freedom march" or as a "subversive uprising" makes a persuasive difference.

Textbook writers have provided lists of adjectives to describe effective phrasing; the lists read like the Boy Scout Laws: lucid, precise, specific, economical, vivid, animated, energetic. Some even say graceful, but this surely must be an outmoded, Victorian attribute of style. To these lists the word *unexpected* should be added. Listeners need more surprises; the expected puts them to sleep. And, perhaps above all, phrasing should be appropriate. Alexander Pope summarizes essential characteristics of style in five compact lines:

> But true *Expression* like th' unchanging *Sun,*
> *Clears,* and *improves* what e'er it shines upon,
> It *gilds* all Objects, but it *alters* none.
> Expression is the *Dress* of *Thought,* and still
> Appears more *decent* as more *suitable.* . . .
> ("Essay on Criticism," lines 315–319)

Rhetorical devices contribute vividness and energy to persuasion. When confronted with the assignment of saying something memorable when stepping upon the moon, Neil Armstrong used antithesis: "That's one small step for [a] man—one giant leap for mankind." Edwin Aldrin contrived an oxymoron: "magnificent desolation." When John Glenn made America's first flight around the earth, John F. Kennedy acknowledged the event with an analogy: "This is the new ocean and the United States must sail on it." When asked if he were being discriminated against at the Democratic Convention of 1968, Eugene McCarthy replied with an analogy: "We haven't been frozen out, but there's an awful lot of ice on our edge of the pond." When trying to persuade his frontier companions to contribute their fair share to a disagreeable task, Abraham Lincoln found an analogy: "Let each man skin his own skunk." The stock market manipulator, Jim Fisk, used a similar analogy to tell his Wall Street colleagues what to do on Black Friday in 1869: "Let each man carry his own corpse." When initiating her assaults upon pre-prohibition saloonkeepers, Carry Nation used personification: "I'll make Hell howl."

The Persuader's Manner

David Starr Jordan once observed that "no man can shout and at the same time tell the truth." Although this may be hyperbole, shouting establishes a poor atmosphere for persuasion. Benjamin Franklin tells how he consciously set about to enhance his effectiveness by avoiding "all direct contradictions of the sentiments of others and all over-positive assertions of my own." When someone "asserted something" that he thought to be in error, Franklin denied himself "the pleasure of contradicting him abruptly, and showing immediately some absurdity in his proposition." He soon found the advantage in his changed behavior: "The conversations I engaged in went more pleasantly. The modest way in which I proposed my opinions procured them a readier reception and less contradiction. I had less mortification when I was found in the wrong, and I more easily prevailed upon others to give up their mistakes and join me when I happened to be right." When he founded the Junto Club in Philadelphia, the charter provided that debate was to be conducted in the sincere spirit of inquiry after truth, and "all expressions of positiveness in opinions, or direct contradiction, were after some time made contraband, and prohibited under small pecuniary penalties." Contentious people, Franklin later concluded, "get the victory sometimes, but they never get good will, which would be more use to them."

The Listener's Responsibility

Listeners should be alert critics, not amiable sponges. Units on evidence and reasoning[15] should alert consumers of persuasion to the hazards of faulty analogy, evidence, and reasoning. Persuasive speeches should be followed by a meet-the-press type of confrontation. Persuaders should be cross-examined. The speech class is thus not a word-play land of adolescent show-and-tell, but a lively intellectual testing ground. The student persuader should be expected to find representative examples; to select, organize, and phrase evidence and argument; and then be prepared to refute the strongest contrary position. In describing the job of the schools, President Nathan M. Pusey of Harvard has outlined objectives that are appropriate for teaching persuasion: "to educate free, independent, and vigorous minds, capable of analyzing events, of exercising judgment, of distinguishing facts from propaganda, and truth from half-truth and lies."

NOTES

1. Gary Cronkhite, *Persuasion, Speech and Behavioral Change.* Indianapolis: Bobbs-Merrill, 1969, p. 12.

2. James A. Winans, *Public Speaking.* New York: Century, 1921, p. 194.

3. Charles H. Woolbert, in *Quarterly Journal of Speech*, Vol. 5, 12 ff., 101 ff., 212 ff.
4. William Norwood Brigance, in *Quarterly Journal of Speech*, Vol. 17, 329 ff.; Vol. 21, 19 ff.
5. Henry L. Ewbank and J. Jeffrey Auer, *Discussion and Debate: Tools of Democracy*. New York: Appleton-Century-Crofts, 1941, p. 20.
6. Allan H. Monroe, *Principles and Types of Speech*. New York: Scott, Foresman, 1935.
7. Thomas M. Scheidel, *Persuasive Speaking*. Glenview, Illinois: Scott, Foresman, 1967, p. 60 ff.
8. Gerald R. Miller, *Speech Communication, A Behavioral Approach*. Indianapolis: Bobbs-Merrill, 1966, pp. 72–75.
9. A. E. Phillips, *Effective Speaking*. Chicago: Newton, 1908, pp. 63–78.
10. Cronkhite, *Persuasion*, pp. 178–186.
11. Kenneth Burke, *A Rhetoric of Motives*. Berkeley: University of California Press, 1969, p. 20 ff.
12. Harry A. Overstreet, *Influencing Human Behavior*. New York: Norton, 1925, pp. 16–19.
13. Kenneth Burke, *A Grammar of Motives*. Berkeley: University of California Press, 1969. p. 59 ff.
14. Cronkite, *Persuasion*. pp. 191–198.
15. Edward Jenkinson, ed., *Teacher's Guide to High School Speech*. Indianapolis: Indiana State Department of Public Instruction, 1966, pp. 92–111. This volume is available only from the Speech Communication Association, Statler Hilton Hotel, New York, New York 10001.

REFERENCES

Auer, J. Jeffery. *The Rhetoric of Our Times*. New York: Appleton-Century-Crofts, 1969. See especially Chapter 23, "The Persuasive Speaker and His Audience," for a succinct and illuminating analysis.
Cronkhite, Gary. *Persuasion, Speech and Behavioral Change*. Indianapolis: Bobbs-Merrill, 1969. An impressive survey of what current experimental research has concluded about the persuasive process.
Johannesen, Richard L. *Ethics and Persuasion*. New York: Random House, 1967. Thirteen essays with differing points of view on the "ethical responsibilities of a persuader in contemporary American Society."
Miller, Gerald R. *Speech Communication, A Behavioral Approach*. Indianapolis: Bobbs-Merrill, 1966. An informed discussion of the communication process with a clear explanation of models of speech communication.

Minnick, Wayne C. *The Art of Persuasion,* 2d ed. Boston: Houghton Mifflin, 1968. A rhetoric of persuasion "built on non-Aristotelian premises."

Scheidel, Thomas M. *Persuasive Speaking.* Glenview, Illinois: Scott, Foresman, 1967. An explanation of the persuasive process and an analysis of the elements in the process. Emphasis is upon the dynamics of persuasion.

On Teaching Parliamentary Procedure

J. CALVIN CALLAGHAN
Professor of Speech
The University of North
Carolina at Chapel Hill

Perhaps the first question to be posed at the outset of a course in parliamentary procedure is whether this subject is to be examined at all. As soon as the bell ceases to toll, the teacher should invite a student to move "that we study parliamentary procedure." After a second has been made, another student should move "to amend this motion by adding the words 'accepting its prerequisite democratic principles and processes.'" Ample debate on the amendment should ensue, with no cloture until argument pro and con is exhausted. Then a vote. If this amendment is defeated, the motion itself is surely lost, and the class should turn to some less controversial facet of speech instruction.

Ordinarily, I should vote for a more inductive approach: study the rules, and *from* them infer the postulates that undergird. The brighter students will prefer the excitement of such self-detection. Or perhaps generic tenets should both alpha and omega be. But first principles first is demanded by the days in which we live.

This *obiter dictum* is penned in the spring of 1970, when the fashionable criterion for all educational endeavor is "relevance."

81

Probably no object of study may be *less* "relevant" today than deliberation by due process.

Many young men and young women in our culture honestly hold that a law need not, ought not, be obeyed if it is "unjust"—unjust, moreover, in the individual judgment of each person contemplating that law. It exists to be violated, knowingly, intentionally—in conscience and with penalty paid, some concede; with impunity, according to others.

Yet suppose in a business session a member were to rise and declare: "The motion we just passed to close debate is not a just motion. It contravenes a minority 'civil' right; it permits a majority to oppress. I voted against it. I'm not going to sanction it. I'm going to keep on talking." Or: "Those who just voted to overrule the decision of the Chair are in patent error. Moreover, their motives are suspect. I demand that we continue as our president has decreed." Such a meeting can only adjourn: for its process is that of anarchy, and proceeding parliamentarily is precisely an attempt to preclude anarchy. At some point, though with safeguards, a minority must bow to the will of the majority. Conflict, yes—but under control.

"Law and order" is often today an obscenity, and in the context in which some people sometimes speak it, it merits opprobrium. But parliamentary procedure is founded on—if you will pardon the distinction—parliamentary "law." *In,* rather than *out of,* "order" is a prime requisite, as well as a phrase. And not all parliamentary tactics incorporate "justice": witness the killing of a resolution, without debate, through adulteration of the motion to table; or even foreclosing vote on a matter if two-thirds "object to consideration." Seminal in the parliamentary process is a hoary Anglo-Saxon habit: we obey a law until we can persuade a majority of our fellows to amend or rescind it. As Thomas Jefferson contended in his *Manual,* quoting, though not verbatim, John Hatsell:

> And whether these forms be in all cases the most rational or not, is really not of so great importance. It is much more material that there should be a rule to go by, than what that rule is; that there may be a uniformity of proceedings in business, not subject to . . . caprice . . . or captiousness.

Before any student agrees to study procedure, he must freely consent to this axiom.

Procedure prescribes, as its method of problem-solving, discussion, debate, information, and persuasion. It manages a system for minds that are and remain open, until closed by decision. Participants welcome new evidence and novel inferences; quietly, objectively they contemplate "wrong" ideas *before* deeming them wrong. They stand willing and able to hear rival points of view, for they sense that the right freely to speak implies a corollary duty to listen efficiently. Yet most schools today have registered some students who—with integrity—find this frame of reference outmoded, its genesis in an "establishment" dangerously dilatory and unconcerned. Decisions are more morally reached viscerally, through passion and pressure, through force psychological, even physical. Solving social problems and effecting improvements by "going through the motions" is an anachronism, out of tune with our times. In a society dedicated to "the death of authority," parliamentary procedure cannot live, nor indeed need it even be learned.

I exaggerate, of course—though not facetiously. The cliché has it that we teach students, not subjects. The indirect object of the verb *to teach*, the youth learning, is the major concern of us all. So with him we begin. Does he prejudge study of our parliamentary heritage "irrelevant," a waste of his time? If so, I don't think I should compel him to resist it, and by resistance vanquish. I should wait until someday he somehow comes to appreciate the *product* of democracy: then he will profit from mastering its *process*.

But in order initially to vote whether to contemn or commend the bedrock doctrines which parliamentary law invigorates, a class must first ferret out what these self-evident truths are. If consequently it opts to study the rules, it may *de*ductively connect each particular application to these general premises.

Like the field of speech itself, which is in part a science and in part an art, parliamentary procedure embraces both substance and skill. Viable instruction in it comprises mastery of content-knowledge, plus practice in participating and presiding. I eagerly second almost anything anyone might aver about the value of learning by doing. If I had fully adequate *time*, which curricula never seem to provide, I should stress substance and skill equally. Probably some items (precedence of motions, for example) can be better learned through drill. But if a choice must be made, I would sacrifice skill for substance.

To the unit of study in procedure should be allotted an irreducible minimum of twenty class periods, preferably thirty. If a teacher can contrive more, drills may be conducted, maybe a few "games" played. Students active in school, church, or community life, however, can procure their "practice" in a setting more relevant than the classroom. Others may form an informal club, designed solely for parliamentary recreation. "Where the action is" can best be extracurricular, realistic rather than role-played. Classtime priorities in this unit should be:

first: philosophy and concepts and attitudes and principles and methods in parliamentary law;
second: the motions—
           (a) major (for example, all subsidiary motions)
           and if time permits,
           (b) minor (for example, call for the orders of the day,
           or opening and closing of polls);
third: drills.

If rationales and rules be known, the rest of one's life is a laboratory for learning by doing.

Students undoubtedly have a lot of fun during a parliamentary drill, and I have no qualms whatsoever about letting learning be "a fun thing." Yet students must perceive procedure in its context, not as a frolic, but as a serviceable democratic-decision tool which groups have at their command—and should employ more adeptly, more circumspectly than sometimes they do. Unless students discern the hierarchy of motions as a die with which a congress or council or club casts its collective will—whether the magnitude of the outcome be war or peace, sale or purchase of property, baked-goods sale or dance—unless students recognize the pertinence of this discipline to their vocational and avocational life, they do not deserve its dividend of fun.

Procedure should not be a course *per se,* rather a unit integral in a larger, broader object of scrutiny. A student should approach it not as an entity or end in itself, but as ancillary always, apposite at a particular stage of the process by which human beings in groups, cooperatively rather than competitively, work out solutions to their problems. The unit in procedure should follow those in discussion, debate, and persuasion, for it climaxes and integrates all three.

Problem-solving, choosing with wisdom among reasoned options, is probably the matrix for most intentional communication above the status of social amenity or persiflage. No problem truly *exists* until an unconcerned group becomes concerned, aware that *something* is wrong. Such a group is thus motivated to discover *what* is wrong and to define and analyze the nature and causes of the difficulty it feels, the dissonant imbalance that upsets and subverts its Pippa-like bliss. Problem-solving begins with a whimper rather than a bang.

Research ensues; talk appraises. Ultimately emerges a long list of conceivable ways to eliminate the causes or mitigate the effects of the pesky problem. Criteria are adduced which a satisfactory solution must meet (the "best" solution, for example, will not be a solution at all if we cannot possibly secure the funds to execute it). So far our group has been working within the format of discussion. In all likelihood a number of solutions satisfy these criteria. Which is "best"? Perhaps the most productive of all methods of testing the validity of any solution is to subject it to the pro-con analysis and appraisal of debate—debate in any of its forms.

One form is parliamentary: a main motion or resolution simply submits a solution to some problem. If a "second" member of the group agrees that this proposal deserves to be evaluated, it is. Speeches long and short, formal and informal, are delivered—one at a time. All are persuasive, some by being merely informative. Although traditionally we refer to *discussion* on a motion, technically we are engaging in *debate,* arguing for or against, estimating the advantages and disadvantages of the action the motion programs. We have at hand a mechanism for improving the proposal: the motion to amend always seeks to perfect, to change for better rather than worse. We can even move to "substitute" a variant, germane proposal—an attempt to reach an identical destination by an alternate route—and thus assess the "comparative advantages" of rival plan and counterplan. We can commit our resolution to a smaller group, for further investigation and reflection, for refinement of method or means.

With this motion of ours, we can do lots of things. But at short or long last, because talk subsides or because two-thirds of us want to get it over with, we vote. Not always does this guarantee the "right" solution to all our problems: our Eighteenth Amendment, it transpired, was a "wrong" solution, which we regretted and repealed, But until human evolution mutates a philosopher-king, majority rules remains our most practicable process for managing controversy.

The unit in parliamentary procedure offers the speech teacher a genus compacting all the species of communication his students have been studying. What better review, or test, of a year's work?

During this unit, the word that should be heard around the classroom more than any other is *why*. A teacher should ask it continually. Soon students will start predicting and preempting its challenge: then they will be truly ready to study this subject.

If I could, I should forbid any student to *memorize* any datum of parliamentary law. Its rules are not mastered by rote, though they can and should be *learned*. We should ask *why* in order to remember, as well as to comprehend, *what*. Sterile on a quiz is the imperative: List all motions that cannot be reconsidered! A more defensible examination question would be a situational one that permits—yea, compels—a student to reason an answer from premises he is supposed to know. For example:

> A meeting, operating under Robert's rules, is debating a crucial resolution. You have already spoken to urge defeat of this resolution, twice. Suddenly you discern a danger in this resolution that no one has yet designated. The group is entitled to learn of this disadvantage before voting, yet you cannot speak again. There are at least four motions you can move that, if

passed, would enable you to deliver this speech you judge essential. How can you procure additional debating time?

As Max Beberman has written: "Teaching is not lecturing or telling things. Teaching is devising a sequence of questions which enables kids to become aware of generalizations by themselves." The query is always *why*: Why does this make sense rather than nonsense?

Why is the motion to adjourn undebatable? If it could be discussed instead of immediately voted upon, if to vote on it we might have to muster a two-thirds majority to close debate on it, would it be fair or feasible thus to require a meeting to remain in session until two-thirds of its members desired to end it?

Why is a question of privilege of the assembly awarded precedence over one of personal, or individual, privilege? Is it democratic to rank the whole as greater than one of its parts?

Why is it that a single person, one only, can raise a point of order? Why no second?

Why must the motion to lay on the table be undebatable? If we could discuss it, what would be the effect on the lower-precedence motion to close debate?

Why is there no such motion as "lay on the table until our next meeting"? What two motions are being confused? Why is it dangerous thus to let a motion to "table" prevent discussion of the wisdom of postponing decision?

Why do we require a two-thirds vote to "limit debate to twenty more minutes," yet only a simple majority to amend that motion by striking out "twenty" and inserting "thirty"?

Why is amendment by filling a blank a useful, though seldom used, procedure?

Why can nominations be reopened by a simple majority after it has taken a two-thirds vote to close them?

Why should a motion to reconsider stop all action on a resolution until it can be voted on again? What exceptions to such a restriction might be necessary? What if an approved invoice has already been paid by the treasurer?

Why did Robert decide that to move reconsideration of a motion a member must have voted with the side "prevailing" on that motion? Why did it appear logical to assume that unless one person had changed his mind there was no reason even to consider reconsideration? Why did this reasoning *not* apply, however, to the seconder of reconsideration? Then, what tactical solution to this restrictive provision is obvious, and how does having someone initially vote with the "other" side vitiate this restriction? So why, among other reasons, did Alice Sturgis abolish this senseless rule in her *Standard Code?*

Why can certain motions and requests be introduced without recognition by the Chair, even interrupting a speaker who has been granted the floor?

Why may a seconder vote against the motion he has seconded? What does his second veritably denote?

Why is a chairman's stating of a motion so crucial a point in progress of action on any motion? Whose property was it before this statement? Who "owns" it now? How does this affect its withdrawal or modification?

Why is the Chair's restatement of a motion just before he puts it to vote another crucial point in its progress? Up to what point may debate on it occur?

Why might Robert have been justified in permitting a presiding officer to vote if his vote would affect the result—a rule quite different from sanctioning his vote only in case of a tie? *Does* this enable a president to "vote twice"?

Why can't a vote be made unanimous retroactively, even by a unanimous vote to do so?

Why does an ex officio member (of a committee, for instance) possess all the rights and responsibilities of any other member, including that of voting? What does *ex officio* mean? What about an "honorary" member?

Why should quorum sometimes be a precise number, sometimes a percentage, occasionally "the number of members present?"

Why? Why not? And never let us fear occasionally to reply:

Why? Why, because Robert said so, and his *Rules* we have adopted for our governance. There isn't any *logical* reason.

For example, why should the motion to table be awarded the highest precedence of all subsidiary motions. I could more readily justify eliminating it. In fact, Robert W. English has proposed that motions to table, to postpone definitely, and to refer, all be combined into a single *incidental* motion to "*de*fer," each amendable into either of the other two forms of "deferring." Why might this be quite feasible? How might it improve the conduct of a meeting?

At first blush parliamentary motions seem to present utter chaos. Hence whenever cosmos does exist, it must be detected. Even when it does not, we should create it. Witness:

All privileged motions are undebatable. Whenever a presiding officer states a privileged motion, immediately he should say: "All in favor say *aye*." Why memorize anything save this fact?

In *all* motions there is an inverse relationship between the right to interrupt a speaker and the requirement of a second.

No incidental motion or request can be amended. True? Almost, but not quite. Probably the principle is worth remembering if one can recall that there are four, exceedingly minor, exceptions. If a bright student is interested in these exceptions, let him look them up.

No incidental motion may be debated? True, if one can remember the single exception: an appeal, universally debatable under the Sturgis code, though Robert dissents in five special circumstances.

When the seven subsidiary motions (I once contended that actually there are fourteen, and I now believe the correct number to be fifteen) are arranged in precedence high to low, a line drawn between limit-or-extend-debate and postpone-definitely is a line of *debatability*—debatable below, undebatable above. A student who induces this verity is on his way to learning-without-memorizing debatability data.

When the privileged motions are listed in high-to-low order of precedence, a line drawn between recess and question-of-privilege is a very significant line:

Above it —
    a motion must be moved;
    this motion requires a second, and
    it may not interrupt a speaker;
    the whole group decides the issue, and the
    vote required is always a simple majority.
Below it —
    lie requests rather than motions;
    none requires a second; all may interrupt a speaker;
    the decision is rendered by the presiding
    officer—subject, as always, to appeal.

Observe also that no privileged motion may be reconsidered except the "top" one (to fix the time to which to adjourn, and amendments thereto).

The precedence of the so-called return motions (take from the table, reconsider, rescind, *et. al.*) offers a stimulating research project for report to a class by one of its "curious" students.

Subsidiary motions might be more fully comprehended if they were classified on bases in addition to precedence: for instance, into those that alter content, those that delay decision, and those that expedite procedure. Which of them may *not* be reconsidered? Is a mnemonic detectable?

Students may enjoy classifying the "unclassifiable" incidental motions, by asking for each: incidental to *what?* To the presiding process, to voting, to elections, to action on a motion? Then may be introduced the incidental motion that appears in no code, no textbook: "Any other incidental request or motion, introduced while some other motion is pending." Can a class conceive some examples?

Actually, the longer one studies parliamentary motions and rules, the more "law and order" one discerns in and among them. If a teacher and his students believe only in aggressive teaching and passive, "receptacle" learning, then that teacher should probe and promulgate for his pupils the cosmos in the chaos. I prefer to hope, however, that any teacher reading this sentence will somehow find some way to stimulate at least many of his students to research and report some of the great quandaries of parliamentary law, thus to profit from that "involvement" without which learning is sterile. I have a colleague who can count on at least one or two or three queries per class from his wide-awake students. His dedicated-teacher response: "That's a good question. Look it up, and tell us all the answer tomorrow."

One of our students, with a little luck and lots of labor, may someday become an assemblyman or congresswoman, or presiding officer of the United States Senate. A colleague of mine once had in his class a young man whose name was John F. Kennedy. One never knows. Yet I wouldn't count on it for 99.9 percent of the faces confronting me each autumn.

During parliamentary units of speech courses in secondary schools, the objective emphatically should not be to train every student to be a legislator. The rules of a "house" he will learn if ever need be. The primary outcome should be competent, knowledge-able participation in business sessions of ordinary community clubs and voluntary boards—though if time permits, some attention ought to be directed to problems of presiding. Such intricacies as when the effect of the motion to table is exhausted, and its distinc-tion between organizations that meet more or less frequently than quarterly, may be ignored without scruple. A student need learn only *how* and *where* to research petty points, if and when they ever become applicable. As Joseph F. O'Brien counseled, in a note

"To the Reader" at the outset of his *Parliamentary Law for the Layman:*

> Always remember that the rules were made for man and not man for the rules. Know your basic principles well, but use as few rules as the situation will permit. . . . Few organizations will require their members to know all the rules of order. . . . Many societies can function well through effective use of the main motion, the motion to amend, and the motion to commit (including committee procedure). Adapt the strictness of your procedure *to the group's unity or division on the issue at hand, to its size, and to its knowledge of parliamentary law.*

Having conceded this, however, I am not sure this is enough. Some additional attitudes toward procedure must be formed—in many instances, unfortunately, re-formed.

Many young men, if from no other source than their fathers, and many young women, if from no other source than their office-holding mothers, presume that the only man who ever wrote on the subject of parliamentary law was that famous Rivers and Harbors Army engineer, General Henry M. Robert.

No student should be taught to disparage Robert: his exquisite skill as a presider, the enormous contribution of his book, pouring into a vacuum in his time a code ably and aptly adapted to the needs of organizations he saw all around him, distilled from legislative practice though not always legal precedent, from vast and valuable experience on engineering boards and in church and community groups, and from extensive correspondence with persons less well informed than he. Let us here record an undeniable fact: when nowadays a person refers to "the proper procedure," he undoubtedly means the Robert prescription. Groups that have no bylaws, or no parliamentary authority, "look it up in Robert" whenever an impasse occurs. The paramount authority of *Robert's Rules of Order (Revised* or *Newly Revised*), though it may be decried, cannot successfully be denied.

On the other hand, no student should be indoctrinated into daily genuflection before the shrine of the Reverend Robert: god he is not.

The lineage of parliamentary law is long. To be convinced of its ancient (1200 B.C.?) Hebrew, Greek, Roman, Norse, and Anglo-Saxon origins, plus British and American adaptations, one should settle down in an armchair some evening with Joseph F. O'Brien's chronicle, "The Historical Development of Parliamentary Discussion" (reprinted in three parts in *Parliamentary Journal,* October, 1966, January and April, 1967, if you don't happen to have copies of *The Thomas Jefferson Parliamentarian,* in which originally it appeared).

Through no fault of his or ours, Mr. Robert's best seller became unduly influential. There have been, are, and will be other codes. In future there may be, undoubtedly will be, *better* codes. Gregg Phifer, former Parliamentarian to the Legislative Assembly of the Speech Communication Association, submits Alice F. Sturgis' *Standard Code of Parliamentary Procedure* as his "personal favorite," on the basis of six numerated criteria. His article in the *Parliamentary Journal* of July, 1967, might profitably be reported to a class—though in all fairness, I suppose, it should be followed by James W. Cleary's addendum in April, 1968, defending Robert's *Newly Revised* edition.

I urge that students of parliamentary procedure become aware of the flexibility of a discipline often thought to be unalterable. Perhaps in the whole long history of parliamentary law, this is the most exciting era in which to teach it. It is one of ferment: and one's students should acquire a sense that it is. There is prevalent today, among both laymen and expert parliamentarians, a belief that procedure must soon, in some way, be simplified and modernized. The great paradox among today's currents and undercurrents of change, the crowning dilemma, is precisely that while authoritative rules are the very essence of efficient procedure, there exists no person, no association or committee or consortium, with authority to decree revised, modern rules. All sorts of interesting innovations are evolving, but with no legislature to enact them, no judiciary to enforce them. Until a new "Robert" comes along, we must communicate to our students our status of flux, and invite them to join in the process of amendment now in vogue.

One way to begin is with curiosa; for example, the note on the previous question, that Robert inserted on pages 117–118 of his

Rules of Order Revised as an inventory of "the great changes which this motion has undergone" since 1604. This affords an opportunity to insist on one more change, accepted now by all save diehards: phrasing this motion meaningfully as one to "close debate and vote immediately." Also this may provide the occasion for clarifying one of the impressive parliamentary confusions of our times: between "Question!" or "I call for the question!" and "I move the previous question." For whenever a presiding officer permits a single member yelling "Question!" to terminate for all the privilege of evaluative and persuasive debate, he is committing probably the most traumatic of all presiding errors—and far too many chairmen confess this sin.

By blending lecture and discussion, you may convince students that "what is right" is not always a simple query. There are levels, a hierarchy, of jurisdictions governing what you can or cannot parliamentarily do. Constraining all is the law of nation and state, sometimes through a charter or certificate of incorporation. Nothing illegal can be done, even though sanctioned by constitution or custom, or even by a Robert rule. Robert did not always follow the law. He created rules that satisfied *him*—witness some of his two-thirds-vote requirements. Courts have overruled him, quashed actions taken under rules he prescribed. Parliamentary law, in the final analysis, is what the judges say it is.

Constraining at a lower level are the organization's constitution, bylaws, and standing rules. A constitution cannot be violated or suspended; it can only be amended or repealed. Any contrary action is void. One article in every constitution should designate a specific parliamentary authority; then this code will govern all procedures except where constitutional provisions conflict. A salutary exercise is to ask each student, near the end of the unit, to draft a set of bylaws for some organization to which he belongs; to include as parliamentary authority whatever textbook he has studied in the unit; to review this code sedulously; and to emend in his bylaws every rule or procedure that, in his judgment, is not suited to the efficient functioning of this particular organization.

Another regulator of propriety in procedure, not always acknowledged, is the force of custom and tradition within the organization itself. A few things *should* be done merely because they always have been. Normally a secretary's minutes will not summarize the content of the debate on every resolution; but there may be excellent reasons why this has become conventional in a society, in, rather than out of, order. Similarly, sometimes diplomacy, the maintenance of compatible human relations among members, may define what is fitting, hence proper. Primary always is the principle: let the will of this assembly be achieved.

Sundry assignments may be devised for students manifesting too high a DQ (Dogmatism Quotient) as the unit nears its end. Let three of them make detailed analyses of Jefferson, Cushing, and Sturgis codes (or those of Demeter or Hellman or Reed or Waples, to suggest alphabetically four more), then report on every difference between Robert and the manual surveyed. Or let a class conduct a half-hour business session experimentally: with cloture by a simple majority, or with such motions as table or refer or reconsider ineligible. Actually to observe effects, advantages and disadvantages, run a drill in which a point of order, or an appeal, or a question of privilege, or a "call for division" is for the moment proscribed.

Or an assignment that, I have found, reaps capital gains: Take all the motions in whatever textbook you have studied and assume that you must cut their number in half. Which ones can you afford to eliminate? Which ones are you forced to retain? How, through some motion retained on your list, can you attain the same goal as that of one you discarded? If you retain point of order, for instance, for what other requests could it substitute? If you were to eliminate secondary amendments, allowing only one primary at a time, what profit and loss would accrue?

Or put to a class the challenge Ray E. Keesey addressed to a regional meeting of the American Institute of Parliamentarians in New York City on April 19, 1969. Dr. Keesey chalked on a blackboard thirteen motions. Then he said: "Now just suppose these were the only available motions in a parliamentary code. Is there anything we couldn't do that sometime we'd have to do?" To stress in this inquiry the irrelevancy or precedence, list the thirteen motions alphabetically:

adjourn	main	refer
amend	point of order	rescind
appeal	postpone	suspend rules
control debate	recess	withdraw
	reconsider	

In any event, by whatever means, let no student complete this unit believing parliamentary rules to be either immutable or inviolable.

In a winter of a teacher's discontent, in a yeasty era in which his students grope toward maturity, in an interval during which his subject searches for modernity, in this epoch of undoubted flux, surely teaching parliamentary procedure cannot be adjudged a sinecure, devoid of anxiety or pain. By no means is this an exact science. Plus-or-minus signs hover over every law one lays down. Exceptions hound every universal essayed.

Yet for precisely these reasons, before this essay adjourns, may I move that teaching students this subject is surely fun? More rewarding, perhaps, than the imparting of any other facet or form of human problem-solving communication?

If your "Aye" has it, if with you this motion carries, is there any further business?

REFERENCES FOR FURTHER READING

Bosmajian, Haig A., ed. *Readings in Parliamentary Procedure.* New York: Harper & Row, 1968. A collection of eleven essays and ten court decisions, many of which widen a teacher's perspective; e.g., on the "evolution" and "legal side" of procedure, on the history of "the majority principle" and quorum, on the ubiquitous motion to amend, on the presiding of Henry M. Robert.

Demeter, George. *Demeter's Manual of Parliamentary Law and Procedure.* Blue Book edition. Boston: Bostonia Press, 1969. Evolving from a lawyer's extensive experience as a parliamentarian, this is an indispensable reference for many of the minor, even picayune, queries students raise, and for step-by-step solution of parliamentary problems. Its counsel is based on law and legal precedent.

Hellman, Hugo E. *Parliamentary Procedure.* New York: Macmillan, 1966. A brief, eminently clear, simplified exposition of the rules, occasionally innovative, concerned with *why* as well as *what;* recommended for those who find Robert unreadable.

Jones, O. Garfield. *Senior Manual for Group Leadership.* Rev. ed. New York: Appleton-Century-Crofts, 1949. A highly useful at-a-glance chart-manual for swift reference, plus some rather naive lesson drills and "contests."

Parliamentary Journal. Published quarterly (Jan., April, July, and Oct.); Vol. 1, No. 1, appeared in March, 1960. Every teacher of procedure should examine every issue; a majority of its articles are worth reading. If unavailable in a library, a subscription is a perquisite of membership in the American Institute of Parliamentarians (4453 Beacon St., Chicago, Illinois 60640).

Robert, Henry M. *Parliamentary Law.* New York: Century, 1923. Pages 399–543 print Robert's replies to 390 questions, selected from his correspondence.

Robert, Sarah Corbin, et al. *Robert's Rules of Order Newly Revised.* Glenview, Illinois, 1970. A standard work no teacher dare ignore.

Sturgis, Alice. *Sturgis Standard Code of Parliamentary Procedure.* 2d ed. New York: McGraw-Hill, 1966. This modern code is deemed by many to be superior to that of Robert.

Parliamentary procedure, by the way, is one subject which lends itself well to that modern system of individualized instruction labeled "programmed learning." So far, to my knowledge, only three published books have employed this device. None can I inordinately praise. But if a student were experiencing difficulty with this subject, he might catch up with his peers by working his own way through:

Lehman, Warren. *Parliamentary Procedure.* Garden City, New York: Doubleday, 1962.

Gray, John W., and Richard G. Rea. *Parliamentary Procedure: A Programed Introduction.* Chicago: Scott, Foresman, 1963.

Wiksell, Wesley. *How to Conduct Meetings: A Programmed Instruction Manual on Parliamentary Procedure.* New York: Harper & Row, 1966.

On Teaching Discussion

ERNEST G. BORMANN
Professor of Speech
University of Minnesota

Speech teachers are experiencing a reawakening of interest and enthusiasm in regard to the study of group discussion. When I was a university student shortly after World War II, interest in group discussion was high among speech teachers. In my junior year I renounced intercollegiate debating as trivial and unethical and decided to devote my time to participating in intercollegiate discussion meetings, which were popular at the time. In those days discussion inferred the scientific application of reason to human problems. The debater was an advocate defending his position tenaciously and switching indiscriminately from side to side, while the discussant adopted an attitude of open-minded inquiry and searched for the facts.

After several years I became disillusioned with the study and teaching of group discussion. Courses in discussion often lacked content, and the exercises seemed superficial and irrelevant to student needs. Today, all that is changing. The traditional stream of group discussion as training in group problem-solving and citizenship has been supplemented by the discovery of the small group by many disciplines in the behavioral sciences. A new generation of scholars oriented to empirical investigations of small group process has given added impetus to the field.

The time has come for the new emphasis, where it has not already done so, to find its way into the units on discussion in our high school speech courses. In this essay, I propose to consider some of the ways in which the recent emphasis on group methods can be integrated into a unit that keeps the best of the tradition of problem-solving discussion as training for citizenship in a representative democracy.

The urbanization of America and the emergence of the highly developed modern industrial state explain the growing enthusiasm for discussion. Several recent developments within the context of urban and corporate life have encouraged the increase in, and importance of, group discussion in contemporary society, and have brought it to where it is most widely used and where it is one of the most important forms of public address.

The pace and style of contemporary American society put a premium on the informal and spontaneous, as opposed to the elaborate, slow, and ritualistic. In the nineteenth century, Webster might speak several hours to large crowds at Bunker Hill or Plymouth Rock. He might speak for several days in the Senate. People thronged to hear him and listened with rapt attention as his Ciceronian style gradually and copiously enveloped a subject. The pomp and ritual of the nineteenth-century oration went out of style at the turn of the century, and by 1920, while the lecture, the sermon, and the political stump speech were still important, the role of the formal speech and of debate in the formation of important decisions was waning. Increasingly, legislative assemblies made important decisions in committee. This was true not only of governmental assemblies but also of other assemblies as well. The complex corporate organizations, that were developing in all areas of life, relied upon conferences and meetings for more and more of the work of the organization. The business conference became a way of life for the managerial class. Every church, labor union, fraternity, sorority, and high school faculty had a number of standing and special committees to investigate, to decide, and to implement policy.

Meantime, the rise of the electronic media put a premium on spontaneous give-and-take public address. The set speech does not hold the radio or television audience's attention as does a discussion. People tend to watch television in small clusters of two or three in the kitchen, living room, or den. The broadcast media filter out much of the surrounding persuasive climate of the rally situation, such as the cheering audience, the flags and buntings, and the bands. The shouting speech that may be effective in Madison Square Garden or in the convention hall looks grotesque on the small home screen. As a result, more and more important public discourse takes place in interview and discussion formats on radio and television.

Teachers of public speaking and directors of forensics studied carefully the rise of discussion in public affairs in the years after World War I. They were among those most interested in the changing forms of public address, and when the study of discussion was introduced into high school and college curricula, it was introduced, for the most part, as a unit in a speech course.

Soon separate courses in discussion became part of the college and university speech curricula. Discussion is still frequently part of a high school speech course that deals with other forms of public address. Conceivably, with the addition of small group theory to the work in discussion and with the growing awareness of the importance of group discussion to the management of the modern organization, the high schools will give added attention to providing separate courses in discussion and group methods. My approach in this essay, however, is to assume that for most high school teachers the discussion material will be a unit in a course that includes the other forms of speech.

Teachers of speech are concerned with the role of public discussion as a means for social control. Discussion serves to inform the citizens in a representative democracy of basic problems and to give the people an opportunity to hear all sides of a controversy. The first emphasis, therefore, in the discussion course has been on achieving change and order in a democratic society. The course that converted me to the importance of group discussion as a form of public address had this emphasis. It contained considerable material on the practical matters involved in organizing and presenting discussion programs. It included material on the various formats useful for show-type discussions, such as the radio round table, the symposium, and so forth. The course also included, however, a theoretical rationale for public discussion as a decision-making tool in a democracy, and that was one of its more important, attractive, and enduring features. Public discussion is, in many respects, the best way to mold public opinion and make decisions. The unit in discussion is one of the important parts of the curriculum that gives the students basic and explicit training for citizenship.

Public discussion differs in important ways from other forms of social control. Dictators can control society by force, by decree supported with force, and by fiat. Society can be controlled by lawgivers and lawmakers backed up by law enforcement personnel or the military. Public opinion can be engineered by campaigns of persuasion. Mores and custom may serve to control society.

Changes can result from dictatorial control, from persuasion, and from direct action, such as marches, demonstrations, protests, general strikes, and other tactics in response to the age-old strategy of "into the streets." Discussion differs from all of these other techniques of social change and control in that it implies that discussants must be free to present and hear all positions and that the citizen must be allowed to make up his own mind on the basis of the public interplay of ideas.

Public discussion is closely related to many democratic values. One need look no further than John Stuart Mill's classical formulations in defense of freedom of speech in his essay *On Liberty* to see how closely discussion and freedom of speech are interrelated. According to Mill, all opinions and arguments should be allowed a full hearing, and if all points of view are presented, the people will select truth from error. Mill's argument is elaborate and skillful, but it essentially asserts that repressing unpopular ideas is unwise because they may contain elements of truth. Even if the unpopular ideas are false, it is unwise to censor them, because the old familiar truths lose their vitality unless they are periodically challenged and defended.

The rationale for discussion as an important and praiseworthy technique of social control assumes that the citizen can rule wisely if he is given an opportunity. Public discussion gives a person a chance to hear all sides of important public questions. Some citizens may not act wisely even when they have participated in a thorough discussion of an issue, but in the long run, the informed majority will rule more wisely than the most enlightened of despots. On occasion, students in a class studying discussion will express a different opinion. They suggest that they do not want to discuss a topic dealing with some aspect of American foreign policy because they cannot get the necessary information. If the experts in the administration who have access to classified information cannot solve the problem, they argue, how can students in a speech course do so? Perhaps the complexities of the modern world make the basic assumptions of discussion and representative democracy untenable. But students who reject these assumptions should be made aware of the implications of such a stand. If the citizens cannot be the rulers, then they must put their trust in experts. In short, if the citizens do not decide, then an elite group of decision-makers rules the country and employs experts in mass persuasion to manipulate public opinion in support of their decisions.

Some students challenge discussion as a viable technique for social change by turning their back on it and resorting to direct action. They substitute for discussion, with its analysis of problems, and for development of solutions and their evaluation, the protest march, demonstration, picket line, and rally. Again, students who reject discussion as too slow or ineffective in changing society should be made aware of the implications of their position. If they fail to discuss a problem with those who disagree with them, the opponents will be forced to adopt the tactics of direct action. Major issues that divide society will then tend to be contested in the streets by partisan mobs. Confrontations between mobs in the streets are liable to incite passions and violence.

The second assumption of discussion, which grows from the first, is that the individual has an innate worth and dignity. The individual is important and is not to be viewed as a cog in the machine of the group, the organization, or the state. The individual thus has a right to have a hand in determining his own destiny. A person ought to be consulted about decisions that affect his welfare. Even though he may choose unwisely, a person has the right to make certain decisions, and this right is, in Jefferson's words, "an inalienable right."

The question of individual worth and dignity is equally relevant in the study of group methods. Effective groups are highly cohesive, and their members make personal sacrifices for the good of all. Groups often demand total commitment from their members, thus causing tension between individual and group welfare and between individual and group goals. When one evaluates a group, therefore, both effectiveness and member satisfaction must be considered. Two equally effective groups may differ as to excellence because one provides its members with greater personal satisfactions than the other which sacrifices its personnel for the sake of group goals. The industrial corporation ought not to be judged by its profit margin alone but also by its contribution to the quality of life experienced by its members.

Finally, group discussion as a technique of social control assumes that while man may act irrationally, he also is capable of behaving reasonably. People do make decisions on the basis of sound conclusions drawn by valid reasoning from the facts. Discussion further assumes that there is virtue in the process of inquiry. Inquiry assumes an open-minded and objective search for facts, a careful examination of possible courses of action, and a decision based upon thorough consideration of all alternatives. The work in group discussion is an important part of the curriculum where the process of inquiry is studied directly, although one always hopes that it is exemplified in the entire curriculum.

The discussion courses in the years immediately following World War II were attractive because of their emphasis on freedom of speech, on discussion as a mechanism for social control, and on the training for citizenship. I found the open-minded and tolerant attitude of the discussant searching for truth more attractive than the closed mind of the advocate fighting tooth and claw to uphold or attack a debate resolution. Some class time in a unit on discussion ought to be devoted to the study of the rationale for free speech and its relationship to discussion. Sections of Mill's essay serve as an admirable basis for such study. Perhaps a free speech controversy in which the community censors a speaker or an example of direct action in the streets can serve to furnish the teacher with case study materials to raise pertinent issues in class. The process of inquiry and the relationship between discussion and debate in the democratic process might be included early in the unit on discussion. These materials have withstood the tests of time and have contributed to the education of many students of discussion.

My disillusionment with courses in discussion came after I taught them for some time and discovered that they consisted largely of exercises in which students picked a topic, met briefly to plan what they would do, and then came to class and presented a show-type discussion. Too often the groups met for so brief a time that the normal social rewards that pull people into groups never materialized, and the students seldom spent enough time studying the topic to become involved and interested in the subject. Class discussions were too often remote and irrelevant to the students. Uninformed participants exchanged opinions and hypothetical examples, or they expressed prejudices in desultory and unorganized programs that were unenlightening and dull for the audience. Many discussion courses lacked substance, and students took them because they were easy.

I was not alone in my disillusionment with discussion. Teachers of speech often viewed discussion as a necessary but unimportant part of the curriculum and specialized in some other area of public address, such as argumentation, persuasion, or rhetorical theory.

Ironically, as the wave of enthusiasm for discussion was receding in departments of speech, other academic disciplines were discovering the complexity and importance of the small group as a social entity worthy of study. Investigators in many disciplines began intensive study of small groups, preparing the way for the addition of a solid theoretical base of group theory to the important rationale of discussion as inquiry and as a method of democracy.

Since World War II, disciplines such as industrial, educational, and social psychology and sociology began offering courses in group dynamics, human relations, and the psychology of small groups. Group techniques came to be widely used in clinical psychology, psychiatry, speech correction, and social work. By the 1960s, a widespread technique for management training in business and industry was the use of group sessions to make well adjusted people more sensitive to others and more aware of the social dimension of group interaction.

The work at such centers as the National Training Laboratory on Group Development at Bethel, Maine, evolved into sensitivity training by means of T-Groups. T-Groups, or training groups, are set up with a trainer to counsel the group. The members of the training group talk about the here and now. An important part of the discussion relates to the group procedures as they develop, and participants are encouraged to discuss the way they feel about the group and about one another. The individuals in the T-Group become more sensitive to the kinds of people they are and to how they affect others, by making an open and direct appraisal of the social dimension of the group.

Similar to the T-Group approach, but with a somewhat different emphasis, has been the work at centers such as the Esselin Institute and the Western Behavioral Sciences Institute, both in California. Often called encounter groups, these sessions remain therapy-oriented and emphasize personal growth as do the T-Groups, but in addition to discussions of the here-and-now they also often include non-verbal games to break down interpersonal barriers, establish personal trust, and encourage encounters.

The main difference between group dynamics, T-Group and encounter group work, and human relations courses on the one hand and group discussion courses on the other is that the former focus upon the group social interactions while the latter consider both the social and task dimension of group problem-solving. T-Group training and encounter groups often are directed toward making individuals more aware of their behavior and its effect on others. Group discussion is directed at helping people work cooperatively to solve common problems.

Leaders in the field of discussion did not ignore the new developments relating to group work taking place in other disciplines.

They kept the better part of the tradition of problem-solving discussion as training for citizenship, and added to that foundation a theory of group process based upon the voluminous research results published in the 1950s and 1960s. A new generation of scholars trained in empirical investigations of small group process have made discussion and group methods one of the most challenging and exciting areas in the field of speech.

The high school speech teacher should retain the best of the material relating to discussion as training for citizenship while concentrating on the task-oriented small group in all of its ramifications throughout our society. The latter concern includes the importance of group discussion to what John Kenneth Galbraith calls *The Modern Industrial State.*

In today's corporate society, decisions are made, work is done, and power is transacted in small group meetings. One can do worse than to think of the modern organization as a more or less tightly knit collection of small task-oriented groups. Task-oriented groups conduct much of their internal business by meetings, and when they cooperate or compete with other groups within or outside the parent organization, their representatives meet with representatives from other units. When important organizational decisions are made affecting a substantial part of or the entire organization, these decisions are often made in group discussion.

Indeed, John Kenneth Galbraith argues that the highly developed nations rely on a pool of knowledgeable people who know how to organize and sustain the modern corporation for their economic well-being. The basic mechanism by which the modern corporation achieves its power to control resources and the environment is the group discussion. Group meetings provide a context for high level communication efficiency. Discussing a problem face-to-face, where feedback can be encouraged and where both nonverbal and verbal communication is possible, provides a means for integrating specialized knowledge.

The key to the industrial state is the ability of the modern organization to take talented but ordinary people who have been deeply but narrowly specialized and bring their skills and knowledge to bear on complicated projects. The power transactions of our time take place in face-to-face group discussions, and the future promises to see an acceleration of the trend as more and more of the underdeveloped and developing nations of the world learn to sustain elaborate corporate structures. If we are, therefore, to educate our high school students for the world in which they will live, we must prepare them to work productively in group discussions.

Educating students about organizational systems, small group theory, and the importance of discussion in a representative democracy is an important but large task. The teacher planning a unit on discussion for a high school speech course cannot cover all of these topics in depth. Nor need he do so. Perhaps the day is coming when our high school curricula will contain courses devoted solely to group discussion. In the meantime, the teacher ought to introduce the student to the basic notions and lay the groundwork so high school graduates can build their competence either with the aid of advanced college courses or on their own as they work with groups after they leave the high school speech class.

A unit on discussion in a high school English, speech, or language arts course should begin the student's education about the complexities and importance of group discussion in contemporary society and about the dynamics of group process. Lectures, assigned readings, and classroom discussions are among the most useful teaching methods for such education. The discussion units should also provide the student with some training in the techniques of discussion. Training is best provided by participation in group discussions under supervision of teachers.

The discussion unit, therefore, ought to both train and educate. A student can be drilled in the fundamentals of voice and articulation. The result of drill in exercises to improve the vocal quality and the clarity of articulation is a trained voice. Education differs from training in that it equips a person to make wise choices. A person may be trained to have a clear, flexible, and expressive voice and yet be uneducated about group process and thus make unwise choices about what to say in the meetings. An educated student can make wise choices about what to say and do to improve a group when alternatives present themselves during the course of a discussion.

Choice implies *conscious* competence. The student who is consciously competent about group discussion not only makes a good decision when faced with a choice but also is aware of what he is doing and why. Unconscious competence might come from trial and error. A person may succeed in a given discussion without understanding why. When formerly successful methods fail in a new group, the individual does not know why he failed nor what corrective action might be taken in the next session.

The nature of the material in a discussion course is such that it must be understood intellectually (that is, well enough to answer examination questions correctly), but it must also be appropriated by the whole person so that the student can *apply* the concepts and theory of small groups while working in a group. Learning at the deeper level of appropriation of insight and skill requires time and involved participation, under supervision, in groups so that a person can absorb the knowledge at an emotional as well as an intellectual level.

One of the important goals of the discussion unit should be to bring the students to a realization of the complexities of group process. Even a transitory meeting, that on superficial analysis seems to be a simple matter of sitting around talking about a topic for an hour, is a complex social event. An embryo group can include role-testing and specialization, the development of leadership functions, and the emergence of rudimentary features of group culture. An introduction to the complicated factors of social and task interaction can bring about a change in students' attitudes and a recognition on their part of the importance and difficulty of group process.

Another important goal of the discussion unit is to introduce the student to the basic concepts of group process. Understanding the content of group theory, composed of basic concepts, terms, and their process interrelationships, is part of the student's education. The person who understands group process is able to work with, lead, and improve groups because he can work with the grain of natural process rather than against it. For example, one uneducated in group process might prescribe the goals of equal participation by all members of all groups in all situations. Prescriptions of this sort are not very helpful, because with some notable exceptions (show-type discussions for audiences) groups cannot evolve role-structures that enable all members to participate equally. Task specialization inevitably takes place in task-oriented groups, and one feature of that specialization is that some members talk more than others.

One might expect considerable insight and change of attitude as a result of a unit on discussion. In terms of behavioral change, the unit on discussion must have rather modest goals. Working productively with groups is as complicated as playing golf or basketball and requires at least the equivalent time and effort for training to change behavior. Of course changes in behavior are the ultimate goal of instruction in an area such as discussion and group methods, and such changes are a result of that integration of education and training that characterizes the appropriation of knowledge. The student must have both an understanding of what to do and the technique to do it.

Given the general goals of a unit on discussion, what content might best lead to achieving an adequate level of both education and training? The following suggestions are meant to be provocative rather than prescriptive. They represent one way to plan and organize a unit on discussion rather than *the* way to do so. Probably there is no one best way to teach a unit on discussion. Each small group must work out its own salvation by developing appropriate social and work norms and its own culture. What may work for one group does not work for another. The same holds true for class exercises and teaching techniques for a given instructor. The good course is often the result of a teacher developing a personal approach and modifying or creating exercises and assignments that excite and involve the instructor. If these comments stimulate the reader to new and creative innovations, they will have served their purpose.

I would begin a unit on discussion with a few periods devoted to placing the task-oriented group into its social, political, and economic context. The instructor might then devote a week to such topics as the forms of discussion, preparation for and participation in group meetings, the importance of listening, the need to become involved in the give-and-take of the dialectical process, and the characteristics of a good participant and a good discussion moderator. During this time, students could be preparing for show-type discussions to be presented before the class. The panel discussion, with members talking back and forth much as they would in conversation except that the group has a purpose and a plan for their talk, is a good format for the first assignment. Small group meetings tend to take the form of the panel discussion, whether they are task-oriented problem-solving sessions, briefing sessions, or instructional meetings.

Training in discussion should begin, I think, with the principles of participating in and moderating discussions. For several sessions, the class can study the guidance skills useful in leading a group. The instructor may quickly describe such skills as asking questions, terminating monologues, drawing out the reticent members, keeping the agenda, summarizing, dealing with conflict, and seeking consensus.

The student should begin early to adapt his other training in speech, English, or the language arts to small group communication. One can expect considerable transfer of such skills as gathering information, testing evidence, analyzing issues, organizing and developing ideas for oral presentation, and delivering ideas effectively in a group meeting.

The communication process consists of the components of a *message,* the *source* of the message, and a *receiver* or listener. The components interrelate through channels that transmit the messages back and forth between source and receiver. One often thinks of chemical metaphors for the concept of process, but I prefer an electrical figure to explain communication. If a positive line (source) approaches a negative one (receiver), sparks (messages) fly back and forth until the two lines meet. In somewhat the same fashion, a discussant makes a comment and the listeners feed back verbal and nonverbal cues until, under ideal conditions, an adequate meeting of the minds is achieved.

Feedback consists of the cues, verbal and non-verbal, that the source and receiver provide one another to indicate how effectively the process is going on and how close they are to understanding. Unless the person initiating a communication event gets contrary cues from the receiver, he will assume that his communication has succeeded. A more realistic attitude is to assume that the first attempt to communicate will fail. Feedback thus refers to the questions, comments, facial expressions, and so forth, that indicate what the listener has understood from the comment. The concept of feedback is important in the fields of cybernetics and computer technology. Take the instance of a person trying to program a computer. The program (message) is encoded on cards and fed into the machine. If the computer does not understand part of the message, the machine prints out an error statement (feedback). The programmer then rephrases his program and punches out new cards and puts them back into the machine. Thus, the programmer and the computer work together until the program is errorless. The machine then understands completely the directions it is to follow in the processing of data. The computer is a difficult listener to please. It feeds back every error and requires a level of perfection that human discussants seldom achieve. If more discussants listened carefully and, like computers, stubbornly requested that messages be debugged, the process of small group communication would be as tedious and time-consuming as is computer programming. On the other hand, careful listening and conscious feedback on the part of group members would improve the quality of data processing in most meetings.

The small group setting maximizes the potential for high fidelity communication because it not only provides for continuous feedback but also employs the most direct and impressive communication channels—those of sight and hearing. (Of course group members may perceive nonverbal messages through other senses, such as touch, smell, and taste.) Within the confines of a small group meeting, the usefulness of the powerful nonverbal messages is enhanced. Nonverbal communication refers to the process by which information is conveyed by the way a person talks and acts, over and above (or in place of) the messages encoded in his words. The way something is said and the actions that accompany it are more believable than the sentiments expressed by the words. To paraphrase Emerson, the *way* you say it speaks so loudly that I cannot hear what you say. If a participant exhibits such behaviors as slouching in a chair, leaning back, leaning forward, dozing, frowning, nodding or shaking his head, laughing, crying, smiling, or smirking, these behaviors may be perceived by others as nonverbal messages. Pitch inflections, grunts, groans, pauses, may all communicate messages to others in the group.

Feedback is continuous in a group discussion because of the nonverbal dimension of communication. Every member of the group can provide nonverbal feedback to the individual making a comment, even as the person speaks. A person tells the group or another participant something. He then watches and listens as the others provide messages (verbal and nonverbal) to give him a reading on what they got out of his comment. The speaker can then compare the desired level of communication with what he interprets from the feedback to have been the actual amount of understanding. He may then send out additional messages designed to bring the communication on target.

If the instructor spends a class period or so emphasizing the importance of feedback and nonverbal communication in the group meeting, he can help students adapt their skills and understanding of speaking, research, and so on, to discussion in the small group context in other units and courses.

Quite often the training in participating and moderating discussion is not very novel or subtle. Just as the basketball coach may find his comments to the untrained player consisting of such platitudes as "You want to develop a jump shot that is difficult to guard and that is very accurate," so the teacher of discussion may find himself saying, "You must keep an eye on the agenda and not let the group get too far off the track. You should, however, give them enough freedom to explore some tangents if it seems to you that the discussion is productive." Even so, one does not argue that a good coach is unnecessary in learning how to play basketball. Having said the obvious about shooting accurately, the coach then puts the basketball in the hands of the player and has him shoot at the basket while the coach watches. The untrained player soon discovers that playing well is more difficult than describing how to play. A student soon finds that leading a discussion is much more difficult than describing how it should be done.

When the coach has had a chance to check a player's form, he will often comment about what the boy is doing. He may say, "You are getting good accuracy but your shot is too easy to guard. You hold the ball in front of you and too low. Try it with a higher jump and hold the ball up more." The coach may demonstrate as well as describe. In somewhat the same way, the instructor in a course in discussion will comment to a student moderator on his skill at summarizing or his failure to terminate an unproductive digression.

Some supervised practice in discussion is very useful, and I would use it in a unit in the high school course. Teaching discussion in this way, however, is very time consuming. To do a proper job of it, the instructor must give each student an opportunity to take part in a discussion and must provide evaluations, suggestions for improvement, and further opportunity to practice under supervision. In this respect the basketball coach and the forensic director have a better opportunity to develop excellence than do teachers of discussion. If high school students could practice the art of group discussion several hours a day, beginning with drills and exercises in the basic fundamentals and gradually working into realistic discussion situations, we might create star discussants as we now create star basketball players and superior debate teams. Of course, varsity teams are elite groups, and even under optimum conditions, not every high school student could be made into a star participant in discussions.

On the other hand, group discussions are so vital and ubiquitous a part of the life of each student that the opportunity to drill on the fundamentals is often available. Students daily participate in a variety of discussion situations. They may discuss a novel in an English class; they may discuss plans for a school dance in a committee meeting; they may discuss religion in a church group; they may discuss who shall have the car on a given evening in the family group. Observing and participating in groups outside of class may provide a student with opportunities to drill on fundamentals without appreciably lengthening the unit on discussion. Occasionally someone suggests that the entire high school faculty should help the English department teach composition by assigning term papers and going over them carefully for errors in grammar and diction. I do not suggest that the entire faculty should assist the instructor who is teaching discussion, but I do believe that discussion techniques are useful in teaching many courses, and certainly the speech course. If small group techniques were more widely used in teaching the students, skills could be greatly improved. Discussion groups can be used in teaching public speaking by having students meet in small groups to discuss and rehearse their speeches. After receiving the group's suggestions and criticisms, the student speakers revise their speeches before delivering them to the entire class. Students can also use discussion groups to work up readings for oral interpretation units. Production groups can plan, script, cast, and rehearse radio and television shows, or present cuttings from plays. Within the context of the speech class, the instructor has many opportunities to use group discussion as a teaching technique.

Beginning the speech course with the unit on discussion and using small groups as a teaching method in the other units allows the teacher to continue to drill students under supervision in discussion principles throughout the term. During the evaluation of each subsequent assignment, the instructor can spend a little time on the discussion skills of the participants.

The recent trend toward modular scheduling in high schools across the country puts a premium on teaching by means of small group techniques. What is useful in the speech, English, or language arts class can be expanded to many other courses in the curriculum. The training aspect of the work in discussion can be continued in some other classes, if group techniques are used in their teaching.

After the preliminary training in group participation and leadership, the next topic ought to be small group theory. The goals of this part of the unit ought to be: (1) to present a description of the nature of the small group; (2) to explain the concepts of co-hesiveness, role, status, norm, and leadership; (3) to describe the process by which groups develop roles, status hierarchies, and leadership; and (4) to clarify the process of group decision-making. The instructor should not try to give the students a complete and sophisticated treatment of group process in a week or ten days. One can, however, educate the students to the point where they can employ the basic concepts and terminology to under-stand, classify, and label their group experiences. To achieve the latter effect, the last part of the unit on discussion should provide the students with an opportunity to analyze a more extensive group experience than the one provided by a show-type panel discussion.

One good way to provide students with an opportunity to ap-ply theory in practice is by placing them in a leaderless group discussion with a clear objective and a specific deadline. The best size for leaderless groups is five, and they should not be larger than nine. Each group is provided, if possible, with a tape re-corder and a place to meet that provides some privacy. The task of the groups is to select a topic of importance relating to school, community, state, national, or world affairs, phrase a suitable question for discussion, investigate the problem, and write a report of their solution to the difficulty. A good way to increase cohesiveness and draw the students into the group process is to assign a group grade shared by all. Some class periods should be devoted to group meetings, although the groups may be allowed to hold additional meetings on their own outside of class.

If a teacher does not have enough tape recorders to transcribe each session of each group, it is helpful to record as many sessions as possible. If the class divides into three groups and the assign-ment of the work meetings lasts for three days, then each group can be recorded once even if the teacher has only one tape re-corder to use in the class. To assure uninhibited group develop-ment and intelligible recordings, the teacher ought to provide a separate meeting place for each group for their work sessions, if possible.

The students will benefit from writing a diary about their

experiences, after each meeting. They can respond to such questions as: What happened to me in the last meeting? and What happened to my group? The instructor should make it clear that the diary comments are privileged information and will be kept confidential, and he should encourage the students to make frank and candid comments. If possible, the instructor should discuss the group experience with each student in an individual conference. The diary reports are helpful in providing information for the individual conferences.

After the groups complete their committee assignments, the instructor should use several class periods to analyze and evaluate what happened during the previous meetings. A brief review of the concepts and theories that were introduced before the leaderless group discussions, with some applications to the group experiences, will make the terminology more relevant to the student's needs. The groups should next meet in separate sessions and make case studies in which they discuss their procedures, their successes, and their failures during the leaderless group discussion assignment. The students should consider not only the socio-emotional dimensions of their meetings but also the task procedure. (People tend to become fascinated by the social interactions and neglect the task area when they conduct a postmortem of a group.)

The following questions are illustrative of the issues that can profitably be raised in a group postmortem. Did some members begin to specialize in certain tasks and to develop roles? Did some members gain in status and influence? Who assumed the guidance functions? Was there contention over leadership? Was the leadership question settled? If so, how? What norms emerged in the group? How did the group make decisions? How was information processed? How was factual data collected and processed? How were opinions submitted and evaluated? How were solutions recommended and tested? (The tape recordings of the meetings are very helpful to the groups as they study their first projects.)

Some instructors who employ the leaderless group discussion may want to begin the unit with a discussion of group process and give the committee two objectives. In addition to the written report, which is given a common grade, the groups can prepare a show-type panel discussion on some aspect of the topic that has been the subject of intensive investigation. The virtue of putting the investigating first is that the students have a much firmer grasp of the content of the program than they often do if they quickly prepare for the panel shows earlier in the term. If the instructor does not have time for the leaderless group discussion and the group case studies in class, a similar result can be obtained if each student makes a field study of a non-class group. I prefer that the student be a participant of the group under study, but the teacher can provide a sound educational experience by assigning nonparticipant observations as well.

Participating in and observing a group that has a task its members perceive as relevant and important provides the student with an opportunity to apply the concepts of group discussion to the real world. Students who have worked together on an important project gain a greater appreciation of the complexities of group process and the relevance of the material to their daily lives. If the unit on discussion provides the students with a frame of analysis to apply to the new groups they join, then they can go on to apply this understanding to develop greater proficiency in one of the most important, and potentially one of the most frustrating or gratifying, of their daily experiences, that of working together with others in the context of a small group.

When one succeeds in introducing students to the nature of discussion and group methods at this level of complexity and relevance, the resultant excitement, insight, dedicated work, and appreciation can make the teaching of discussion one of the most gratifying experiences in the entire speech curriculum.

REFERENCES

An important aid to the teaching of a unit on discussion in the high school course is the *Teacher's Guide to High School Speech,* published in 1966 by the Indiana Department of Public Instruction, in cooperation with the Indiana University English Curriculum Study Center. (It is available from the Speech Communication Association.) That book cites a number of sources on teaching methods and several standard college textbooks as background material suitable for teaching high school discussion (pp. 36, 40). In addition to those sources, I would refer the reader to several recently published college texts, to some reference books containing summaries, syntheses, and bibliograhies of small group research, and to a few manuals and workbooks that are suitable for high school students' use in a unit on discussion.

Almost any recently published standard college textbook on discussion will present the basic theoretical foundations of discussion and group methods. See particularly:

Borman, Ernest G. *Discussion and Group Methods.* New York: Harper & Row, 1969.

Gulley, Halbert T. *Discussion, Conference, and Group Process,* 2d ed. New York: Holt, Rinehart and Winston, 1968.

Sattler, William M., and N. Edd Miller. *Discussion and Conference,* 2d ed. Englewood Cliffs, New Jersey: Prentice-Hall, 1968.

Taken together, these three books represent recent publications reflecting the changing emphasis in the field of discussion and group methods. *Discussion and Conference* was first published in 1954 as a standard text in the tradition of the early courses in discussion. The 1968 edition contains several new sections devoted to group methods, including such topics as "The Elite and the Many," "Groups and Their Characteristics," and "Adaptability in Leadership."

The first edition of *Discussion, Conference, and Group Process* was published in 1960. It was one of the early books that added material drawn from research in small groups to the problem-solving discussion as inquiry and as training for citizenship. The revised edition updates the conclusions drawn from research studies and brings the book more closely to the contemporary emphasis.

Discussion and Group Methods amplifies and develops the ideas outlined in this essay. It covers the traditional discussion materials that have survived the challenge of new ideas, and builds upon that foundation a coherent small group theory composed of concepts and principles that are both supported by the newer research and adaptable to the problems of teaching discussion and group methods. It presents the findings of a research program at the University of Minnesota in group discussion.

Research in the field of small groups has matured to the point where bibliographies, summaries of important studies, and surveys drawing conclusions from the literature are available as reference works. Among those most useful for the teacher of speech in the high schools are:

Cartwright, Dorwin, and Alvin Zander, eds. *Group Dynamics: Research and Theory,* 3rd ed. New York: Harper & Row, 1968.

Collins, Barry E. and Harold Guetzkow. *A Social Psychology of Group Processes for Decision Making.* New York: Wiley, 1964.

Hare, A. Paul. *Handbook of Small Group Research.* New York: Free Press, 1962.

McGrath, Joseph E., and Irwin Altman. *Small Group Research: A Synthesis and Critique of the Field.* New York: Holt. Rinehart & Winston, 1966.

Group Dynamics and the *Handbook of Small Group Research* serve as excellent introductions to the nature, limits, and scope of small group research. The Cartwright and Zander book, first published in 1953, was one of the early collections of outstanding research reports. Updated in 1960, the current edition (1968) contains several essays synthesizing research results, but the book concentrates on presenting complete reports of some of the better small group studies. Hare's handbook is primarily a descriptive survey of the literature. The book contains a bibliography of over one thousand items. The author states that the book represents a first "excursion" through the research literature in order to make available to students and teachers a catalogue of the field.

A Social Psychology of Group Processes for Decision Making is a synthesis of a large number of empirical studies in order to draw conclusions about the group processes. In somewhat the same vein, the McGrath and Altman book contains essays of synthesis, bibliographical items, and also an essay evaluating and criticizing the shortcomings of the research literature on small groups.

While the research literature relating to small groups is voluminous, the publications suitable for the high school student studying a unit on discussion are considerably fewer in number. Several brief, clear, and sound manuals written for discussion and leadership workshops, management training programs, short courses in leading and participating in meetings, and for use in conjunction with a standard textbook for lower division college students may be adapted to the needs of the high school student. See, for example, the following:

Bormann, Ernst G. *Workbook for Work Groups.* Minneapolis: Gordon Press, 1966.

Brilhart, John K. *Effective Group Discussion.* Dubuque, Iowa: Wm. C. Brown, 1967.

Potter, David, and Martin P. Anderson. *Discussion: A Guide to Effective Practice.* Belmont, California: Wadsworth Publishing, 1963.

Effective Group Discussion is a brief and clear account of the fundamentals of leading and participating in discussions. The book is aimed at the beginning student rather than at researchers and advanced students and presents an excellent simple treatment of first principles. The Potter and Anderson workbook is, according to the preface, primarily a classroom tool to be used as a supplement to a text or as a major teaching aid in a class that emphasizes practice. However, the Potter and Anderson manual does contain brief essays on preparing for discussion, improving participation, leadership, and problem-solving in discussion, as well as many rating blanks and questionnaires.

Workbook for Work Groups was written to provide a brief, practical, and sound group process booklet for management training seminars, workshops in group process and leadership, and short courses for discussion participants. It includes sections on cohesiveness, roles, leadership, and small group communication.

On Teaching Argumentative
Speaking and Formal Debate

Every daily newspaper and news broadcast confirms the fact that we are living in an age of confrontation between dissenters facing defenders of the establishment, as well as in an age of polarization between hawks and doves, blacks and whites, impoverished and enriched, teachers and learners, and men and unliberated women. Unhappily, these confrontations have not meant logical, structured, or even polite clashes over the issues at stake. Instead, they have pitted agitators against each other in emotional shouting contests that seem more concerned with recriminations than with resolution of problems and that rhetorically demonstrate what Richard Hofstadter called "the paranoid style in American politics."

Walter Lippmann might have been writing about 1970 when, fifteen years ago in *The Public Philosophy*, he sadly noted that "what has been lost in the tumult is the meaning of the obliga-

---

* This chapter is a slight revision of a portion of "Part Two: The Advanced course in Speech" in *Teacher's Guide to High School Speech* edited by Edward B. Jenkinson (Indianapolis: Indiana State Department of Public Instruction, 1966).

The members of the state-appointed committee who wrote the book include: J. Jeffery Auer, Indiana University; Mrs. Adeline Nall, Fairmount (Indiana) High School; Victor M. Powell, Wabash College; Miss Juanita Rucker, Chrysler High School, New Castle, Indiana; Mrs. Juanita Shearer, Brazil (Indiana) High School; Ronald F. Reid, University of Massachusetts; Harry H. Wilfong, Warren Central High School, Indianapolis, Indiana; and Edward B. Jenkinson, Indiana University.

Teacher's Guide to High School Speech is available from the Speech Communication Association. Copies cannot be purchased from the Indiana State Department of Public Instruction.

tion which is involved in the right to speak freely. It is the obligation to subject the utterance to criticism and debate. Because the dialectical debate is a procedure for attaining moral and political truth, the right to speak is protected by a willingness to debate:" This is the crux of real confrontation: *the espousal of contrary views by equally qualified debaters using equal amounts of time in the same hall and to the same audience.* The real strength of free speech lies in the mandate that those who are to decide must first hear each side. "For in the absence of debate," Lippmann warns, "unrestricted utterance leads to the degradation of opinion. By a kind of Gresham's law the more rational is overcome by the less rational, and the opinions that will prevail will be those which are held most ardently by those with the most passionate will."

These views are of course centered upon debate in the public forum, where debate is, as John F. Kennedy called it, "a testing of ideas" before public policies are determined. Is school debate different? Is the teaching of argumentative speaking in the secondary school classroom different? Only in one major sense: in the public forum the public policy is the payoff, but in school debating it is the learning experience (as *training* for participation in the public forum) that has immediate value.

From the standpoint of both teacher and student, this is a difference about what learning experiences are most appropriate to what level of development, not a substantive conflict about ultimate goals. We accept as almost axiomatic the notion that we learn to do by doing. Of course there are other methods. We also learn by watching others or by reading instructions. But we spend millions of dollars on laboratory space and equipment on the theory that students learn more even by fumbling through experiments than by watching others do them efficiently or by listening to teachers tell what will happen. Even though a teacher could, perhaps, tell a student all about something in two minutes, we believe the young experimenter will learn more and retain it longer by spending, say, two hours learning for himself.

We cannot, of course, draw a perfect parallel between debate and the laboratory method. But for the kinds of problems with which each is designed to deal, both approaches apply the laws of logic in a rational analysis. We cannot "try out" a proposed National Health Insurance plan on selected citizens, as a new drug may be "tested" on laboratory mice. The first is clearly a non-laboratory problem. Thus the conclusion we reach about it is distinguished by not being labeled a law or a scientific truth but an opinion arrived at through the rigor of debate.

Even the teacher of speech who is inexperienced in debate will know about the tools of rhetorical inquiry or analysis: he will have an understanding of logical validity, and he will know how to reason from evidence to a conclusion. Such a teacher may find useful a general treatment of argumentative speaking and formal debate, as they may be offered in secondary programs.

Argumentative Speaking

The student's first step is to learn the nature of an argumentative proposition, a task that is complicated by the fact that the term *proposition* is used in two different senses. In logic, a proposition is a verbalized judgment. Thus any assertion—from a simple statement such as "It is raining" to a highly controversial idea such as "The public school system should be federalized"—is a proposition. In argumentation, however, the term *proposition* is used differently. In a single speech, the proposition is the central idea, the main assertion that the advocate is trying to persuade his audience to accept. In debate, it is the central idea that one side wishes the audience to accept and the other side wishes the audience to reject.

Argumentative propositions grow out of some controversial question (issue). We do not ordinarily give speeches trying to persuade someone that the Declaration of Independence was signed on July 4, 1776, or that the earth revolves around the sun— these facts being too well known to be controversial. However, we do give speeches about controversial subjects, and, to be persuasive, we advance reasons for our point of view. In argumentation, our main reasons for believing a proposition are usually called *contentions.* The relationships among questions (issues), propositions, and contentions can be clarified by using examples like these:

QUESTIONS

MAIN QUESTION: Did John Doe kill his wife?
SUBORDINATE QUESTIONS:
  1. Did he have a motive to kill his wife?
  2. Did he have an opportunity to kill his wife?
  3. Are there any witnesses to testify that he killed his wife?

ARGUMENTATIVE SPEECH

PROPOSITION: John Doe killed his wife.
CONTENTIONS:
  1. He had a motive to kill his wife.
  2. He had the opportunity to kill his wife.
  3. Competent and unprejudiced witnesses saw John Doe kill his wife.

In this example, a general question gives rise to subordinate ones. By answering various specific questions, we have a better idea how to answer the general one. The proposition is simply an affirmative or negative statement answering the general question, and the contentions are answers to the specific questions. And, of course, the contentions should be based upon the available evidence.

Although theorists are not in universal agreement as to how best to classify propositions, most teachers of argumentation use the traditional division of fact, value, and policy. Many teachers concentrate on teaching propositions of policy, a practice that can be justified because questions of policy involve questions of fact and value. Others prefer to begin by teaching students to argue propositions of fact and value and then to work on propositions of policy. Either approach can get good results; but since one or the other must be used, let us decide arbitrarily to begin with factual questions in the procedures suggested below.

ARGUMENTATIVE SPEAKING ON QUESTIONS OF FACT

Students often have difficulty distinguishing between facts and propositions of fact. Unfortunately, it is exceedingly difficult to define a "fact," but a "proposition of fact" can be defined quite clearly. A proposition of fact is simply an assertion about the nature of reality. Thus the statement, "The world is flat," is a proposition of fact; it asserts that the world has a certain characteristic. The use of such obviously false propositions of fact is sometimes the best way of helping students to understand that propositions of fact are not the same as facts; they are simply assertions about reality, which can be either true or false.

More particularly, a proposition of fact asserts or denies (1) that something exists or occurs ("It is raining," "Flying saucers exist," "John Doe shot his wife last Monday," "The Senate will pass the housing bill next month"); (2) that something has certain characteristics ("The world is *flat*," "John Doe *deliberately* killed his wife"); or (3) that something has certain relationships to other things or events. The third type of factual proposition is difficult to teach, primarily because there are so many kinds of relationships that can be asserted. Some of the common relationships are: (a) similitude and dissimilitude ("John is *bigger* than his brother"), (b) time ("The Emancipation Proclamation was issued *after* the Civil War had started"), (c) space ("The ionosphere is about twenty-five miles *above* the surface of the earth"), and (d) causality ("Crime comics *cause* juvenile delinquency").

Many questions of fact are best settled by empirical observation, not by argumentative speaking. For example, the best way to determine whether it is raining outside is to look out the window, not to debate the question. However, when evidence is incomplete and inconclusive, opinions often differ; therefore, students should be taught to compose and analyze speeches on controversial factual questions and to be guided to the realization that empirical evidence often leads to differing opinions.

No clear-cut formula will work for organizing and developing argumentative speeches on all propositions of fact, but students should be encouraged to follow certain general procedures. First, the terms of the proposition should be defined clearly. For example, if someone argues that juvenile delinquency is caused by crime comics, the speaker should define clearly what he means by *juvenile delinquency* and by *crime comics.*

Second, the student should develop the habit of analyzing a general question by raising specific questions. For example, in the illustration used above, the general question of whether John Doe killed his wife gives rise to several specific questions: "Did he have a reason or motive to kill her?" "Did he have the opportunity?" "Are there any witnesses to the alleged killing?" Similarly, if the general question asks, "Do crime comics cause juvenile delinquency?" such specific questions as the following are relevant: "To what extent do juveniles read crime comics?" "Do those who read crime comics commit more acts of delinquency than non-readers?" "Do readers have other characteristics, different from non-readers, which might be related to delinquent behavior?" By raising such specific questions, the debater is able to locate the issues that must be resolved and to prepare his case accordingly.

ARGUMENTATIVE SPEAKING ON QUESTIONS OF VALUE

Propositions of value assert that something is good or bad; for example, "John Doe is a good man" or "Murder is evil." Some students have difficulty detecting propositions of value because many statements imply goodness or badness without actually using the words: for example, "It's a neat picture" or "He's a nice guy." Furthermore, it is often difficult to determine whether a proposition is meant as a factual assertion or as a value judgment: for example, when someone says, "The United States is a democracy," he is making a factual statement about our form of government, or (since most Americans think that democracy is good) is he implying that the United States is good?

One of the best ways of making the distinction between propositions of fact and those of value is to ask students to think in terms of a stimulus and a response. For example, an apple is a stimulus and our liking (or disliking) the apple is our response. The apple possesses certain characteristics—redness, crispness, and so forth —and if two persons perceive accurately, they will observe the same characteristics. Yet one person might respond favorably to the apple ("I like it" or "It's good"), while another might respond unfavorably ("I don't like it" or "It's bad"). Propositions of value do not assert that something has a certain characteristic; instead, they state the speaker's response to it. Factual propositions are about the nature of reality; whereas propositions of value are about our responses to reality.

Propositions of value are not confined to simple and rather trivial matters of taste, such as liking or disliking apples. Assertions about what is ethical and unethical, moral and immoral, beautiful and ugly are also propositions of value. Determining the truth of factual propositions is not too difficult if a sufficient amount of evidence is available. But how does one establish or deny a proposition of value? The answer to this question is not easy, but students should learn the nature of criteria and how to apply them. They should understand that criteria are standards for evaluation.

For example, suppose a speaker decides to support the proposition, "Lincoln was a great man." As a first step in analyzing this proposition, the student should establish criteria of "greatness." Similarly, if a proposition asserts that "Legalized abortion is moral" or "The federal system of government is outmoded" or "Present restrictions on law enforcement officers are undesirable," students should formulate criteria by which to judge morality, outmoded systems of government, or desirable restrictions.

Having formulated appropriate criteria, the student then attempts to apply them to the facts of the case. For example, having formulated criteria of greatness, the student should examine the facts about Lincoln's life to see which ones show that he meets the criteria and which ones show that he fails to meet them. In brief, analyzing propositions of value involves formulating criteria and applying them to the facts of the case.

ARGUMENTATIVE SPEAKING ON QUESTIONS OF POLICY

Propositions of policy are assertions that something should (or should not) be done. They call for the adoption of certain courses of action. For example, "The United States should discontinue farm price supports" and, at a less esoteric level, "I ought to eat lunch this noon" are propositions of policy.

As mentioned previously, many teachers concentrate on assignments involving propositions of policy because of custom and because analysis of facts is involved in analyzing policy questions. Indeed, one of the most important points for students to learn is that policy questions are resolved by studying the relevant facts and values. For example, suppose that a student advocates the use of seat belts in automobiles. The usual argument advanced to support this policy is that seat belts reduce the chances of injury in the event of an accident—an assertion about future fact. But also implicit in the argument is the value that one attaches to preserving his own life. Propositions of policy inevitably involve considerations of both facts and values.

Most textbooks in argumentation provide a list of the stock issues involved in propositions of policy. Although the lists vary slightly, the following is representative:

1. Is there a need for a new policy?
2. Will the proposed new policy solve the need?
3. Would the advantages of the new policy outweigh the disadvantages?

Simply giving the students a list of stock issues, however, is not sufficient. Students need to learn how to apply the system to specific propositions, and the national interscholastic debate propositions are often used for this purpose.

Let's consider the proposition, "The federal government should prohibit the requirement of union membership as a condition of employment." After determining precisely what this proposition means and what present governmental policy is, the student should ask himself: "What is the need for a new policy?"

In analyzing the issue of need, the student ought first to determine the goals of present policy. It is at this point that considerations of value become relevant. After all, our values determine our goals, and we may find a need to change present policies if they are based upon unwise goals. However, even if the goals of present policy are sound, the question arises, "Is the present policy failing significantly to attain the goals?" And, if so, does the failure result from some inherent feature of the policy, or does it result from other circumstances? In other words, is the problem inherent in the policy? In short, students should be taught to analyze the issue of need by asking these questions:

1. Are the goals of the present policy valid?
2. Is the present policy failing significantly to attain the goals?
3. Is the failure a result of some inherent feature of present policy?

In applying these questions to the proposal to prohibit union membership as a condition of employment, the student should ask himself what goals the present policy is trying to achieve and whether the goals are valid. Affirmative speakers might, for example, argue that the present goal is to encourage union membership and that such a goal is unwise, or they might argue that the goal of protecting individual rights is not being achieved. Conversely, opponents of the proposition might argue that the encouragement of union membership is not really a goal or that it is a worthwhile goal, or that the goal of protecting individual rights is satisfactorily achieved under present policy. Regardless of the specific pro and con arguments, analysis of the issue of need involves considering the goals of the present policy and the success of the present policy in achieving them.

The second main issue in a proposition of policy concerns practicality. Phrased as a question, the issue is "Will the proposed new policy solve the need?" A number of topics are relevant to this issue. If the policy requires an administrative agency, students should consider whether an adequate administrative structure can be organized, whether competent administrative personnel can be procured, and whether the law is enforceable. Not all policy proposals, of course, require administrative agencies, but when they do, such questions are relevant.

A major consideration regarding practicality, of course, is whether adoption of the proposed policy would remove the inherent factors that cause the present policy to fail. For example, one debate team, in affirming the proposition, "Resolved: That the United States should adopt a program of compulsory health insurance for all citizens," argued that the present system of private voluntary health insurance was deficient because private systems do not pay all medical costs. Then, in its proposed plan for health insurance, the team advocated a scheme in which the government would pay only part of the individual's medical costs and the individual would pay the rest. Clearly, this team had not corrected the situation that it considered a problem in the present system. Thus, even if it had been able to show that it had an administratively feasible proposal, it would not have been able to defend successfully the practicality of its proposal in solving the alleged need.

Finally, students should learn to compare the advantages and disadvantages that would result from adoption of a new policy. The advantages, of course, result from the solution of certain problems. But even if a proposal would solve certain problems in the present system, its adoption might create other problems. Stated another way, the adoption of a policy to attain certain goals might prevent the attainment of other goals.

For example, to attain the goal of protecting society against criminals, we might find it advantageous to permit police officers to search anyone they felt like searching, wire tap phones indiscriminately, abolish the rules of evidence, and take other drastic measures that would result in more convictions. Adoption of such policies, however, would interfere with the right of privacy. Consequently, the adoption of policies designed to achieve the goal of protecting society against criminals must be weighed against the goal of protecting the individual right of privacy; conversely, policies designed to protect the individual must be weighed against the goal of protecting society.

Similarly, the advantages of proposals calling for new governmental expenditures must be weighed against the goal of economizing. The advantages of a proposal calling for governmental regulation of the economy must be weighed against the goal of preserving a free market economy. In short, students should be taught to determine the total effect of adopting a new policy and to assess the effects in terms of various goals.

In selecting goals and determining their relative importance, students are again involved in making value judgments. They should learn that it is often necessary to consider the worth of various goals, some of which are contradictory, and to determine which goals are most important.

Suggested Activities

1. Give students a list of statements and ask them to classify them as propositions of fact, value, or policy.
2. Have students prepare a brief on an argumentative proposition, either the national interscholastic debate proposition or one selected specifically for classroom use. The brief should include a comprehensive listing of all possible need arguments, the major types of solutions that are compatible with the proposition, the major possible counter-plans, and all possible disadvantages, together with all possible counterarguments.
3. Conduct a class discussion on either one of the national interscholastic debate propositions or on a proposition selected specifically for classroom use. The discussion outline should include the following topics:

    I. The meaning of the proposition.
        A. What terms are ambiguous or technical enough to require definition?
        B. What definitions of these terms are given by authoritative sources?
    II. The present policy.
        A. Description of the present policy.

    1. What goals is the present policy designed to achieve?

    2. What methods are used under present policy to achieve these goals?

  B. Evaluation of the present policy.

    1. Are the present goals valid?

    2. Are present methods successful in meeting current goals?

    3. Are weaknesses in the present situation due to inherent features of present policy?

III. The proposed solution.

  A. Is the proposal administratively feasible?

  B. Is the proposal enforceable?

  C. If feasible and enforceable, would the proposal solve the inherent problems of present policy?

IV. Advantages versus disadvantages.

  A. What disadvantages might result from adopting the proposed policy?

  B. How do the advantages of solving present problems compare in importance with the disadvantages that might result from adopting the new policy?

4. Have each student select some subject-matter area and prepare and present three argumentative speeches, one on each of three types of proposition. As a prelude to the unit on formal debate, each speech could be followed by a short rejoinder given by another student.

5. Assign each student an oral critique on one or more speeches. The speeches should be evaluated on the basis of the adequacy of analysis. Either contemporary or historical speeches are useful for this purpose. For teachers preferring historical speeches, the following are useful:

Abraham Lincoln, "Address at Cooper Union," available in Marie Hochmuth and Wayland Maxfield Parrish. *American Speeches.* New York: Longmans, Green, 1954, pp. 284–304.

Daniel Webster, "The Murder of Captain Joseph White," available in Hochmuth and Parrish, pp. 122-178, and A. Craig

Baird. *American Public Addresses,* 1740-1952. New York: McGraw-Hill, 1956, pp. 46-53. Excellent background, including lengthy excerpts from the testimony given at the trial, is provided in Howard A. Bradley and James A. Winens. *Daniel Webster and the Salem Murder.* Columbia, Missouri: Artcraft Press, 1956.

Formal Debate

Many teachers like to use one or more of the national interscholastic debate propositions for classroom debates. Others prefer to select their own resolution or to have the class make a selection. In either event, the teacher should be familiar with the criteria of a good resolution and may wish to discuss these criteria with the class.

First, the resolution should have two good sides. A debate on the factual proposition, "The world is flat," would be a waste of time; the affirmative obviously could not construct a sensible case. Some students find it difficult to understand that a debate resolution can have two good sides because they have an unfortunate tendency to think in "either . . . or" terms. They tend to think that a proposition is either all true or all false and that an examination of the facts will reveal it to be one or the other.

Unfortunately, life is not so simple. True enough, we can best determine the color of a house simply by looking at it, not by debating the question; but how are we to know whether John Doe killed his wife? Or whether crime comics cause juvenile delinquency? or whether John Quincy Adams made a "deal" with Henry Clay to gain the presidency in 1824? Such factual questions are often debatable because they cannot be resolved by simple observation and because evidence is inconclusive or contradictory. Furthermore, not all propositions are limited to considerations of facts. Intelligent people often disagree about questions of value—witness contemporary debates on the morality of abortion or wire tapping. And even experts often are at odds on matters of policy —witness contemporary debates on foreign policy and economic legislation. Whenever evidence is inconclusive, and intelligent and informed opinion is contradictory, a debate proposition will probably have two good sides.

Second, it is usually better to phrase a debate resolution affirmatively. Negatively worded resolutions are seldom as productive as affirmatively worded ones. For example, a debate on the proposition, "The mayor-council form of government in Centerville should be abolished," would probably result in a consideration of alleged weaknesses of the mayor-council form of government, and the audience might be left wondering what form of government the affirmative side thinks is better. It would be preferable to debate a proposition such as, "A city-manager form of government should be adopted by Centerville." An affirmative proposal lends itself better to a comparison of the advantages and disadvantages of two or more policies. Negatively worded resolutions, on the other hand, give opponents of the status quo an opportunity to criticize present policy without a corresponding responsibility to suggest a better policy.

Third, debate resolutions should be worded in an unprejudiced manner. For example, the proposition, "Problems resulting from the present system of international monetary reserves should be solved by establishing a system of adjustable world monetary reserves," gives the affirmative the crucial issue of whether the present system is defective (or at least implies that such is the case) and leaves open only the solution for debate. It would be better to phrase a proposition calling for an adjustable world monetary reserves system and let the adequacy of the present system also be debated. Similarly, loaded words ought to be avoided.

Fourth, propositions for formal debate should contain only one proposal. A resolution calling for two or more proposals is likely to result in a confusion of arguments. In general, issues become more clear-cut if only one main idea is debated at a time.

Finally, resolutions should be worded so that the affirmative advocates a new proposal. Although this principle is more a custom than a theoretical necessity, it works better within the context of the usual debate format. The affirmative speaks first in the usual format. If the affirmative is supporting present policy, what is it to say? It could, of course, praise the merits of present policy, but a better debate results if the defenders of the status quo present its merits after it has been attacked by the proponents of a new policy. In other words, existing beliefs and policies are presumed to be satisfactory, and the advocate of something new is under the burden of persuading listeners to accept the new idea.

Suggested Activities

1. Have the class select a subject-matter area for classroom debate and have each student prepare one or more resolutions within the subject-matter area. If you prefer to use one of the national propositions in class, have the class phrase other propositions within the same subject-matter area.
2. Have the class discuss the national debate resolutions in terms of the criteria of a good resolution.

ANALYZING THE MEANING OF A DEBATE RESOLUTION

Because language is inherently imperfect, any debate resolution, no matter how precisely worded, contains a certain element of ambiguity. The debater's first step, therefore, is to determine as clearly as possible just what the resolution means.

Students were introduced to the methods of defining terms in the basic course. However, it might be well to review the basic characteristics of a definition—classification and differentiation—and to review the methods of definition, such as using synonyms, examples, and dictionary definitions. In addition, students should be taught (1) the requirements of a good definition and (2) the sources of a good definition. These matters are especially important for debaters, who must define the terms of a resolution before they can debate it intelligently.

Definitions should be more specific and clear-cut than the term that is being defined. Furthermore, definitions should be reasonable in light of present usage. For example, a number of years ago the national intercollegiate debate resolution called for the establishment of a "federal world government." One debate team, more ingenious than sensible, discovered an old theological doctrine that went under the name of "federal." The team proceeded to define "federal world government" as a worldwide theocracy based upon the principles of federal theology. Such a definition might have made sense when federal theology was well-known (in the seventeenth century), but such a definition is not reasonable today.

A standard source of definitions is, of course, the dictionary. Many debate resolutions, however, involve technical terms; therefore students should go to technical sources. If a proposition contains legal terminology, students should go to legal dictionaries; if it contains economic terminology, they should go to economic textbooks, and so on.

Many high school students (and adults, for that matter) get upset if authoritative sources disagree on the meaning of terms. Many interscholastic debates are marred by one team's maintaining that a term means one thing, the other team's maintaining that it does not—and both citing authorities for their position. Semanticists remind us that terms do not *have* meanings; people *assign* meanings to terms. Consequently, it is quite possible that different authorities will assign different meanings to the same term. Thus, students should not be encouraged to find *the* meaning of a proposition, but rather, they should be encouraged to find the various meanings that authorities give to it. In formal debate, the affirmative, since it is proposing a proposition, ought to have the right to debate a proposition on the basis of any reasonable definition; and the negative should be sufficiently flexible to adapt to any reasonable definition.

Suggested Activities

1. Assign a three-minute speech of definition in which each student defines a term related to the resolution for classroom debate. The terms could be technical (*gross national product, union shop, balance of payments*) or a glittering generality (*justice, free enterprise, democracy*). (For a discussion of a method that helps students define words, see chapter 7 of *Writing As a Process of Discovery* by Edward B. Jenkinson and Donald A. Seybold. Bloomington: Indiana University Press, 1970.)

2. Assign a three-minute speech of definition in which groups of students are assigned different techniques of definition, such as definition by authority, by example, or by comparison.

DETERMINING THE ISSUES IN A DEBATE RESOLUTION

The stock issues in a proposition of policy were considered in the unit on argumentative speaking, but a brief review of them is often helpful before students begin analyzing a debate resolution. A debater should have a clear understanding of what is meant by need, practicality, and advantages versus disadvantages before he starts to construct a debate case.

The debater should also understand certain theoretical concepts. He should understand the concept of presumption, which means that the status quo (present policy) already occupies the ground and that the advocate of a new policy (the affirmative) must therefore assume the burden of overthrowing present policy. In other words, the affirmative must show why a new policy should be substituted for the present one; it has a burden of proof, or, as it is often termed, a burden of persuasion. Its burden is sometimes called the risk of non-persuasion since, if the affirmative fails to persuade the listener, the status quo will continue.

The affirmative's burden is met with a *prima facie* case: that is, a case which reasonable people would consider persuasive in the absence of refutation. Once the affirmative fulfills its burden by presenting a *prima facie* case, the negative has the burden of rebuttal: that is, the duty of responding to the case. Both sides, of course, have the duty of responding to its opponent's arguments as a debate progresses, but the burden of proof remains with the affirmative.

Theoretically, affirmative debaters must succeed in establishing their contentions on all three of the main issues if they are to fulfill their burden of proof. After all, why should we accept a new policy simply because present policy is defective? To demonstrate a need is insufficient; we want a policy that will be practical in solving the needs. Furthermore, even if the affirmative could present a practical plan for solving present problems, we would not want it if it would create more disadvantages than it would solve.

In short, the affirmative must show a need *and* the practicality of its proposal *and* that the advantages of the proposal would outweigh any disadvantages that the negative might allege. Clearly, the negative has the opportunity to make choices in fulfilling its burden of rebuttal. It could, for example, agree to the issue of need but argue against the practicality of the affirmative's proposal. In other words, the stock issues are only potential issues; they do not become actual issues unless there is disagreement between the two sides.

No pat formula exists for telling students which arguments to use in a debate case. However, affirmative debaters should be encouraged to select the contentions that will be the strongest in light of the available evidence and the audience's beliefs and values. Similarly, the negative should be encouraged to determine which issues are the most vulnerable to attack and to concentrate its attack on those points.

Suggested Activities

1. Assign students to prepare briefs on the resolution selected for classroom debate. Each brief should include a comprehensive listing of possible need issues, practicality issues, and issues concerning possible advantages and disadvantages.
2. Assign a "need" speech in which the student states a need contention and develops it with evidence and reasoning.
3. Assign a "disadvantages" speech in which the student states a disadvantage, explains how and why adoption of the resolution would result in the disadvantage, and supports his argument with evidence and reasoning.

CONSTRUCTING THE CASE

What are the duties of the affirmative and negative debaters? Rather than separating the duties of each side, the statements that follow have been structured around the duties of each debater in his order of speaking in a typical school debate: the first affirmative speech, the first negative speech, the second affirmative speech, and the second negative speech.

The first affirmative speech sets the pace for a formal debate. If this speech is composed well, chances are high that a good debate is under way. Assuming that a good debate is dependent upon the first affirmative speaker, let us examine in detail each of his duties: (1) introduction, (2) statement of the resolution, (3) definition of terms in the resolution, (4) brief summary of the entire affirmative case, (5) explanation of the status quo, (6) demonstration of the inherent weakness (need for a change) in the status quo, and (7) summary of the speech.

The introduction is little more than an attention step. To stimulate a listener, the first affirmative speaker must make some sort of ear-catching statement related to the solution. The introduction could be a shocking or surprising quotation, an almost unbelievable fact or statistic, or an interesting example. The introduction must fulfill its purpose of getting the attention of the audience; otherwise the debate will begin on a sour note. Thus, the first speaker should communicate effectively from the very beginning so that the listener will automatically want to listen to the debate.

After the listener's interest has been aroused, the affirmative speaker is now ready to state the resolution. Many beginning debaters often forget to state precisely what they are talking about, thus leaving the teacher, judge, or audience bewildered. The resolution should be stated slowly, distinctly, and clearly. In some instances it could be repeated for the sake of emphasis.

The debater must never insult the intelligence of his audience; thus in defining the terms of the resolution, he should define only those terms which could become controversial. For example, take the term international organization"—what does the affirmative mean by these two words? Does he mean an organization formed by two countries, four countries, or all the countries of the world? A degree of fair play or ethics is involved in defining terms; thus the affirmative debater should be as clear and meaningful as possible. A debater who relies upon skimming the terms indeed is missing the real objective of debate.

A good debater will summarize the entire affirmative case before he begins describing the status quo. He will tell his opponents what his need contentions are and give a brief summary of the plan that his colleague will propose to satisfy the inherent needs. By giving a complete summary of his case, the affirmative gives the negative team and his audience a clear and well-organized preview of what is to come. The next step is to explain the status quo. The explanation and the illustration of needs for a change can be, and are often, combined.

After the status quo has been explained, the first affirmative debater should emphasize the weaknesses by bringing them to the foreground and clearly labeling them "needs for a change" from the present state. Usually two to four major needs are sufficient; however, in some cases perhaps only one major need is desirable—in others, perhaps as many as six. The needs should be pointed out one by one and probably numbered; for example, "Need number one is. . . ." "Need number two is. . . ." And so on. After each need is developed, the affirmative debater should summarize it before continuing to his next need contention. If this practice is followed, the organization of the first affirmative speech will be clear to all concerned.

After the last need in the affirmative's case is completed, a good debater will summarize very briefly what he has said and, if at all possible, conclude by relating back to the introduction or attention step.

After the first affirmative's speech, the first negative's duties are clearly set for him. He should (1) accept or reject the definition of terms, (2) summarize the first affirmative's speech, indicating the approach to be taken by the negative, (3) refute each affirmative need contention one by one, (4) rebuild the status quo, and (5) summarize the entire first negative speech.

Before examining the above points, let us examine the negative approaches that may be pursued. First, the negative may defend the status quo. In this approach, the negative will clash directly with the need contentions of the affirmative and/or the practicality of the affirmative plan. Second, the negative may use a "patch and repairs" case. In this approach, the negative clashes with the *inherency* of the needs, and purposes modifications of the status quo. The modifications should solve the problems without changing the inherent features of present policy. Third, the negative may present a counterplan in which the need is admitted and a substitute solution is proposed.

Keeping the varying approaches in mind, we can now consider the duties of the first negative speaker. Perhaps the first duty of the negative is to agree or disagree with the definition of terms in the resolution given by the affirmative. Generally speaking, accepting the term is a common courtesy; however, if the negative justly feels that the affirmative is unclear or using a trick in his definitions, it is only logical for the negative speaker to reserve the right to challenge the terms until the affirmative defines them more accurately. If the negative speaker makes no reference to the definition of terms, it is automatically assumed that the terms are acceptable. If a negative team rejects the definition of terms, the debate could develop into a quibbling controversy, causing the main issues to be avoided.

The second duty of the negative speaker in presenting his case is to summarize what has been said by the first affirmative speaker and to make quite clear what approach he will use in his adaptation to the affirmative case. If he plans to defend the status quo, then he should so state; if he plans to acknowledge weaknesses in the status quo but argue that they are not inherent and can be solved by a few moderate changes, then he should so state; if he plans to agree with the affirmative's need contentions but offer a more desirable solution, then again he should so state.

Third, if the status quo is being defended, the negative should refute each affirmative need contention one by one. It is the duty of the first negative speaker to take each need contention given by the affirmative and refute it with evidence and reasoning. If the negative wishes to modify the status quo or to offer a counterplan, he should explain clearly the nature of his proposals and then show how they can solve the needs.

Fourth, the negative should rebuild the status quo (unless, of course, a counterplan is being presented). Although the refutation of the need contentions is a rebuilding to the status quo, it is very important for the negative to relate his refutation to the status quo by pointing out that the avowed needs are not inherent and do not exist to any appreciable degree. Thus the negative speaker has not only refuted the affirmative's argument but has re-established the effectiveness of the status quo.

Finally, the first negative speaker should summarize, for the sake of clarity and emphasis.

The responsibilities of the second affirmative speaker are (1) to summarize what has been said by the first negative, (2) to refute the negative's arguments, (3) to rebuild the affirmative need contentions, (4) to present the affirmative plan that will meet or satisfy the affirmative needs, and (5) to summarize the entire second affirmative speech. To go into detail on most of these points would be to repeat what we have already said.

It is not uncommon to hear a debater proposing a plan that has little to do with the affirmative needs. It is the duty of the second affirmative speaker to relate his solution to the need contentions: "Need number one is . . . and the affirmative's proposal will solve this need. . . ." In short, the proposed plan must meet the needs in the most effective way without introducing new evils.

The second negative speaker should (1) summarize the entire debate at this point, (2) locate, analyze, and refute the major issues, (3) refute the practicality of the affirmative plan, (4) re-establish the negative case, and (5) summarize the entire speech. Perhaps it should be noted that the negative should analyze the plan from the standpoints of unworkability, impracticality, and undesirability. If a negative team is using a counterplan, then it is its duty to show the advantages of its plan over the solution offered by the affirmative.

Suggested Activities

1. Have each student prepare an affirmative case on the resolution selected for use in class.
2. Have students outline and evaluate the affirmative case presented in a debate that has been printed.

REFUTATION

Debate is distinguishable from other forms of public speaking because it provides opportunity for refutation. Without an opportunity to defend one's own arguments and to attack those of one's opponents, there is no debate. Refutation is essential in debate, but it is one of the most difficult arts for students to learn.

Many of the principles that undergird the art of refutation have already been discussed. If students know how to evaluate evidence, reason logically analyze propositions, and construct *prima facie* cases they have already mastered the basic principles of refutation. Consequently, students will have been exposed to the fundamentals of refutation before actually engaging in it—at least this will be true if the teacher organizes his course in the same way that this course of study is organized.

Nevertheless, students often have difficulty applying the principles of argumentation to the specific task of refutation. Consequently, the teacher will need to help them to apply these diverse principles to the single task at hand. And it goes without saying that an important way of helping them is to give them much practice and to criticize their performances. In addition, specific instruction should be given in the purposes, the basic methods, and the organizational techniques of refutation.

The purposes of refutation are simple and easily explained. In essence, the debater's task is to rebuild his own arguments and to destroy those of his opponent. For the audience, this process of tearing down and rebuilding arguments serves a valuable purpose: it helps the listener to understand the issues and to make an intelligent judgment concerning them.

There are so many methods of refutation that a comprehensive list is almost impossible to compile. However, the teacher should familiarize the student with the basic methods. First, the importance of effective listening and careful note-taking should be stressed. Many a debater has had difficulties because he answered an argument that he thought his opponent developed but which, in fact, his opponent did not. Careless listening often causes debaters to misinterpret what their opponents said.

Second, debaters should be taught to think in terms of chains of argument, rather than simply in terms of individual arguments. For example, an affirmative case supporting a policy proposition consists essentially of three major contentions—there is a need for a new policy, the proposed policy will solve the need, and the advantages of adopting the proposal will outweigh the disadvantages —and (theoretically, at least) *all* of these arguments must be made to establish the proposition. Theoretically, therefore, the negative can admit two of the affirmative's arguments and concentrate on refuting only one of them. Similarly, to establish a disadvantage of the affirmative proposal, the negative must show that the adoption of the policy would have a given effect *and* that the effect would be harmful. The affirmative can *either* deny that the effect would accrue, *or* deny that the effect would be harmful, *or* argue that the degree of harm would be less than that of maintaining the status quo.

Once a student develops the habit of thinking in terms of chains of argument, rather than simply in terms of individual arguments, he can employ three specific methods of refutation:

1. He can look for unstated assumptions—links in the chain, which his opponent did not state but which must be valid for the conclusion to be established—and attack the assumptions if they are vulnerable.
2. He can agree to certain arguments but show that they are irrelevant to the major point that his opponent is trying to establish.
3. He can admit certain arguments but show that the conclusion depends upon other arguments in addition to the admitted ones, and concentrate his attack on the weak link in the chain.

Once a debater learns to search for the weak link in an opponent's chain of argument, he avoids the errors of trying to refute strong or irrelevant points and trying to cover more than he has time to cover; instead, he seeks out fatal flaws and drives a wedge into them.

What are some of the methods of attacking crucial weaknesses?

First, the opponent's evidence can be attacked. If the source of the evidence is incompetent or highly biased, the worth of the evidence is suspect. For example, in debating a proposition concerning labor unions, the debater can attack statements of opinion by either industrial managers or union officials because the sources are likely to be biased. A good debater will point out these biases and introduce counterevidence from more objective sources.

Nor is testimony of opinion the only type of evidence whose source can be questioned. Statistical surveys conducted by biased sources are often deficient. We all know the story (perhaps apocryphal) of the tobacco company that sent free cartons of its cigarettes to medical doctors and then sent interviewers around a few days later to ask physicians what brand of cigarettes they were smoking at the time. Small wonder that "most medical doctors" smoked the company's brand. When statistical surveys are used, debaters should determine how the evidence was gathered. Was a representative sample used? Were leading questions asked? Any significant weaknesses along these lines can be emphasized in refuting the opponent's evidence.

Similarly, biased sources often employ questionable measuring sticks in statistical studies. The selection of one type of measurement often leads to one conclusion whereas another type leads to another. For example, suppose that a given community has very few wealthy people living in it along with few medium-income people and many poor people. Someone who wished to show that the community had a high income could do so by computing a *mean* average (adding all of the incomes and dividing by the number of income-earners). Mean averages are always affected by extremes, and the few wealthy people would artificially raise the "average community income" to a high level. Conversely, someone who wished to show that the community had a low income could do so by computing a *median* average (ranking all of the incomes and determining the mid-point). A debater should determine precisely what measurements were used and, if they are questionable, expose their weaknesses in refutation.

Examples taken from biased or incompetent sources are often questionable. For instance, a number of years ago the national intercollegiate debate proposition called for a national right-to-work law; some debaters used examples of "unfair labor practices" that had been taken from an article in a popular magazine, one which is usually superficial and biased in its reporting. Good debaters soon discovered that all of the examples cited in the article involved court cases, and they studied the opinions rendered by the courts. They found that "unfair labor practices" were involved —but the accused parties in every example had been found innocent! It is easy to imagine the effect of the debaters' citing the judicial opinions to refute the examples cited from the popular magazine.

Second, in addition to countering an opponent's evidence, a debater can refute by exposing weaknesses in interpreting the evidence. To establish a conclusion, a debater must reason from evidence to the conclusion, and a rebuttalist can expose weaknesses in his opponent's reasoning.

Third, if the opponent generalizes, the debater can refute by showing that the particular instances are insufficient in number or are non-representative of the category being generalized about. This method is more effective if the rebuttalist also presents counterexamples.

In some instances, the examples cited by the side that is generalizing are not presented to show that the generalization applies in *all* instances; instead, the generalization is qualified by saying that "X is sometimes true," or "X is true of many cases," or "X is often true." In such cases, the use of counterexamples is not too effective; the opponent has already protected himself against counterexamples by qualifying his generalization. However, the rebuttalist can sometimes minimize the generalization by showing that it holds true in only a few instances or by showing that the seriousness of the situation is insignificant. Conversely, the person making the generalization can maximize it in rebuttal by showing that the number of cases is large or by making the seriousness of the situation vivid.

The techniques of minimization and maximization do not involve the truth of generalizations as much as they involve the listener's feelings about them. Suppose, for example, that a given state had a labor force of ten million people, five-hundred thousand of whom were unemployed. One debater, asserting that this situation constituted a problem could say that "Many people are unemployed, some five-hundred thousand in all—many of whom are married and have dependents." Another debater might say that "Only five percent of the labor force is unemployed." Some listeners would probably regard the situation as a problem whereas others would not; and the relative skill of the two debaters in maximizing and minimizing the situation could affect the listeners' reactions.

Fourth, if the opponent argues from analogy, the rebuttalist can show that the analogy is too dissimilar to justify the conclusion. For example, one speaker in an argumentation class attempted to show that an "honor system" would work in a large university because it had worked in one of the military academies. His opponent argued that, even if the honor system had worked well, the situations in military academies and large universities are too dissimilar to justify the conclusion. Here again some minimization and maximization are involved; for no two situations are exactly alike. One debater can legitimately point to similarities while another can legitimately emphasize differences. The task of both sides, during the rebuttals, is to persuade the listener that the differences are more significant than the similarities, or vice versa.

Fifth, if the opponent argues from general principles to conclusions about specific instances, the rebuttalist can point out deductive fallacies. However, as we have already mentioned, the nature of deductive argument is complicated and technical for high school students, and the various fallacies of deduction are therefore difficult to teach. Nevertheless, good students can be taught to cast deductive arguments into syllogistic form and to recognize the fallacy of the undistributed middle. For example, suppose a debater asserts that "X union practices discrimination against racial minorities," and supports the point with the general principle, "Most labor unions are discriminatory." Cast into syllogistic form, the argument is as follows:

Major premise: Most labor unions are discriminatory.
Minor premise: X is a labor union.
Conclusion: X is discriminatory.

However, the middle term, *labor unions,* is undistributed in this syllogism; that is, only a part of the category of labor unions is alleged to be discriminatory. Consequently, the conclusion does not follow from the premises. Technically, the syllogism contains the fallacy of the undistributed middle term.

Another form of the fallacy follows:

Major premise: All teachers work in school buildings.
Minor premise: Miss Smith works in a school building.
Conclusion: Miss Smith is a teacher.

If the minor premise said that Miss Smith is a teacher, it would be valid to conclude that she works in a school building. However, this syllogism is invalid. Since "(people who) work in school buildings" is the major term, it is possible that the major category contains particulars that do not fall within the middle term. To put it more simply, Miss Smith might be a secretary who works in a school. Although few debaters cast their arguments into syllogistic form, a good rebuttalist is able to point out deductive fallacies.

In summary, instruction in refutation should emphasize the importance of careful note-taking and listening. The student should be taught to think in terms of chains of argument, rather than in terms of individual arguments; he should look for unstated assumptions, irrelevant points, and weak links in the chain. He should learn how to expose weaknesses in either the evidence or the reasoning presented by his opponents.

Many students, even though familiar with the points just mentioned, have difficulty presenting effective rebuttals. They often become disorganized, hence confusing to the audience Therefore, a review of the principles of effective organization will be helpful. Some teachers like to give their students an organizational formula for refutation. The following is helpful for negative debaters:

1. State the general position being taken with regard to the opponent's arguments.
2. Indicate which of the opponent's arguments will be contested and which will not.

3. Point out why some of the arguments will not be contested (for example, they are irrelevant or, since the conclusion depends upon additional arguments, they are not crucial).
4. Refute each of the opposing arguments in the same order that they are presented. In refuting, (a) state the argument being refuted, (b) summarize the counterarguments that will be developed, (c) develop each of the counterarguments, (d) summarize the counterarguments, and (e) make a clear transition to the next major argument that is to be refuted.

The same basic approach can be used by an affirmative debater to rebuild his case after it has been attacked. However, his rebuttal should be in terms of his own case. He should restate the original case summarily and then state the first argument in the case, summarize the answers against it, and attack the answers much in the same way described above.

Like all formulae, these will not work in all situations. Teachers should not insist pedantically that students follow these schemes. But mastery of them will be helpful to students, at least as a beginning.

Suggested Activities

1. Divide the class into pairs. One student should present a single argument and the other should refute it. Then have the students reverse roles.
2. Have each member of the class bring a newspaper editorial to class, summarize it, and refute it.
3. Have the class analyze a debater's refutation of "need" contentions in a debate that has been printed.

Cross-Examination

Many high school speech teachers like to give their students training in the art of cross-examination. Such training is crucial if students are to compete successfully in interscholastic debate tournaments. Furthermore, training and experience in cross-examination are valuable for all students.

Although valuable, the art of cross-examination is extremely difficult to master. Many unskilled debaters permit cross-examination periods to turn into disorganized arguments and, even worse, into sessions where legitimate questions are evaded and insults are exchanged.

Because cross-examination is difficult and can easily lead to unethical tactics, the teacher must assume responsibility for comprehensive and accurate instruction in the art. The first step is to explain clearly the purposes of cross-examination. The purpose is not to give speeches or to browbeat the opposition. Rather, the purposes are (1) to gain information (for example, to determine the opponent's stand on an issue, the source of a piece of evidence, or the meaning of a term); (2) to assist the debater in developing his own case (for example, to gain admission of an assumption on which an argument rests); or (3) to expose weaknesses in the opponent's line of argument (for example, to expose fallacious reasoning or inconsistencies).

Equally important is instruction in the ethics of cross-examination. Students should understand that the cross-examination period in a debate belongs to the questioner, not the respondent (that is, the person being questioned), and that the respondent should therefore keep his answers brief and to the point. They should understand that it is legitimate to discredit arguments and evidence but that it is not legitimate to discredit the other debater. They should understand that speeches are not in order. If the questioner secures a damaging admission, he should wait until his next speech to comment upon it; and if the respondent sees the point that his opponent is trying to make, he should resist the temptation to refute it until his next speech.

Only when students understand the purposes and ethics of cross-examination are they ready to learn the fundamentals of asking and answering questions. The main principle of effective questioning is that the debater's questions, like the points in a speech, should be organized so that an argument or counterargument is developed clearly. Like the points in a speech, the questions should lead to a conclusion.

Some poorly trained debaters attempt to get their opponents

to admit the conclusion in the course of one or two questions ("Don't you agree that there's a need for a change?"). A respondent will seldom admit the questioner's conclusion, especially a broad one concerning need or practicality. Consequently, the questioner should set up a chain of small points or pieces of evidence. For example, a number of years ago, the national intercollegiate debate proposition called for giving Congress the power to reverse Supreme Court decisions. One affirmative team argued that many Supreme Court decisions have the effect of making policy, a situation that constitutes a problem because judges lack the executive and legislative experience to make good policy. The cross-examination conducted by the negative went something like this:

Q: Who is serving on the Supreme Court at present?
A: Earl Warren, who is Chief Justice, Tom Clark, Hugo Black . . .
Q: Could you tell me something about Justice Warren's background?
A: Well, I'm not familiar with his entire life; he was Governor of California.
Q: Pretty active in Republican politics, wasn't he?
A: Oh yes.
Q: Could you tell me something about Justice Clark's background?
A: Well, he was Attorney General during the Truman Administration.
Q: Could you tell me something about Justice Black's background?
A: Well, he was a Southerner, appointed by Roosevelt.
Q: Did he hold any public offices before his appointment?
A: Yes, he was a Senator.
Q: Now let's see. Warren is an ex-Governor, Clark an ex-Attorney General, and Black an ex-Senator. Right?
A: Yes.
Q: Wasn't one of your main points that Supreme Court Justices lack legislative and executive experience?
A: (gulp) Yes.

Note that the questioner led to his conclusion in much the same way that an argument in a speech is developed. Bits of evidence were drawn out, a summary of the evidence was given in the next-to-the-last question, and the conclusion was implied in his last question.

Note too that the cross-examiner stopped when he did. Unskilled debaters are prone to push too far by asking something like, "Well, in light of what you have just admitted, why do you still believe that?" Such a question, of course, gives the respondent an opportunity to present his own evidence and reasoning.

Since the cross-examiner should attempt to make two or three crucial points during a cross-examination period, it is important for him to know what points he wants to make before he starts. Prepared questions are almost always necessary, though, of course, debaters should be encouraged to be flexible.

Debaters should be taught to answer questions briefly and courteously. They should, of course, be encouraged to look ahead—to try to determine what points their opponents are trying to get them to admit; but they should resist the temptation to evade or to offer refutation in their answers. Their best protection is to have a logical, well supported case; if they do, their questioners will not be able to expose any fatal weaknesses.

Classroom Debates

One speaking activity usually predominates during a unit on formal debate—obviously classroom debates. We have, however, suggested a number of activities in connection with the various aspects of formal debate, that can serve to ease the student into the debating situation gradually. If these activities are all related to the debate resolution being used in the classroom debates, students should be well prepared for the first full-scale formal debate.

Formats for classroom debates vary widely. Which will be most useful depends upon the length of the class period and the amount of time the teacher wishes to have for criticizing the debate. If time permits, the usual format used at debate tournaments is very good. For shorter debates, adaptations must be made. For example, the following makes a good format for a forty-minute debate:

First affirmative speeech	7 minutes
First negative speech	7 minutes
Second affirmative speech	7 minutes
Second negative speech	7 minutes
First negative rebuttal	3 minutes

First affirmative rebuttal	3 minutes
Second negative rebuttal	3 minutes
Second affirmative rebuttal	3 minutes

The following makes a good format for a fifty-minute debate:

First affirmative speech	7 minutes
Negative cross-examination of first affirmative speaker	4 minutes
First negative speech	7 minutes
Affirmative cross-examination of first negative speaker	4 minutes
Second affirmative speech	7 minutes
Negative cross-examination of second affirmative speaker	4 minutes
Second negative speech	7 minutes
Affirmative cross-examination of second negative speaker	4 minutes
Negative summary	3 minutes
Affirmative summary	3 minutes

The judging of classroom debates helps to motivate students. However, when debates are judged, the judges should be instructed to assume at the beginning that they are neutral toward the debate resolution. This requirement is necessary if debaters who are advocating the side of the resolution with which the judge personally disagrees are to have equal chance. The teacher may wish to do all of the judging himself, but experienced and talented debaters will find the experience of judging valuable.

On Teaching Rhetorical Appreciation

RICHARD MURPHY

Professor of Speech
University of Illinois

We may think of *rhetoric* as something ephemeral—some words, spoken or written for some persuasive purpose of the moment, which soon perish from the earth. The phrase, *mere rhetoric*, is used to condemn language that is empty, overly ornate, or lacking in substance. Actually, types of rhetoric are among the oldest art forms, and speeches have been preserved throughout literature. In the *Iliad*, Homer described "fleet-footed noble Achilles" as speaking "winged words." Thucydides records Pericles speaking at the graves of those who fell in the first year of the Peloponnesian War, 431 B.C.; lines from the speech are recognizable today, for example: "The great impediment to action is, in our opinion, not discussion, but the want of that knowledge which is gained by discussion preparatory to action." The Bible has splendid examples of speeches. The prophets thunder against the sins of the people; the parables of Jesus are simple homilies on man's behavior. The "Voice of the Lord" sounds forth again and again. Did you realize that the Ten Commandments are a speech of "God?"

Speeches often are a mark in the development of culture. It is said that British history begins in 597 when King Ethelbert, speaking to St. Augustine and his group (who had come from Rome to Christianize the Britons) promised them sanctuary: "Since I seem to perceive that you believe the concepts you wish to impart to us to be true and ennobling, we desire that no harm befall you." From that speech came the establishment of Canterbury diocese and a continuous line of archbishops for fourteen centuries. Famous speeches dot our literature and mark cultural achievements. Edmund Burke's speeches for humane treatment of the American colonists by the British have been studied in American schools for two centuries. Who does not know Patrick Henry's "Give me liberty, or give me death" speech to the Virginia Convention in 1775? George Washington's "Farewell Address" of 1796 is an American classic, is read in Congress every year on his birthday, and contains such oft-quoted passages as, "In proportion as the structure of a government gives force to public opinion, it is essential that public opinion should be enlightened." On the sacred land at Runnymede, where the Great Charter was signed in 1215, there is an acre of ground given by the British to the American people. A stone monument to John F. Kennedy marks the spot, and on the memorial stone there is carved a sentence from his inaugural address. The great speech reveals a significant moment in history, a landmark in culture. The great speech preserves for us a microcosm of humanity; a man in high thought and feeling, in a worthy cause, seeking by his word-artistry to make an audience know and care about values in life.

Rhetorical appreciation is not limited to speeches. Any discourse, oral or written, which is directed to getting a response from an audience on some view or action is rhetorical. This appeal may be found in all forms of discourse. In order to understand rhetorical appreciation, it is helpful to identify other main forms of discourse. One form is *poetic*; imagistic and figurative language, usually highly patterned as in the English sonnet, with three quatrains and a couplet, rhyming *a b a b, c d c d, e f e f, g g*. Poetry is a category large enough to include blank verse (iambic pentameter without rhyme, as found in Shakespeare), and even free verse. Traditionally, the appeal in poetic is aesthetic, somewhat removed from everyday practical affairs. We may think of poetic as having to do with seasons, and with birds singing, as in Shelley's "Ode to the West Wind," or Keats's "Ode to a Nightingale." Actually, much poetry is didactic; that is, rhetorical. Shelley's "To the Men of England" has a verse:

> Men of England, wherefore plough
> For the lords who lay ye low?
> Wherefore weave with toil and care
> The rich robes your tyrants wear?

Much of Robert Burns is didactic and therefore rhetorical, as are his lines in "Man Was Made to Mourn": "Man's inhumanity to man makes countless thousands mourn."

Our literature is rich in another form of discourse, the *dialogue,* in which question and answer are used, or rejoinders are made in sequence. Two or more persons may reason together by turn, as in the *Dialogues* of Plato, and Landor's *Imaginary Conversations* (1824-29). A writer who wishes to stand outside the arena may cast his characters in dialogue, much as a puppeteer might manipulate his strings. More formally, the dialogue appears in *debate,* such as in the great debates in Parliament and in the Congress, and in those meetings which are now an integral part of American history, the Lincoln-Douglas debates of 1858. Historically, dialogue and debate are an offshoot of *dialectic,* one of the branches of learning in ancient and mediaeval times. In Plato, dialogue and speechmaking are intermingled.

A fourth kind of discourse is *dramatic;* it contains much dialogue and speechmaking, is episodic in character, and builds to climaxes and conclusions. This form is basic in plays, novels, and short stories, where human events are plotted to bring interest and suspense. The speech often appears, as in Marc Antony's eulogy of Caesar in Shakespeare's *Julius Caesar,* or in Sydney Carton's speech in Dickens' *A Tale of Two Cities.*

These four forms of discourse are often intermingled in a literary work. The various elements can be distinguished, although they cannot be separated without destroying the work. Whenever the author tries to influence people, he is striving for a rhetorical effect; and to that extent, the works or parts of the work may be analyzed according to the principles of rhetoric. Actually the work or its parts must be so analyzed. The explanation is that

in the history of criticism, the rhetorical critics were there first—
our critical vocabulary in all forms is essentially rhetorical.

What a Speech Is

The main form of rhetoric is, of course, the speech. What is a
speech? Is it anything that is spoken? Is someone reading excerpts
from *The World Almanac* making a speech? Not at all! A speech
is a verbal composition, of variable length, fashioned for a specific
or generic audience, usually but not necessarily spoken, and frequently but not always listened to, in which composer, reading
or listening audience, theme, and occasion are interrelated for the
purpose of directing the listener or reader to a point of view
chosen by the composer. In its practical form, such as sales-
manship or soul-saving, a certain amount of success in effect is
anticipated.

Let us amplify this definition. 1. A speech is a verbal composition, usually in prose, although there are sermons in verse, and
sometimes someone rises to the occasion by giving some thoughts
in doggerel. A speech in prose may have rhythm and high imagery
in places. An oft cited passage is a sentence from Lincoln's
"Second Inaugural":

> Fondly do we hope,
> Fervently do we pray,
> That this mighty scourge of war
> May speedily pass away.

Such rhythm in rhetoric usually is the result, not of a conscious
attempt, but of high feeling. Many of Churchill's passages can be
written as poetry. Here is an example from his speech to Commons (June 4, 1940), when Britain stood alone against Fascist
Europe and her troops had been bottled up at Dunkirk:

> We shall not flag or fail.
> We shall go on to the end.
> We shall fight in France,
> We shall fight on the seas and oceans,
> We shall fight with growing confidence
> And growing strength in the air,

> We shall defend our Island,
> Whatever the cost may be.
> We shall fight on the beaches,
> We shall fight on the landing grounds,
> We shall fight in the fields and in the streets,
> We shall fight in the hills;
> We shall never surrender.

Notice the patterned lines, the imagery, the rhythm.

Frequently in speeches, poetic devices may be used. Adlai Stevenson often used alliteration, as in this passage from his acceptance address to the Democratic Convention on July 26, 1952:

> . . . there is the stark reality of responsibility in an hour of history haunted with those gaunt, grim specters of strife, dissention and materialism at home, and ruthless, inscrutable and hostile power abroad.

In general, however, the speech is not poetical in extensive use of rhythm. Longinus noted in the third century, in his *On the Sublime,* that "an over-rhythmical style does not communicate the feelings of the words but simply the feeling of the rhythm," an aesthetic response to sound rather than a "verbal" response to sense. He added that Greek audiences would "stamp their feet in time with the speaker" when he became over-rhythmical. There is a difference, too, in the nature of imagery in poetry and in a speech. Carl Sandburg's "Fog," for example, is a metaphor. You are expected to do nothing about it except "get the picture." William Jennings Bryan, in his famous "Cross of Gold Speech," uses these figures:

> You shall not press down upon the brow of labor this crown of thorns, you shall not crucify mankind upon a cross of gold.

Bryan's figure is not for aesthetic appreciation; he wanted to get rid of the gold standard in currency. The rhetorical image is used to elicit a response from an audience about some action.

2. The speech as a form is of variable length. One of the celebrated English speeches is William Pitt's last speech, given as a

toast in 1805, during the Napoleonic Wars. It is only two sentences long:

> I return you thanks for the honour you have done me; but Europe is not to be saved by any single man. England has saved herself by her exertions, and will, as I trust, save Europe by her example.

On the other extreme, Strom Thurmond spoke in the United States Senate continuously for twenty-four hours, eighteen minutes, August 28-29, 1957.

3. An essential element in a speech is its relation to an audience. A lyric poem is an expression of a person's feelings about something; it is overheard by an audience, not directed to it. A personal essay is a composition growing out of the writer's mood. The speech is a composition in which the composer relates his materials to an audience. In a sense, the audience composes the speech, for the speaker must consider the opinions, the mood, the setting, not primarily of himself, but of the people he is addressing. Where a speech is worked out in extemporaneous fashion, the response of the audience guides the speaker and gives him clues as to what to say. The speaker hopes to articulate the thoughts of an audience more lucidly than they could for themselves. William Gladstone, four times Prime Minister of Britain and a celebrated orator in his time, put it this way:

> The work of the orator from its very inception is inextricably mixed up with practice. It is cast in the mould offered to him by the mind of his hearers. It is an influence principally received from his audience (so to speak) in vapour, which he pours back upon them in a flood. The sympathy and concurrence of his time, is, with his own mind, joint parent of the work. He cannot follow nor frame ideals; his choice is, to be what his age will have him, what it requires in order to be moved by him; or else not to be at all. (*Homeric Studies*, III.)

Charlotte Brontë, in superb self-expression, gave *Jane Eyre* a setting in time and events but addressed it to no audience. As a novelist, Benjamin Disraeli wrote *Coningsby* and *Sybil* as fiction with many social implications, but as Prime Minister of England, he pointed his speeches to definite responses from his audiences.

For example, his speech on the Reform Act of 1867 greatly aided in doubling the number of enfranchised citizens.

Although a speech is usually directed to a particular audience meeting in a specific time and place, it may be designed for a generic audience, people at no particular place but who listen on radio or view on television, or in the days before these media, read the speech in the newspapers. When the President speaks, he may have an audience before him as scenery, but his remarks may be directed mainly to Rome, Moscow, or Paris. Whatever the speaker does, he must have his audience in mind.

4. Although the normal end of a speech is delivery, not all compositions delivered are speeches, and not all composed speeches are delivered. That is, delivery does not make a speech. A poem or an essay may be read or recited. Charles Dickens read cuttings from his novels, but they were "readings," not speeches. Not delivery but form identifies the speech. One of the greatest speeches ever written, John Milton's *Areopagitica,* a defense of free speech and free press, was never given orally; it was, however, titled "A Speech . . . to the Parliament of England." It was designed, on classical models, as a speech and was printed for distribution. Sometimes a speech is composed and then never delivered. In 1895, Mark Twain was scheduled to speak at the launching of a ship, S. S. *St Paul,* in Philadelphia. When the time came the ship could not be moved down the ways; it was stuck fast. The next day Twain sailed for Europe, but gave a copy of his speech to a reporter. It was published twenty-eight years later (*Mark Twain's Speeches,* 1923). There is no reason why one cannot write speeches and put them away in a bureau drawer, even as Emily Dickinson wrote and stored her poems. No doubt many audiences have thought such a repository would be fitting for speeches they have had to listen to.

5. In the speech, a composer, an actual or potential audience, a reading or listening audience, a theme, and an occasion are interrelated. No other form of literature uses such a combination of relationships. The playwright hopes that his work will be seen by many audiences many times and under many conditions. The speech maker works with a particular time and place in mind.

Among the institutions of man, the speech has developed as an essential ritual. The tree is not really planted on Arbor Day unless a speech about it is given. Every important epic in a man's life may be marked by a spech. When he is christened, words are spoken; when he marries, he receives a ritual on his rights and duties; when he retires, he listens to a speech as a traveling bag or watch is about to be presented; when he dies, someone speaks about his life.

Sometimes the speaker can blend the elements of a speech into a work that endures in historical significance. Pericles, speaking at Ceramicus Cemetery, Athens, 431 B.C., at the burial of those who fell in the first year of the Peloponnesian War, described the "open society" of democratic Athens (Thucydides, II. 37, 39): "in our private intercourse we are not suspicious of one another, nor angry with our neighbor if he does what he likes . . . ; our city is thrown open to the world, and we never expel a foreigner or prevent him from seeing or learning anything." This speech has become one of the great documents of democracy. Sometimes a speech carries ideas that set off programs of action. On June 5, 1947, Secretary of State George C. Marshall, speaking at Harvard University, proposed a plan for aiding economic recovery in Europe following World War II. The speech caught the imagination of the country; Congress set up a plan whereby twelve billion dollars were spent on European recovery; the plan is credited with stopping the sweep of Communism in Europe. Sometimes a speech achieves historical significance by the nature of the occasion. Such is Edward VIII's "Farewell Message" of 1936. Unable to marry Mrs. Simpson because of political and ecclesiastical pressure, he abdicated the throne, saying: "I have found it impossible to carry the heavy burden of responsibility and to discharge my duties as King, as I would wish to do, without the help and support of the woman I love." It was a generic speech—only radio technicians and a friend were present in the Windsor Castle room from which it was broadcast—but 500 million people around the world listened to it.

6. The speaker tries to do something to an audience. He may be satisfied with entertaining them, or he may try to bring infor-

mation, as in a class lecture. The most common use of speeches is persuasion. (These aspects of speaking will be discussed later under purpose in speaking.)

7. An adjective frequently applied to speaking is *effective*. Advertisements for popular courses in public speaking may give a money-back guarantee that the student's personality will be improved, that he will have power over people, that he will get a raise in salary. It should be understood, however, that in the great rhetorical tradition, success, in the sense of a speaker doing anything he wants to with an audience, has never been considered a legitimate criterion. The slick salesman may succeed in selling bogus oil stock or even the Brooklyn Bridge. Since classical times there has developed the criterion that a speech shall commonly be judged by what a speaker tries to do, not by how well he succeeds. As Saint Augustine said, "He who seeks to teach in speech what is good . . . when he does this well and properly, he can justly be called eloquent, even though he fails to win the assent of his audience" (*On Christian Doctrine*, XVII). There has always been popular admiration for speakers who could sweep audiences off their feet. Many examples are to be found in preachers. Jonathan Edwards, an eighteenth-century New England preacher, pleaded so graphically about the horrors of hell that his audiences moaned and wept. John Wesley often preached in the open fields, sometimes so "effectively" that members of his audience wept and rolled on the ground. In many communities, evangelists come to town, sometimes setting up a tabernacle, and thousands "hit the sawdust trail." Critical opinion through the ages, however, has given greater recognition to enduring value than to temporary effect.

Literary Qualities in a Speech

We have been discussing elements we normally expect in any speech. However, if a speech is to become literature in the broadest sense, additional criteria must be satisfied. It must be written or recorded in some way, on brain, paper, wax, or tape, for transmission, examination, and appreciation. It should have substance, ethical appeal, universality, moving force and fluency, an artistic design, and humane value. In the speeches that have become literature, whether Burke on conciliation with the American colonies, Lincoln at Gettysburg, or Woodrow Wilson on the League of Nations, a certain amount of failure in immediate effect has been traditional. Let us look at these criteria.

1. Because there may be no written record of a speech, either recorded and transcribed or in manuscript supplied by the speaker, many speeches reputed as "great" have been lost forever. Hence the importance of having some recorded report of a speech so that it may be read, studied, and if deserving, admired and appreciated. It is remarkable that about sixty speeches of Demosthenes, from the fourth century, B.C., have been preserved although some may be spurious. We must be grateful to those through the centuries who have written down words that otherwise would have been lost. There may be only incidental resemblance between such recorded speeches and what was actually said. Pericles' famous speech of 431 B.C. was recorded by Thucydides in 404, twenty-seven years later. The little speech of Edwin's Alderman, given later in this article, was made in 627, but was not recorded until 731 by the Venerable Bede. Patrick Henry's "Liberty or Death" speech was recorded by William Wirt in his *Life and Character of Patrick Henry* in 1817, forty-two years after the speech was made; the biographer was three years old at the time of the speech, and he never met Henry.

The problem of recording speeches is not limited to ancient and past years. Today, an electronic recording instrument may break down, or a stenographer may make errors in his report. In World War II, it was known the Nazis were trying to bomb the House of Commons in London; so Parliament met in secret places without adequate facilities for reporting. The result was that five of Churchill's most fiery speeches were never reported, and notes in his papers must be used to try to reconstruct what he said. (Eventually the House of Commons was completely destroyed by Nazi bombs, but the members were meeting in another place.)

The speech differs from other forms of literature in that there may be a number of kinds of texts. In literature that has been preserved, there may be problems of accuracy. In reconstructing what

Chaucer wrote, there are at least seven texts scholars have studied. These are versions of what Chaucer actually wrote. There may be, too, variations among the original edition and revisions. But in speech texts there is a greater variety. There is the speech as composed before delivery. This appears today in newspaper accounts as the "released" text, meaning reporters have been given a copy of a speech as it may be given later. Often there are many changes, and sometimes the speech is not given at all. President Kennedy released the copy of his last scheduled speech in Dallas, Texas, but he was assassinated before he could deliver it. There is the stenographic text of what the speaker actually said, although this may contain errors. In the Government Printing Office version of President Kennedy's inaugural speech, there are fifteen errors in accuracy. Another version of a speech text may be edited by the speaker himself for publication. In this version the speaker may make few or many changes from what he originally said. Adlai Stevenson, in his Preface to his *Major Campaign Speeches of 1952,* says he used "stenographic transcriptions in most cases," but where these were lacking, he used his own "notes to reconstruct what I said as accurately as possible." He also explained that he deleted "comments about local candidates and local references or jokes." It is very interesting that when a speaker prepares his speech for publication, he usually takes out those specific references to time and place and persons present—references which make the speech specific and real when given. Sometimes when a speech is given in a newspaper, responses of the audience, such as "applause," "cheers," and "interruption," are included. Such helps to interpretation are rarely included in collected speeches. And, as has been mentioned in the case of Patrick Henry's famous speech, someone other than the author may record the speech from what he recalled on hearing it or from the oral tradition of what was said.

Lincoln made five drafts of his Gettysburg Address, although it has never been established exactly what he said on the platform. The first copy, presumably the one he read from, said: "This we may, in all propriety do." The second copy read: "It is altogether fitting and proper that we should do this"—an improvement in diction. In the third copy, he inserted "under God" in the line "that this nation [under God], shall have a new birth of freedom" —thereby heightening the tone of the sentence. The fourth and fifth drafts have minor changes. The fifth is generally accepted as the definitive text and hangs in the Lincoln Room of the White House.

In studying a speech, the teacher should know what kind of text he is using—whether it is something written before delivery, or something never delivered, or a stenographic copy, or perhaps something revised by the author in tranquillity after the tumult and the shouting have died. There is no "best" text; each shows something different. The teacher should not be gullible about some speech he finds in print; he should inquire as to what it is. Often only an excerpt of a speech will be given in anthologies. In this case the teacher should know something about the whole text.

2. An enduring speech has basic substance, weight of idea. It is possible, through artistry and appeal, and the excitement of the occasion, for a speech to be well received yet not much valued a month or a day after the event. Lord Rosebery (in *Lord Randolph Churchill*) has described such a speech when reflected upon later:

> The lights are extinguished; the flowers are faded; the voice seems cracked across the empty space of years; it sounds like a message from a remote telephone; one wonders if that can really be the scene that fascinated and inspired. Was this the passage we thought so thrilling, this the epigram that seemed to tingle, this the peroration that provoked such a storm of cheers? It all seems as flat as decanted champagne.

To endure, a speech must have substance on matters of continuing interest. Sometimes the tensions of the day dramatize speeches into newsworthy events, but the speeches may fade as the events lose their significance. In the Kennedy-Nixon debates of 1960, the confrontation on Quemoy and Matsu had great appeal for the television audience. When Chiang Kai-shek stopped shelling the mainland of China from the islands, the issue was ended and nothing has been heard from it since. On the other hand, the Lincoln-Douglas debates of 1858 are still very much alive, are staged from time to time in the schools, and are read in classes in history, political science, and speech. The reason for this is not only that men of stature spoke directly and with weight of ideas but also that the problems they discussed are still with us. The teacher can help the student distinguish idea from vacuity, and banality from originality, and to distinguish from pedestrian prose a sentence such as Bacon's, which, as described by Alexander Smith (*Dreamthorp*), "bends beneath the weight of his thought, like a branch beneath the weight of fruit."

3. The speech that endures gives us some appeal to the better motives in life. There is appeal to some specific form of equality, truth, freedom, justice—conditions all men admire and want for themselves, but may not be willing to grant to others. There is nothing mysterious about our ethical values. They are values we all cherish as essential to a life of self-respect and freedom. In 1786, Gordon Turnbull published *An Apology for Negro Slavery* (London), containing his remarks on justifications for human slavery. He argued that "Negro slavery is not only consistent with the principles of sound policy, but also with those of justice and humanity." Slaves had been saved, he maintained, from the "grossest ignorance, idolatry, and barbarism" in Africa. Mr. Turnbull had some humanitarian touches; he thought slaves should not be beaten without limit "unless a magistrate be present." And he thought overcrowding on slave ships should be limited in some way. Such justifications of inhuman behavior as a defense of slavery do not endure in literature. Adolph Hitler's appeals for elimination of anyone he did not like, his vast program for murder of millions of Jewish people, his appeals to hate, are curiosities of history. They could never be included in speeches to be venerated and passed on from generation to generation. It is Pericles appealing for the free society, Ethelbert justifying free inquiry, Lord Macaulay pleading for an honest system of elections—these are speeches we care about and preserve.

4. To be great, a speech must go beyond the occasion and the moment; it must present ideas and values that have a universal appeal. John F. Kennedy, in his inaugural speech of January 20,

1961, went beyond time and place in such statements as: "Let us never negotiate out of fear. But let us never fear to negotiate." And, "My fellow Americans, ask not what your country can do for you; ask what you can do for your country." Robert G. Ingersoll made a short eulogy at the grave of his brother in 1879. He spoke, in universal terms, words that could be used at death for any noble person: "He added to the sum of human joy, and were everyone for whom he did some loving service to bring a blossom to his grave he would sleep tonight beneath a wilderness of flowers." Abraham Lincoln dedicated a burial ground at Gettysburg, but he did more than that; he left us a document full of meaning for today. The great speeches are a repository of much of the best that has been thought and said in the history of mankind.

5. The speech with literary quality must move with some sweep and progression, even providing at times dramatic periods. Another way of describing this is to use the word *eloquent*. Matters are put in such a way that an audience is carried along. Shakespeare has caught this in many parts of Marc Antony's speech at Julius Caesar's body. Here is a passage well known:

> I speak not to disprove what Brutus spoke,
> But here I am to speak what I do know.
> You all did love him once, not without cause.
> What cause withholds you then to mourn for him?
> O judgment, thou art fled to brutish beasts,
> And men have lost their reason! Bear with me.
> My heart is in the coffin there with Caesar,
> And I must pause till it come back to me.

6. A speech which is a jumble of words is like piles of dumped brick as compared with a finished building. There are many ways of designing a speech, and these are discussed later. The speech must begin where the audience is, with their thoughts and emotions, and carry them to conclusions the speaker wishes to reach. The Kennedy inaugural, mentioned above, has an artistic design. It is begun with an approach to the immediate audience: "We observe today not a victory of party, but a celebration of freedom." He then describes the feelings of Americans in all parts of the

country: "We shall pay any price, bear any burden, meet any hardship, support any friend, oppose any foe, to assure the survival and the success of liberty." Having tried to unify the immediate audience and the whole of the American audience, he talks to various parts of the world, and asks for a new beginning for peace. He then returns to the immediate scene, pleading for the audience "to lead the land we love." There is an architecture in this speech, as in all speeches that endure.

7. If a speech is to have a lasting quality, there must be appeal to the values we cherish, the imperishable values of man's yearnings. In 1953, Winston Churchill received the Nobel Prize in literature. His citation had this line: "for his brilliant oratory, in which he has stood forward as the defender of eternal human values."

8. As was discussed before, there is the notion that a great speech has to be "successful." Historically, many of our greatest speeches have been failures as judged by the immediate circumstances. Lincoln's Gettysburg speech was thought by many to be inept, and he himself was dissatisfied with the effect. *The New York Times* reported the speech in twelve lines, but gave three columns to a speech by Henry Ward Beecher in Brooklyn. Edmund Burke, regarded as the greatest of the English orators, seldom won a contest in Parliament. He argued for taking the American colonies into the British constitution and predicted independence if the Parliament refused. He was voted down, and the colonies were lost. Woodrow Wilson pleaded for Senate approval of the League of Nations, toured the country until he collapsed, and predicted that rejection of the League would mean a second world war. The League was rejected, and World War II came with all its horrors. The verdict of history is not the failure of Burke or Wilson, but the failure of the British Parliament and the United States Senate.

Kinds of Speeches

There are many kinds of speeches, because speeches grow out of occasions, and many events evoke "appropriate" remarks. One system of classification is by occasion, such as inaugural speech, "keys to the city" speech, speech of introduction, speech from the dock just before or after being sentenced to death. Such a classification may be roughly helpful in understanding a speech, but it is not definitive. Franklin D. Roosevelt's famous Teamsters' Union speech, in which he accused the opposition of maligning his little dog, Fala, was an after-dinner discourse; but actually it was his opening campaign speech in the presidential election of 1944.

Another method of classification is by institutional setting. George Campbell (*Rhetoric*, I, X) classified speeches as those in the courts, in legislative assemblies, and in the pulpit. This method has its shortcomings, too, for it oversimplifies the kinds of speeches. A clergyman may argue a case from the pulpit, and a lawyer may preach a sermon to a jury.

Sometimes speeches are classified according to purpose, such as to inform, to entertain, to convince, or to persuade. This system is hard to apply in that a speech may be a mixture of all purposes. For example, the speaker giving a speech of information usually has a persuasive purpose up his sleeve, although he may not announce it.

The oldest system of classification is still the most generally used. It was made by Aristotle in his *Rhetoric* (I. 3). The classifications are: forensic, deliberative, and epideictic. Forensic speeches are those in which propositions are attacked or defended, and they deal with the past. In the courts, for example, the argument concerns whether the accused did kill so and so in the past. The second classification is called deliberative. Such speeches deal with policy, such as legislation for tax revision, and they apply to the future: The third kind of speech is epideictic—occasional or ceremonial—and the setting is the present. In the funeral oration, for example, the speaker declares what we think of the deceased, now. A fourth kind of speech—didactic, or informative—was sometimes recognized by the ancients, but it was not given much prominence. This is because dialectic—dialogue—was the main instrument of instruction.

There are two forms of speech, prominent in our day, which blend classical types—the lecture and the sermon. At its best, the lecture is a systematic presentation of information, with

artistic touches that bring pleasure and make the hearing somewhat more pleasant than reading a chapter in a textbook. With the
great spread of knowledge in the nineteenth century, the lecture
became a standard form. Thomas Carlyle lectured on "Heroes
and Hero Worship," and his discourses have been widely read
ever since. Ralph Waldo Emerson lectured on "Self Reliance,"
and turned his remarks into essays still read in the schools. In his
enthusiasm for the expanding form of the lecture, Emerson declared, "A lecture is a new literature" (*Journal,* July 5, 1839).
Henry Thoreau lectured on getting back to nature and living in
the woods, and used the materials in such books as *Walden.*
Very popular in America has been the inspirational lecture along
the lines of "You, too, can succeed if you try hard the right way."
A classic of this form is Russell H. Conwell's "Acres of Diamonds,"
given at the turn of the century. The lecturer—a lawyer, teacher,
and clergyman—related stories of good fortune, the title story
being an account of a man who wanted diamonds, and toured the
world without success; when he returned home, he found that
the land he had sold literally had acres of diamonds. Conwell
gave his lecture over six thousand times and made enough money
from it to found Temple University in Philadelphia.

The second form of speech which may be a blend of classical
forms is the sermon. With the spread of Christendom, the sermon
became the most prevailing form of speech. It was given not only
in churches and tabernacles but also in fields and cemeteries. A
speech given in some ritualistic atmosphere and designed to in-
duce faith or to restore or extend it, the sermon has been elo-
quently described by Logan Pearsall Smith (*Donne's Sermons*):

> ...this form of expression is one—since its subject matter is
> nothing less than the whole of life—which gives the widest possible
> scope to a great preacher. He can pour his whole soul into his
> sermon, his hopes, fears, and self-accusations, the furthest flights
> of his imagination, the ripest results of his philosophic meditations,
> all the wisdom of mellow experience, and even the most amusing
> details of satiric observation. The very circumstances of his de-
> livery, the ceremonious solemnity of the church and pulpit, the
> great responsibility of the occasion, give a nobility to his utterance;

and the presence of the congregation, the need to speak directly to the hearts and minds of men and women, lends a certain dramatic intensity to all he says.

Our literature is rich in great sermons. John Donne's sermons, although given more than three hundred years ago, have recently been printed in ten large volumes.

Divisions of Rhetoric

In the classical system, divisions of rhetoric are made in order to know and to understand the processes better. As Ciciro (*De Inventione*, I. vii) classified them, they are: *inventio, dispositio, elocutio, memoria,* and *pronuntiatio.* These are the steps in composing and delivering a speech of any type.

INVENTIO (SUBSTANCE)

Invention is the process of discovering arguments, pleas, or ideas that may influence an audience. These are the substance of ideas. In ancient days the materials of rhetoric were proverbs, maxims, analogies, enthymemes, and examples. Today we also look for evidence, often statistical in nature, and for the testimony of experts, although we still draw heavily on the commonplaces of belief an audience and a speaker may hold together. Longinus (*On the Sublime*, VII), speaking of this aspect of rhetoric, says we are "naturally uplifted by the truly great; we receive it as a joyous offering; we are filled with delight and pride as if we had ourselves created what we heard." The great source of such substance, he says, is "natural high-mindedness. . . . great speaking is the echo of a noble mind."

DISPOSITIO (ARRANGEMENT)

Disposition, or arrangement in a speech, is a second division. Arrangement of details is probably more important in a speech than in other forms of literature. The essay may be an elaboration of a whim of the writer, and may move in any direction the author fancies. The novel may look backward, forward, in both directions, or in any narrative order the writer chooses. The lyric poem may be only an emotional response to a situation, with no discernible plan for an audience to follow. The speech, however, must follow a clear course, for the speaker tries to take an audience from where they are at the beginning to where he thinks they should be at the end. There is always a clearly discernible pattern of arrangement in a speech of literary merit. Details may follow an order of time, or space, from the unknown to the known, from problem to solution, or in some pattern which is particular to the subject being discussed. Sometimes a series of narratives may be the sequence, or one extended example may be elaborated in its many aspects throughout the speech. No matter how we arrange, it is generally accepted that a speech should have an introduction, a discussion, and a conclusion. The introduction provides for putting an audience on common ground with the speaker, for centering attention, and for pointing the way to what lies ahead. The discussion develops the main arguments, pleas, and exposition. The conclusion reviews the journey and dwells upon the place where audience and speaker have finally arrived.

The ancient rhetorician, Quintilian (*Institutes*, III. 9), describes five basic steps in arrangement. They are useful in understanding speeches of many ages. The introduction is called the exordium. This is followed by a statement of facts, the narration, upon which the argument is based, and then by proof of the proposition. Next is the refutation of opposing arguments, and finally comes the conclusion, called the peroration.

As an illustration of such a design, let us look at one of the greatest speeches of all time, Demosthenes' "On the Crown," often called the greatest speech by the greatest orator in all history. It was made in 330 B.C. before a jury in Athens. A man called Ctesiphon had proposed that Demosthenes be presented a crown for his services to the state. Aeschines, a rival of Demosthenes, brought Ctesiphon to trial on the grounds of illegality and Demosthenes' unworthiness. Demosthenes defended his patron, but really defended himself, since he was the subject involved. His exordium sought to gain good will. He then presented the facts of the case on which his arguments were to be based. Next he made what is called a "division," not always included in the classical system, of the arguments he would examine. In the third step (or fourth if you count division), he dissected Aeschines' charges and justified Demosthenes' conduct regarding the welfare of Athens. This is the proof of the speech. Fourth was refutation of charges against Demosthenes. The last part, or peroration, was a comparison of Demosthenes and Aeschines to show who was the really patriotic citizen.

A speaker is not restricted to any particular pattern, but he has to use a clear progression. No audience would tolerate the deliberate misleadings and obscurities found in a mystery novel. A widely used pattern is deduction, moving from a proposition through subdivisions and transitions to a conclusion. A great master of this form was Edmund Burke. In his speech "On Conciliation with the Colonies," 1775, he so arranged his materials deductively that if you were to cut the speech into parts you could reassemble it like a jigsaw puzzle. No matter what form of organization is used, the speaker must give the audience a sense of progression, a sense that they are moving forward, not standing still nor going backward.

ELOCUTIO (STYLE)

Words

Style is concerned with words and how they are used, one of man's basic interests. The child takes great enjoyment in just making sounds, and when he learns to connect words with objects, he has a sense of mastery of the world. As he advances in his use of words, he laughs at his mistakes, he enjoys puns, and if he cannot get the right word, he coins one. One child, unable to master "tongue depressor," called it an "ah stick," because the doctor said to say "ah" when he used one.

Words can be used and manipulated in many ways. Take the old jingle:

> Old King Cole was a merry old soul
> And a merry old soul was he.
> He called for his pipe, he called for his bowl,
> He called for his fiddlers three.

All this says is that one King Cole, an aged person but of good disposition, asked for a pipe to smoke, something to drink, and some music. But note how the effect is increased by the manipulation of the words and their arrangement. The king is not merely a person, but a soul. By the use of repetition, the effect of "merry" is increased. By inverting "three fiddlers" to "fiddlers three," rhyme is sustained. By using "bowl" for a drink of wine, a figure is used, called synecdoche, using the part for a whole—"bowl" for "bowl of wine." And so the jingle has been passed on from generation to generation, although the message, if there ever was one, has been lost.

Words are capable of definite rhetorical effect. "Give me the right word and the right accent, and I will move the world," wrote Joseph Conrad in *A Personal Record*. There is the exact word, the witty word, the novel word, as President Truman's "snollygaster," applied to some of his opponents, and Harold L. Ickes' "curmudgeon," applied to himself. If a word is to be rhetorically effective, it should satisfy three criteria. First, it should be *exact;* it should satisfy the dictionary definition of what is being talked about. Second, it should be *appropriate* to the occasion, the purpose, and the mood and intellectual capacity of the audience. Third, it should be *vivid;* it should heighten the emotional intensity of the idea being communicated. Words are also described as specific and general, abstract and concrete, denotative and connotative. So powerful are words that they have to be restrained by laws against libel and slander. Words are the bricks of rhetorical architecture, and they may be assembled in many designs, held together by the mortar of rhetorical contrivance.

Rhetorical Devices

There are many ways of arranging words for rhetorical effect, and many classifications have been made. One system consists of identifying by *schemes* and *tropes*. In the scheme, words are arranged out of ordinary conversational order, as in "a merry old soul was he," with the subject at the end of the sentence. A trope is a change in the meaning of words, as when, in the King Cole quatrain, "bowl" is used to mean "quantity of wine."

In general, the ways words may be manipulated for rhetorical effect are called *rhetorical devices*. In many periods of rhetorical study, devices were of primary concern. The oldest English rhetoric, The Venerable Bede's *De Schematibus Et Tropis*, written in 701, is a collection of word devices as classified by ancients and as used in the Bible. Had you been teaching rhetoric in the sixteenth century, you might have used Richard Sherry's *A Treatise of Schemes and Tropes Gathered out of the Best Grammarians and Orators* (1550) as a textbook.

To illustrate ways of classifying rhetorical devices, let us take one of the most generally used, repetition. A simple form is mere repetition, called *epizeuxis*. The Earl of Chatham, in defending the colonies in their revolt against England (November 18, 1777), said: "If I were an American, as I am an Englishman, while a foreign troop were landed in my country, I would never lay down my arms—never—never—never." A word may be repeated at the beginning and at the end of a sentence—*epanalepsis* it is called—as in St. Paul's lecture (Philippians 4:4): "Rejoice in the Lord always. . . . Rejoice." Another form of repetition is *ploce*, the same word repeated in each clause, as in the introduction of a speaker, "a man who . . ." You could classify a dozen or more ways of repeating for emphasis, if you were interested in doing it.

Favorite devices in rhetoric, as in poetry, are the metaphor—a figure in which a word or phrase denoting one kind of object is applied to another to indicate a comparison—and the simile—in which things are expressly likened. Martin Luther King used this metaphor in his famous "I Have a Dream" speech before thousands assembled at the Washington Monument: "The Negro lives on a lonely island of poverty in the midst of a vast ocean of material prosperity." Variations of an old simile turn up in speeches: "Democracy is like a raft; it's unsinkable but you always have your feet wet."

The anecdote and the story are much used in rhetorical discourse. In his first campaign concession speech in 1952, Adlai Stevenson, attributing the anecdote to Lincoln, remarked that he felt "like a little boy who had stubbed his toe in the dark. He said that he was too old to cry, but it hurt too much to laugh." The fable and the tale were standard sections in the *progymnasmata,* the books of rhetorical exercises used for training students in classical and mediaeval times.

Rhetorical literature abounds in epigrams and other sayings so well cast one tends to remember them. President Franklin D. Roosevelt said in his first inaugural address: ". . . the only thing we have to fear is fear itself."

Some devices are favorites in oral address, where an audience is present. An example is *epanorthosis,* meaning *correction,* in which the speaker deliberately makes an error for effect: "Did I say *millions* wasted? I meant *billions!*" If one made such a mistake in writing, he would be expected to take a clean sheet of paper and start again. Another particularly oral device is *anacoenosis,* an appeal to the hearer's own judgment. Jaggers, the lawyer in Dickens' *Great Expectations,* was fond of arguing by "putting the case." He would state details in such a way that the listener himself, on appeal, would arrive at Jaggers' own conclusion.

Various forms of questions are much used in oral discourse. Sometimes the speaker asks a direct question and then answers it. "What did my opponent then do? I'll tell you what he did." There is the rhetorical question, which has the answer in the query. "Do you want our beloved country torn by strife and dissension?" asks the orator. Of course the answer is no, and a reply is not needed, but the audience may cry out, "No, no!" There is a form of question called *erotesis,* in which the speaker makes his opponent uncomfortable by hurling a series of impassioned questions at him. Here is part of a sequence from Cicero's treatment of Catiline:

> When, O Catiline, do you mean to cease abusing our patience? How long is that madness of yours still to mock us? When is there to be an end of that unbridled audacity of yours, swaggering about as it does now? Do not the mighty guards placed on the Palatine Hill—do not the watches posted throughout the city—does not the alarm of the people, and the union of all good men—does not the precaution taken of assembling the senate in this most defensible place—do not the looks and countenances of this venerable body here present, have any effect upon you? Do you not feel that your plans are detected? Do you not see that your conspiracy is already

arrested and rendered powerless by the knowledge which everyone here possesses of it? What is there that you did last night, what the night before—where is it that you were—who was there that you summoned to meet you—what design was there which was adopted by you, with which you think that any one of us is unacquainted?

Whether one should bother to identify and classify the hundreds of rhetorical devices and their combinations might be argued. But the student should be taught something about them and their possibilities in order that he may appreciate them. Whether one can name the devices or not, listener and reader may enjoy manipulations of words. Note these from Winston Churchill:

... the iron curtain which lies across Europe (Fulton, Missouri, March 5, 1946).

[Russia] is a riddle wrapped in mystery inside an enigma (October 1, 1939).

Now, this is not the end. It is not even the beginning to the end. But it is, perhaps, the end of the beginning (November 10, 1942).

Phrases

The normal unit of speech communication is a rhetorical phrase, a word or group of words expressing a unit of thought. We may say to another, "O.K.," or "Right," or some current slang word or phrase. The rhetorical phrase may be a word or a group of words —usually not more than five or six—with a key word which in pidgin English could express the idea roughly. "A very beautiful girl," we may say as one passes, although a look and "beautiful" is almost clear enough.

Sentences

When thoughts are completely articulated, especially for recording in writing, the unit of expression is the sentence, a complete predication containing at least subject and predicate; as, "There is a very beautiful girl." Grammatically, sentences are traditionally classified as *simple,* with a single predication; *complex,* with a main clause and one or more dependent clauses; *compound,* with two or more main clauses; and *compound-complex*, a combination of independent and dependent clauses. This classification is arbitrary and is used mainly by grammarians. Rhetorically, according to effect, sentences are described as *loose* and *periodic*. In the loose form, meaning is communicated piecemeal. In the periodic, completion of the main thought is delayed until the end. In the loose form, the effect is reportorial, with events in sequence. The increased effect of the periodic form comes in subordinating elements and in giving the main idea at the last as a climax. Here is an example of each form, two consecutive sentences which show variety—an essential rhetorical element in sentence construction if tedium is to be avoided—from a famous speech by Theodore Roosevelt (*The Strenuous Life*, 1899):

(Loose)   Let us therefore boldly face the life of strife, resolute to do our duty well and manfully; resolute to uphold righteousness by deed and by word; resolute to be both honest and brave, to serve high ideals, yet to use practical methods.

(Periodic)   If we stand idly by, if we seek merely swollen, slothful ease and ignoble peace, if we shrink from the hard contests where men must win at hazard of their lives and at the risk of all they hold dear, then the bolder and stronger peoples will pass us by, and will win for themselves the domination of the world.

Constructing a coherent sentence is not an easy job for most people. As you listen to interviews and impromptu remarks on radio and television, note how frequently the speaker may start a sentence, stop, start another, and have great difficulty getting any sentence ended. If the student does not appreciate a coherent— even artistic—sentence, record him as he talks impromptu or extemporaneously. He may discover, when he hears his discourse played back, that he strings along with "and," "and," "and," or uses fillers such as "well," "you know," "and so on," or even "stuff like that."

It is hard to believe that a speaker and writer of Winston Churchill's quality should have had trouble composing, but he confessed he did (in *My Early Life*). He was kept in "the Third Form three times as long as anyone else," he says; his teacher was "a delightful man, to whom my debt is great." As a result, "I got into my bones the essential structure of the ordinary British sentence—which is a noble thing."

Many orators learn to design long, involved sentences as they work upon an audience, adding here, qualifying there, frequently balancing their periods with gesture, or evolving their climax by the rhythm of their voices. When such constructions are written down, the reader may have difficulty following the thought without the actual presence of the speaker. George Macauley Trevelyan (in his *Life of John Bright*) said of the great English orator, William E. Gladstone: "Gladstone's orations suffer in the reading from a quality which made them delightful to hear, their dependence on the skill of the speaker to effect his escape with grammar intact from the maze of parentheses—an operation safely sustained on that magnificent voice and by those dramatic gestures."

Skilled speakers often write as though they were working out a sentence with an audience. Here are two examples from master stylists, Adlai Stevenson and Edmund Burke. The Stevenson sentence is a long, loose construction, a sort of narrative of events, which appeared in the Introduction of his *Major Campaign Speeches—*1952.

> You must emerge, bright and bubbling with wisdom and well-being, every morning at 8 o'clock, just in time for a charming and profound breakfast talk, shake hands with hundreds, often literally thousands, of people, make several inspiring, "newsworthy" speeches during the day, confer with political leaders along the way and with your staff all the time, write at every chance, think if possible, read mail and newspapers, talk on the telephone, talk to everybody, dictate, receive delegations, eat, with decorum—and discretion!—and ride through city after city on the back of an open car, smiling until your mouth is dehydrated by the wind, waving until the blood runs out of your arm, and then bounce gaily, confidently, masterfully into great howling halls, shaved and all made up for television with the right color shirt and tie—I always forgot —and a manuscript so defaced with chicken tracks and last-minute jottings that you couldn't follow it, even if the spotlights weren't blinding and even if the still photographers didn't shoot you in the eye every time you looked at them.

This can be described as a loose, compound-complex sentence, consisting of sixteen independent clauses connected by "and," expressed or understood. All the compound clauses begin with "you must," expressed or understood. The complex clauses and phrases are all modifiers. The rhetorical artistry of the sentence comes in verbally restructuring the events—if you try reading the sentence hurriedly you will be as breathless and exhausted as though you had gone through a campaign day.

The celebrated sentence from Edmund Burke's *Letter to a Noble Lord* (1796) is a highly rhetorical, periodic construction. The rhythm is emphasized through the use of parallel structure in the various clauses introduced by "as long as." Balance is achieved through juxtaposing the clauses introduced by "as long as" against the clauses introduced by "so long." Since the sentence is periodic, the clauses are arranged so as to reach a climax at the end. Some of the rhetorical devices are indicated in the margin.

Burke was a master of elaborate composition. You may feel this sentence is too elaborate, but it developed from a mood of outrage —a sense of injustice. A simple construction could hardly express his feelings. In his old age, in 1796, as a long-time member of Parliament, he received a pension from the government. The Duke of Bedford, the "Noble Lord," attacked it. Burke was wounded, and replied to his fullest. All the sentence says is that the Duke, with all his holdings and wealth, should be grateful that Burke had defended institutions which made the Duke safe, despite the revolutionary trends that developed from the French Revolution across the channel. Here is the sentence, with an introductory statement and an epilogue.

PROLOGUE: Such are *their* ideas
              such *their* religion and
              such *their* law.

CONTRAST: But as to *our* country and *our* race,
              as long as the well-compacted structure of our
              Church and State
                  the sanctuary,
                  the holy of holies of that ancient law,
                      defended by reverence,

	defended by power,
	a fortress at once and a temple,
METAPHOR:	shall stand inviolate on the brow of the British Sion, —
	as long as the British monarchy,
METAPHOR:	not more limited than fenced by the orders of the state shall,
SIMILE:	like the proud Keep of Windsor,
	rising in the majesty of proportion, and
METAPHOR:	girt with the double belt of its kindred and coëval towers,
REPETITION:	as long as this awful structure
	shall oversee and guard the subjected land, —
	so long the mounds and flats of the low, fat, Bedford level
SYNECDOCHE:	will have nothing to fear from all the pickaxes of all the levellers of France;
	as long as our sovereign Lord the King, and his faithful subjects,
	the lords and commons of this realm, —
METAPHOR:	the triple cord which no man can break, —
	the solemn sworn constitutional frank pledge of this nation
PARALLEL STRUCTURE:	the firm guarantees of each other's being and each other's rights, —
	the joint and several securities
	each in its own place and order,
	for every kind and every quality of property and of dignity—
	as long as these endure,
	so long the Duke of Bedford is safe,
	and we are all safe together, —
CONTRAST:	the high from the blights of envy and the
ALLITERATION:	spoliations of rapacity,
	the low from the iron hand of oppression and the insolent spurn of contempt.
EPILOGUE:	Amen!
	and so be it!
	and so it will be!

Adapted from P. F. Baum, . . . *the other harmony of prose* . . . (Durham: Duke University Press, 1952), pp 174–175.

FABRIC AND TEXTURE

Rhetorical literature usually expresses a mood, or attitude, which may be more or less consistent throughout, and can be called fabric or texture. One way to understand this is to compare style in language with style in clothes. There must be in clothing material some substance such as wool or silk or cotton. But this material is processed in various forms of textural quality. Cotton, the substance, may be muslin, calico, gingham, denim, or corduroy. So words, phrases, and rhetorical devices, basically some form of evidence, may have such textural qualities as irony, wit and humor, invective, or exhortation. We make much use of irony, saying the opposite of the meaning intended; as, "It's a beautiful day," when it is snowing and blowing. "The honorable men whose daggers have stabbed Caesar," said Marc Antony in his funeral oration, and the audience, getting the point, repeated in bitterness, "Honorable men!" Traditional in after dinner speaking is a strain of humor, and such speakers as Mark Twain, Chauncey M. Depew, and Charles Dickens were exemplars of this custom. Audiences love to hear invective and abuse directed at men and ideas they do not like. Benjamin Disraeli, famous novelist and prime minister of Britain, described his opponent, William E. Gladstone, in scathing language:

> A sophistical rhetorician, inebriated with the exuberance of his own verbosity, and gifted with an egotistical imagination that can at all times command an interminable and inconsistent series of arguments to malign an opponent and glorify himself. (July 27, 1878)

Exhoration is a fabric much used in sermons and political addresses. It is difficult to read this famous reflection of John Donne (*Meditations*, XVII) without some brooding and some appraisal of one's own destiny:

> No man is an island entire of itself; every man is a piece of the continent, a part of the main. If a clod be washed away by the sea, Europe is the less, as well as if a promonotory were, as well as if a

manor of thy friend's or of thine own were. Any man's death diminishes me, because I am involved in mankind, and therefore never send to know for whom the bell tolls; it tolls for thee.

Attempts to explain style have been made by hundreds of writers. The observations made here are intended not to be definitive but suggestive. As Alexander Smith said in *Last Leaves*, "To define the charm of style is as difficult as to define the charm of beauty or of fine manners. It is not one thing; it is the result of a hundred things. Everything a man has is concerned in it." Buffon's famous expression (*Discours sur le Style*), "style is the man himself," is a way of putting the personal element in style. One might not agree with Smith that "it is not of so much consequence what you say, as how you say it" (*Dreamthorp*), but you might agree with him that "the enamel of style is the only thing that can defy the work of time" (*Last Leaves*).

MEMORY AND DELIVERY

In addition to invention, arrangement, and style, *memoria* and *pronuntiatio* complete the "five canons" of rhetoric. Memory covers two aspects: stocking the mind with materials and quotations that can be drawn upon when the rhetorical occasion arises, and committing a prepared speech to memory in such a way that it can be delivered as though spontaneous. *Pronuntiatio*, delivery, is an art in itself, involving as it does the expressiveness of the voice and the accompanying range of gesture. However, these two aspects of rhetoric, important as they are, do not appear directly in rhetorical literature and so are not discussed fully in this study.

The Rhetorical Tradition—The Old and the New

The literature of rhetorical theory is a vast realm. References at the end of this essay may suggest some guidelines for teachers who are not too familiar with the tradition. Many famous ancients, such as Plato, Aristotle, Isocrates, Cicero, and Seneca, wrote on the subject. In the mediaeval period, Boethius and Bede are among the illustrious names. In modern times, persons such as Bacon, Gabriel Harvey, Thomas Hobbes, Joseph Priestley, and John Quincy Adams contributed their share to the rhetorical tradition. The study of rhetoric continues, and there are various "new" approaches. In 1936, I. A. Richards called for a "new rhetoric" in his *The Philosophy of Rhetoric*. He wanted less emphasis on belligerence, more on understanding. In his many studies, he analyzed words as symbols in relation to thought and feeling, and gave particular attention to the metaphoric nature of language.

In *A Grammar of Motives*, Kenneth Burke, a major writer in the "new" rhetoric, emphasizes a "dramatistic" approach. Conceiving rhetoric as action, he developed the "pentad," a five-way analysis, as an instrument for explaining the communicative relationship between speaker and listener, writer and reader: (1) the *act* (what took place); (2) the *scene* (the situation, the background); (3) the *agent* (the person performing the act); (4) the *agency* (means and instruments used); (5) the *purpose*. Burke's theories are a combination of old and new: of classical rhetorical theory, Marxist dialectic, and Freudian psychology.

Another significant explorer into new explanations of rhetorical processes was Alfred Korzybski, founder of "General Semantics." In his *Science and Sanity* (1933) he pointed out the dangers in language: how we abstract and confuse meaning, how we confuse words with things (the difference between "maps" and "territories"), and how confusions in language usage result in confused thinking. He argues for "semantic flexibility," for understanding words in an ever changing context instead of trying to make them rigid. Korzybski is rather difficult to read, and if you do not know him, it would be best to start with an interpreter. Irving J. Lee's *Language Habits in Human Affairs* (1941) would be a good place to begin.

Another significant commentator in newer approaches to rhetoric is Marshall McLuhan. In his many writings he has analyzed relations between the "medium"—whether oral, written, or radio or television—and the message being conveyed. He thinks that "the Medium is the Message" (*Understanding Media*, 1964). Once upon a time, society was entirely oral; men *spoke* and *listened* and that was all. Then came ways of recording speech: on wax and clay tablets; with squid juice on papyrus; and then by printing; and in our day, on wax and tape recordings, and the extension of speech through radio and television is so vast that a piece of rhetoric is sent back from the moon: "one giant leap for mankind." How these developments affect communication—the influence of the means of transmission on what we say—has been explored by McLuhan.

Many "newer" approaches to understanding rhetoric are Freudian in nature. For example, Norman N. Holland, in his *The Dynamics of Literary Response* (1968), maintains that literature transforms primitive, childish fantasies into adult, civilized meanings. "The literary work manages . . . fantasy in two broad ways: by shaping it with formal devices which operate roughly like defenses, by transforming the fantasy toward ego-acceptable meanings." The teacher should feel free to explore all possible approaches to rhetorical appreciation. Rhetorical theory has been rather consistently traditional, unlike the avant-garde innovations in poetry, which appear from generation to generation. For example, Allen Ginsberg, in arguing against any pattern or conventional form, maintains that his "own mind . . . has no beginning and end, nor fixed measure of thought (or speech—or writing) other than its own cornerless mystery." So he claims that "the mind must be trained, i.e., let loose, freed—to deal with itself as it actually is, and not to impose on itself . . . an arbitrarily preconceived pattern (formal or Subject)" (*the second coming magazine,* July, 1961).

Why has rhetoric been so traditional and poetry more exploratory? An answer is that practitioners of rhetoric appeal directly to audiences which tend to be traditional in their conditioning to language, whereas poets, especially lyric poets, usually seek self-expression and hence use more individualistic, psychological forms.

The teacher of English might review some of the history of his subject. In the second half of the nineteenth century and the first half of the twentieth, there was a departure from the main concerns in rhetoric. Many teachers emphasized mechanical functions, such as spelling and punctuation—very important—but elements of grammar rather than rhetorical expression. The main concern became the paragraph. For example, in 1909, F. N. Scott and J. V. Denny published *Paragraph-Writing*, subtitled *A Rhetoric*. . . . Through the years much attention was given to themes, and to narration, exposition, and description, with diminishing attention given to argumentation. There are shelves of books titled something like *Rhetoric and Composition*, most of them not concerned with any effect the writing might have on any person other than the paid theme reader; they are neither quite of this world nor of the next. For decades the primary aspect of rhetoric—effect on an audience—was forgotten.

Recently, among the rediscoverers of rhetoric and rhetorical literature are the teachers of English. In 1961, Wayne C. Booth published his *The Rhetoric of Fiction,* in which rhetorical principles were applied for a better understanding of novels. In 1963, the National Council of Teachers of English issued *Toward a New Rhetoric,* a pamphlet with articles on the aspects of rhetorical approaches. In 1969, Edward P. J. Corbett published his *Rhetorical Analyses of Literary Works,* a rediscovery of application of rhetorical principles to the understanding of poetry, and prose forms such as the essay, and drama.

As this essay is written, there is a flow of books on the "rhetoric of confrontation." *The Rhetoric of the Civil Rights Movement,* by H. A. and H. Bosmajian (Random House), and *The Rhetoric of Black Power,* by R. L. Scott and W. Brockreide (Harper and Row) are examples of this movement. There is also an increased publication of specimens of rhetoric by Negroes, such as *The Negro Speaks—The Rhetoric of Contemporary Black Leaders* (Noble and Noble), and *Malcolm X Speaks* (Grove Press). These books indicate the concerns of the times, and also the enduring value of rhetoric as a way of understanding mankind.

Whether the teacher uses the old or the new in exploring and explaining rhetorical appreciation, he has an abundant field to draw upon. He should not feel himself limited by rubrics and arbitrary distinctions and categories.

The teacher always has the problem of attuning his own sense of appreciation to his students, and of getting them to respond. Some students, unusually perceptive and sensitive, will detect and respond to thought and emotion without much help if their attention is called to worthy passages. The mass of the students, however, may seem to the teacher to be like Wordsworth's Peter Bell, untouched by anything beyond the obvious and the literal. To Peter,

> A primrose by a river's brim
> A yellow primrose was to him,
> And it was nothing more.

So the teacher must use all available devices to elicit responses from the students.

Identifying and counting figures of speech, or distinguishing satire, irony, and burlesque, may become rather dull. Sometimes it might be enough to identify the main appeals in the work or passage. Rhetorical appeal, as pointed out by Aristotle (*Rhetoric* 1.2), occurs in three realms. First is *ethos*, the qualities of character revealed in the work. The speaker or author expresses traits of character, either directly or indirectly. According to tradition, the qualities of character we all admire are intelligence, virtue, and good will (see the *Rhetoric* 2.1). The second kind of rhetorical appeal is *pathos*—emotional appeal—words and devices to touch the feelings of readers and listeners. Appeals to the higher motives are respected historically, and low appeals—to opportunism, to venality—are suspect, although in an immediate situation, without perspective, they may be effective. The third appeal is to *logos*, consistent, valid reasoning.

The standard method of teaching rhetorical appreciation is by talking and reading together. Take this example of a speech made in 627 in northern England (recorded in Bede's *Ecclesiastical History of England*, I. 13). The setting was this. Missionaries had come up from the south to convert to Christianity King Edwin of Northumbria. The king called a meeting of his advisers to discuss the matter. The conference was held in Edwin's castle at Alby, probably in the banquet room. It was a cold day in January, a season of wintry snows and sleet. At one point one of Edwin's advisers rose and made this speech:

> The present life of man on this earth, oh king, in comparison to that existence which is not revealed to us, appears to me like the very swift flight of a sparrow, which for a moment flies through the room in which you, your leaders, and ministers on a wintry day are seated at supper around a warm fire, while out of doors rage the whirling storms of wintry rains and snows; the bird entering through one door quickly passes out through the other. For the brief moment it is within the room, it is safe from the wintry blast, but after a moment of calm from the storm, it quickly returns from winter to winter, and slips away from sight. So, for such a little time, seems this present life of man. But what has gone before, and what comes after, we know not. Therefore if this new doctrine can dispel the mystery, there seems to be merit in following it.

Read this together, keeping in mind the times in which it was said. Note the appeals. Is this a speech, or a piece of poetry? How is the simple beauty of expression achieved? (If your students ask if this speech was effective, you can tell them it was; the pagan temples were destroyed and Christianity was established.)

The ingenious teacher can apply many devices for touching up appreciation. One of the favorite devices is parody. By casting a brilliant piece of expression into the mundane, the greatness of the original may be revealed. Note this parody by George Orwell (*A Collection of Essays*). The original is from Ecclesiastes (9:11):

> I returned and saw under the sun, that the race is not to the swift, nor the battle to the strong, neither yet bread to the wise, nor yet riches to men of understanding, nor yet favour to men of skill; but time and chance happeneth to them all.

Here is the parody in "modern English":

> Objective consideration of contemporary phenomena compels the conclusion that success or failure in competitive activities exhibits no tendency to be commensurate with innate capacity, but

that a considerable element of the unpredictable must invariably be taken into account.

One of the most parodied pieces of literature is Lincoln's "Gettysburg Address." Here is a burlesque of Lincoln's first sentence as one writer thought General Eisenhower might have composed it (from *Parodies,* edited by Dwight Macdonald):

> I haven't checked these figures but 87 years ago, I think it was, a number of individuals organized a governmental set-up here in this country, I believe it covered certain Eastern areas, with this idea they were following up based on a sort of national independence arrangement and the program that every individual is just as good as every other individual.

The teacher can divide a class into small groups of four or five, give each student the same idea to be expressed, and then have the compositions read when the group reassembles. The students can try rewriting a good piece of rhetoric to see if improvements can be made. This usually results in some merriment. The teacher can ask each student to bring to class a section of writing he regards as excellent and have him explain his reasons for choosing it.

The main device for appreciation is reading selections orally. Language, whatever kind, is speech, and is most fully expressed when spoken. No devices of punctuation, italics, capital letters, or marginal notes can duplicate the intonations of the voice. Look at these lines:

> What is mind?
> No matter!
> What is matter?
> Never mind!

This may look rather senseless, but if full meaning is given in vocal nuances—bringing out *mind*—*no matter*—*matter* and *never mind*—the contrast becomes clear. As one stands in the Jefferson Memorial in Washington, he may hear a sentence carved in stone being misread: "I have sworn upon the altar of God eternal hostility against every form of tyranny over the mind of men." This is usually read as though the hostility is eternal; actually, eternal should be linked with God—God Eternal.

Then there are, in addition to clarity, all the rhythms and sounds of speech not fully appreciated in silent reading, especially if it is very rapid. An example is a children's book, Watty Piper's edition of *The Little Engine That Could;* there is much sound and rhythm. The little engine had a difficult time getting the train up the mountain. It puffed and snorted, "I think I can—I think I can—I think I can" with decreasing speed as the summit was approached. Then when he made it to the top, and started down the other side, his "I thought I could—I thought I could—I thought I could" came faster and faster as he picked up speed and confidence. The printed page cannot express this, either to child or to adult.

The vast resources of recordings should be drawn upon. Although the ideal arrangement is to have the whole class listen and then respond together, some teachers save time by having students go to a listening room, perhaps at the library hour. The recording is most useful if a printed text is available, and many recordings are issued with printed copies. Another resource is film. Some sound films are available, such as the National Educational Television two-part series on satire, with lecture and illustrations (Indiana University Audio-Visual Center). The rhetorical effectiveness of a film as a whole may be assessed, but it is difficult to make specific analyses of a film in class.

The principles and suggestions given in this essay have a historical background. Whatever the teacher does, he should have some historical perspective for what he is doing. The intention, however, is not to limit the students' study to the past. Nor is the intention that teachers should lecture their students on matters covered here. One of the great hindrances to imaginative teaching is the teacher's proclivity to give to his students the materials he received in college or graduate school. The teacher should use this knowledge to make adaptations to his particular students. How much theory, how much practice can be determined only by the teacher. He should keep in mind, however, that knowing why one likes or dislikes something is a higher form of appreciation than liking or disliking or being indifferent to something by mere tropism. The teacher should keep in mind, too, the future life of the student. He may never again read an esoteric lyric under assignment, never again an obscure novel; but he will be constantly exposed to rhetorical appeals, whether in political speeches, sermons, pamphlets and tracts, or letters to the editor of the newspaper. His life will be much richer if he can analyze these appeals and respond to them in a critical-appreciative manner, and sort the shoddy from the worthy.

REFERENCES

Acknowledgment

In this essay I have drawn upon three of my previously published articles: "Teaching Rhetorical Appreciation of Literature," *The English Journal*, Vol. LV (May, 1966), 578–82; "Problems in Speech Texts," in *Rhetoric and Poetic*, ed. Donald C. Bryant, Iowa City: University of Iowa Press, 1965, pp. 70–86; "The Speech as Literary Genre," *Quarterly Journal of Speech*, Vol. XLIV (April, 1958), 117–27.

Grateful acknowledgment is made to Duke University Press for permission to reprint the arrangement of the sentence by Edmund Burke.

Collections of Speeches

Baird, A. Craig. *American Public Addresses—1740—1952*. New York: McGraw-Hill, 1956. Speeches from Jonathan Edwards to Adlai Stevenson.

———. *Representative American Speeches*. New York: H. W. Wilson. An annual collection since 1937–38. Now edited by Lester Thonssen.

Bryant, D. C., C. C. Arnold, F. W. Haberman, R. Murphy, and K. R. Wallace, eds. *An Historical Anthology of Select British Speeches*. New York: Ronald Press, 1967. Speeches from 597 to 1940, with detailed prefaces and notes. Emphasis on completeness and accuracy of texts.

Copeland, Lewis, ed. *The World's Great Speeches*. 2d rev. ed. New York: Dover, 1958. Paperback. Comprehensive selection of ancient, continental, British, and American speeches.

Fielding, K. J., ed. *The Speeches of Charles Dickens*. London: Oxford University Press, 1960. A skillfully compiled collection with authenticated texts. Gives opportunity to compare Dickens' themes, such as poverty, exploitation, with treatment in his novels.

Goodrich, Chauncey A. *Select British Eloquence* [1852]. (Facsimile reprint, with an introduction by Bower Aly.) Indianapolis: Bobbs-Merrill, 1963. A classic treatment of speeches.

Hill, Roy L., ed. *Rhetoric of Racial Revolt.* Denver: Golden Bell Press, 1964. Contains speeches by celebrated Negro speakers, such as Frederick Douglass, Booker T. Washington, Langston Hughes, Malcolm X, and Martin Luther King.

Linkugel, Wil A., R. R. Allen, and Richard L. Johannesen. *Contemporary American Speeches.* Belmont, Calif.: Wadsworth Publishing, 2d ed., 1969. Notable speeches arranged by forms, with an index of rhetorical principles.

Peterson, Houston, ed. *A Treasury of the World's Great Speeches.* New York: Simon and Schuster, 1954. Paperback. Significant speeches with dramatic settings.

[Rhys, Ernest] ed. *English Historical and Political Orations from Ethelbert to Churchill.* Rev. ed. New York: Dutton, 1960. Collection of historically significant British speeches, first issued in 1915, but lacking setting and sources.

Woodson, Carter G. *Negro Orators and Their Orations.* Washington D. C.: Associated Publishers, 1925. Also available in reprint from Russell and Russell, New York. Speeches by Negroes, from 1788 to 1918.

Wrage, E. J. and Barnet Baskerville. *American Forum—Speeches on Historic Issues, 1788–1900.* New York: Harper & Brothers, 1960–62. 2 vols. Emphasizes the historical significance of the speeches.

Classical Rhetorical Theory

Aristotle. *The Rhetoric.* Translated by Lane Cooper. New York: Appleton-Century-Crofts, 1932. Issued as a paperback in 1960. Mr. Cooper prepared this edition as a student textbook, for use today. Most enduring and copied of all the rhetorics.

_____. *On Poetry and Style.* Translated by G. M. A. Grube. Indianapolis: Bobbs-Merrill, 1958. Paperback. The famous *Poetics,* with the theory of purging the passions of pity and fear through tragic drama.

Bede. *On Schemes and Tropes.* Translated by G. H. Tanenhaus. *Quarterly Journal of Speech,* Vol. XLVIII (October, 1962), 237–53. The first English rhetoric although originally written in Latin in 701 A. D.

Mainly figures of speech drawn from the Bible. This is the only translation.

Cicero. *De Inventione.* Translated by H. M. Hubbell. Cambridge, Massachusetts: Harvard University Press, 1949. An early, incomplete work of Cicero, restricted to invention, but very influential in rhetorical theory.

_____. *De Oratore.* Translated by E. W. Sutton and H. Rackham. Rev. ed. Cambridge, Massachusetts: Harvard University Press, 1959. A very significant rhetoric, giving Cicero's more mature views, written in dialogue form.

[Cicero]. *Rhetorica Ad Herrenium.* Translated by Harry Caplan. Cambridge, Massachusetts: Harvard University Press, 1954. Authorship unknown, but attributed to Cicero for many centuries. Systematic and precise rhetoric very influential historically.

Longinus. *On the Sublime.* G. M. A. Grube, ed. Indianapolis: Bobbs-Merrill, 1957. Paperback. Longinus is the supreme ancient rhetorician in applying appreciation to rhetoric.

Saint Augustine. *On Christian Doctrine.* Translated by D. W. Robertson, Jr. Indianapolis: Bobbs-Merrill, 1958. Book IV contains strictures on rhetoric and truth, with treatment of simplicity in style. Very influential work in applying rhetorical principles to preaching, and generally useful.

Quintilian. *Institutes of Oratory.* Translated by H. E. Butler. Cambridge, Massachusetts: Harvard University Press, 1953. 4 vols. Very detailed treatment of all aspects of rhetoric, centered on the education and training of the orator, "a good man skilled in speaking."

Modern Rhetorical Theory

Blair, Hugh. *Lectures on Rhetoric and Belles Lettres* [1783]. Ed. H. F. Harding. Carbondale: Southern Illinois University Press, 1965. Widely used, influential rhetoric, treating taste, style, figures of speech, composition, kinds of speeches, with copious examples drawn from poetry, drama, and prose.

Campbell, George. *The Philosophy of Rhetoric* [1776]. Ed. Lloyd F. Bitzer. Carbondale: Southern Illinois University Press, 1963. One of the most influential rhetorics, with an emphasis on psychology.

Priestley, Joseph. *A Course of Lectures on Oratory and Criticism* [1777]. Ed. Vincent M. Bevilacqua and Richard Murphy. Carbondale: Southern Illinois University Press, 1965. Written by a famous scientist for use in high schools, the book is interesting for what was studied in the eighteenth century.

Whately, Richard. *Elements of Rhetoric: Comprising an Analysis of the Laws of Moral Evidence and of Persuasion, with Rules for Argumentative Composition and Elocution* [1828]. Ed. Douglas Ehninger. Carbondale: Southern Illinois University Press, 1963. Particular attention to the logical aspects of rhetoric, and a very famous treatment of "natural" delivery.

Contemporary Rhetorical Theory

Burke, Kenneth. *A Grammar of Motives*. New York: Prentice-Hall, 1945.
————. *A Rhetoric of Motives*. New York: Prentice-Hall, 1950. Two of Burke's many books on rhetoric, which combine classical, Marxist, and Freudian theories in application to the contemporary scene. Both books are available in a combined, paperback edition. Meridian Books. Cleveland: World, 1962.

Holland, Norman N. *The Dynamics of Literary Response*. London: Oxford University Press, 1968. Concern with involvement by application of Freudian psychology.

Korzybski, Alfred. *Science and Sanity* [1933]. 3d ed. Lancaster: Science Press, 1948. Korzybski has written extensively on the relations between language and living. He is the founder of "General Semantics."

McLuhan, Marshall. *Understanding Media* [1964]. London: Sphere Books, 1969. Paperback. McLuhan's many writings have explored the relations between speech and the medium in which it is expressed, whether in simple communication or through film, radio, and television.

Richards, I. A. *The Philosophy of Rhetoric* [1936]. New York: Oxford University Press, 1965. Richards' theories on language have been very influential. This is one of his clearer statements on rhetorical expression.

Applications of Rhetorical Theory

Auer, J. Jeffry, ed. *The Rhetoric of Our Times*. New York: Meredith Corporation, 1969. Paperback. A collection of readings and studies which apply various aspects of contemporary rhetoric.

Beaumont, Charles A. *Swift's Classical Rhetoric*. Athens: University of Georgia Press, 1961. Applications of rhetorical theory to a better appreciation of Jonathan Swift.

Booth, Wayne C. *The Rhetoric of Fiction*. Chicago: University of Chicago Press, 1961. An influential book in the rediscovery of rhetorical practice by teachers of English.

Cooper, Lane. *The Art of the Writer.* (Originally published in 1923 as *Theories of Style.*) Ithaca: Cornell University Press, 1952. Selections from famous works of criticism, such as Herbert Spencer's "The Philosophy of Style," and M. De Buffon's address containing the statement, "Style is the man himself."

Corbett, Edward P. J. *Rhetorical Analyses of Literary Works.* New York: Oxford University Press, 1969. Paperback. A collection of rhetorical analyses of literary works, including poetry, essay, drama, novel. Contains, for example, T. O. Sloan's "A Rhetorical Analysis of John Donne's 'The Prohibition,'" and Kenneth Burke's "Antony in Behalf of the Play."

Crocker, Lionel. *Rhetorical Analysis of Speeches.* Boston: Allyn and Bacon, 1967. Contemporary speeches analyzed with marginal notes on rhetorical devices used.

Gorrell, Robert M., ed. *Rhetoric: Theories for Application.* Champaign, Illinois: National Council of Teachers of English, 1967. Articles on applications such as "Teaching the Rhetorical Approach to the Poem."

Lanham, Richard A. *A Handlist of Rhetorical Terms—A Guide for Students of English Literature.* Berkeley: University of California Press, 1968. Definitions of rhetorical devices from apostrophe to zeugma, with illustrations.

Linsley, William A. *Speech Criticism: Methods and Materials.* Dubuque, Iowa: Wm. C. Brown, 1968. Seven essays on contemporary criticism, with American speeches from Jonathan Edwards to Martin Luther King, Jr.

Macdonald, Dwight, ed. *Parodies.* New York: Random House, 1960. A sprightly collection from Chaucer to the present.

Sister Miriam Joseph, C.S.C. *Shakespeare's Use of the Arts of Language.* New York: Columbia University Press, 1947. Explains the power of Shakespeare in terms of rhetorical analysis, and demonstrates he was a master of rhetoric.

Murphy, James J., ed. *Demosthenes' On the Crown.* New York: Random House, 1967. An intensive study of a very famous speech.

Shaw, W. David. *The Dialectical Temper—The Rhetorical Art of Robert Browning.* Ithaca: Cornell University Press, 1968. An examination of Browning's ability to engage an audience and control its responses by using dialectical irony and the devices of legal and religious rhetoric.

On Teaching Speech Criticism

DONALD W. ZACHARIAS

Associate Professor of Speech
University of Texas at Austin

"There were so many people there and then when I paused for the first time, there was that really remarkable deep silence. That was impressive." Reliving this memorable moment in his address to 1,500 scientists and students at a Massachusetts Institute of Technology conference was Professor George Wald, Nobel Prize-winning, but little-known, Harvard professor of biology. Shortly after the March 1969 conference, the Boston *Globe* reprinted Wald's speech from a tape recording and was besieged with requests for 85,000 reprints. The *New Yorker* published 3,000 words of it and gave out 55,000 reprints.

The speech, entitled "A Generation in Search of a Future," had clearly propelled Wald into the business of making more speeches. His new fame brought him fifty letters a day from admirers. Invitations to speak came from colleges, peace groups, and businessmen. Perhaps not since the days of "Single-Speech Hamilton," remembered for his one major presentation in the British Parliament, has any speaker received such unexpected acclaim for one speech. Why? What circumstances were at work to produce widespread response to Wald's ideas? Was his speech a superficial explanation of national confusion over Vietnam, peace, and political change? Should his analysis of contemporary affairs be accepted? What made his speech one that people continued to play and discuss at parties months after it was delivered? What impact has it had upon American society?

These are the kinds of questions that a citizen-critic should be able to answer, because he will be bombarded throughout his life by speeches requesting his endorsement of public policies. Early in his education he needs to be given the analytical tools for dissecting the anatomy of a speech situation. Just as his training in mathematics and biology gives him an understanding of nature's laws, so training in rhetorical criticism can help him understand the process of man's trying through speech to make changes in society nonviolently.

If you were to ask your students for their impressions of what they were supposed to be trained to do after they finished their first speech course, you would undoubtedly get a conglomeration of answers. Most of them, however, would fit into the category of improving their personal ability to communicate in public and in private. These are reasonable and acceptable answers, since speech education has traditionally focused on improving personal skills in communication while neglecting the important task of showing students why a society values public speaking or what kind of speaking is of greatest value to the society. Recent events in the civil rights movement, peace movement, political conventions, and student activism have shown the importance of the spoken word, used in conjunction with rallies, television, placards, and threats of force, in advocating change. Teachers of English and speech on all levels must begin teaching their students how to be intelligent consumers of oral discourse, and not merely hope that some day their best students will undertake the analysis of a speech in a graduate seminar.

Unfortunately, the mercurial nature of criticism makes it difficult to teach high school students how to carry on this activity. There is no book of dots that a student can connect to see how a critical essay is supposed to look. There is no cookie cutter or micrometer to give him for measuring the dimensions of a speech. What you can do is instill an appreciation and sensitivity for the role speech-making plays in community, national, and international affairs. And you can help your students discover the appropriate principles for assessing the value of speeches. The remainder of this chapter is devoted to assisting you in these goals.

In the beginning you will need to awaken a better understanding of why people make speeches. Unlike authors of beginning speech textbooks who stress the process of preparing speeches, the critic asks why a speaker spoke and why he spoke as he did. The rhetorical critic asks the basic question: What function did a speech or group of speeches perform for society? He is concerned with making value judgments about the worth of specific speeches and speakers and not merely with determining whether a speech was successful or unsuccessful. For him the division of oral discourse into informative and persuasive speaking is totally inadequate, since these terms do not describe accurately conditions that produce speeches or meaningfully characterize the utterances of speakers.

Some critics prefer to use the labels of fact, policy, and value for classifying speeches. These categories have considerable merit if you wish to focus chiefly upon the text of the speech, but they are of only limited value if you wish to study the entire speech situation, a practice that is required for the kind of criticism discussed here. An alternate classification based upon situations or exigencies requiring speeches seems more useful when teaching criticism. But before discussing these various kinds of speeches, you will find it necessary to discuss the general characteristics of a rhetorical situation.

Traditionally, rhetorical critics have considered the speaker, speech, audience, and occasion the basic elements of any speaking situation. Much writing in professional journals, in fact, still tends to follow this pattern of analysis. Literary critic Kenneth Burke has developed a pentad of agent, agency, act, purpose, and scene for analyzing discourse. Communication researchers refer to the sender, message, channel, and receiver. Political scientist Harold Lasswell suggests that the student of communication study who says what in which channel to whom and with what effect.

Although any one of these approaches has merits, a preferable method of analysis is one based upon the postulate that the act of making a speech depends upon the interaction of a condition requiring a speech, rhetorical strategies developed and planned by the speaker, and audience reactions. These are similar to the three basic elements in a rhetorical situation, or the process that Edwin Black calls a rhetorical transaction. All of them need to be explored in greater detail to show their interrelationship and the kinds of issues discussed by critics.

You may wish to approach teaching the characteristics of a condition that evokes a speech by having your students list the common speech situations they encounter. Their list would probably include classroom lectures, sermons, talks by the principal, speeches by candidates for class offices, pep talks, convocation speeches, and televised addresses by the President or by a candidate for state office.

The next step is to examine each of these situations in light of the six characteristics of a speech situation, developed by Lloyd Bitzer and offered here in an abbreviated form.

First, a speech is given in response to an existing condition. The circumstances may be as uncomplicated as the presentation of an athletic trophy to the school or as complex as an address by the President to the American people on the Cuban missile crisis.

Second, whatever the situation, it invites the speaker to respond. He feels compelled to use oral discourse as a means for changing the existing disharmony and getting things the way they should be.

Third, the situation prescribes an appropriate response. Some situations will clearly dictate the purpose, theme, matter, and style of the response. The same speaker may display a wide range of responses when confronted by different rhetorical situations. Consider, for instance, the variations in a speech by a presidential candidate at his party's nominating convention, on the campaign circuit, and in a nationally televised address after he is in office and you can easily see how the situation shapes the discourse.

Fourth, the people and events involved in the situation are real, as opposed to those found in fictitious speeches in novels and dramas.

Fifth, the components of the situation exhibit patterns that are simple or complex and more or less organized. Richard Nixon's acceptance speech at the Republican National Convention called for an uncomplicated pattern of ideas stressing the usual party platitudes and goals. Hubert Humphrey, on the other hand, faced a bewildered and belligerent audience exhausted by days of divisiveness. Certainly the parameters of order and disorder were working in contrasting ways to shape the discourse of the two nominees.

Finally, the condition that evokes a rhetorical response comes into being and then either matures or decays or matures and persists; conceivably it may persist indefinitely.

Consider the circumstances surrounding President Lyndon Johnson's address to a joint session of Congress and to the nation following the assassination of President John F. Kennedy to discover the influence of a situation upon the discourse. The immediate situation after the President's death was one of shock, horror, and disbelief. Next came fears that his death was part of a plot to overthrow the government, and then followed the growing anxiety about replacing the vigor and strength that he had shown. In short, events in Dallas left Americans stunned, anxiety-ridden, and leaderless.

Numerous speeches were made in response to the assassination. Critics, in fact, have analyzed sermons preached in Dallas following the tragedy. There were, of course, the usual tribute speeches made in Congress, but this plethora of speeches failed to relieve the grief of the nation. The situation demanded a speech from the new President.

Determining the appropriate or fitting response was difficult. Where was the speech to be delivered? What should be recalled about the President? What promises should be made? What should be the tone of the speech? These were questions the speaker had to consider; and critics, too, asked them in making their judgment about the speaker after he spoke.

The situation surely was real, but in this instance the response was intensified by having President Johnson go before Congress as his live audience for an address transmitted to Americans and people throughout the world. Also the situation, while complex in its implications, took on a ceremonial pattern. The American customs for mourning, interment, and honoring a deceased national leader gave the situation some degree of organization. Finally, this rhetorical situation existed for a short time. It came about suddenly, persisted with great intensity for a few days, and then expired. Though the references to President Kennedy were to be many during the following months, the time for eulogizing was brief.

You will notice certainly that this examination of the rhetorical situation did not provide an evaluation of President Johnson's speech. It was important preliminary work, nevertheless, because it will give the critic who did his homework well a clear understanding of the forces at work to produce a speech. Moreover, it will reveal the complexity of speechmaking to the beginning student and will, perhaps, give him information to use when making his evaluations. He may well discover that the situation under scrutiny did not require a rhetorical response but merely the execution of a nonverbal act by the people involved. If this is his conclusion, he has discovered a situation requiring what is popularly mislabeled "action not rhetoric."

Closely related to the characteristics of a legitimate rhetorical situation is the question of what kinds of responses are evoked by them. It seems desirable to describe briefly five categories of responses to assist the beginning critic in understanding the product of these situations. From a critical viewpoint, most contemporary speeches can be placed into one of five categories: instruction, advocacy, conciliation, image, and ritual. Although a speech may contain a blending of several categories, it will be marked by characteristics that enable a critic to determine its real purpose. His ability to crack the speaker's code and make this assessment separates him from the common audience member who may be too directly involved in the speech situation to respond critically.

Speeches of instruction are commonly known as those designed to inform, to report, and to explain or describe. The emphasis is upon clarity, vividness, and reliable evidence. Listeners are supposed to leave the speech situation better informed but not neces-

sarily encouraged to take any specific action. Lectures, sales reports, oral book reports, and technical demonstrations all belong
to this category. The critic, however, must decide how to classify
the speech, since the speaker may consider his presentation informative when, in fact, it is one of advocacy or even ritual. For
instance, a speech on the relationship of smoking and lung cancer
may be presented with such vividness and clarity that listeners
perceive a message demanding that they stop smoking. What a
speaker perceives as informative is actually persuasive for his
hearers. Yet this raises no ethical question since the speaker and
his listeners value truthfulness and good health. Suppose, on the
other hand, a representative of the tobacco industry gave a speech
to inform on the relationship of smoking and health. In judging
the value of this speech, should the critic be more concerned
about whether the talk is actually a persuasive speech disguised
as an informative one? In this manner you can raise questions
about how a speech of instruction varies from one of advocacy.

In a society that prides itself on debating questions of public
policy, the speech of advocacy is the most common. Candidates
harangue annually on issues from fluoridation to foreign aid, and
audiences return again and again to be exhorted. The classic
Kennedy-Nixon debates of 1960 attracted an estimated 85 to 120
million viewers and affected the voting of numerous Americans.
No one expected either candidate to convert the other to his point
of view, but their encounters heightened interest in national
issues. Unlike the speech of instruction, speeches of advocacy
are expected to be one-sided and highly exhortative. Listeners
are supposed to feel, understand, and change in the manner desired by the speaker. Critics assume that advocates are identified
either by their professions or by their membership in organizations as special-interest pleaders. An attorney represents his
client in the most favorable light. Officers of the state teachers
association argue for the improvement of the schools. Officials of
NASA request more money for the space program. Obviously,
advocacy, with all its deficiencies, is valued as superior to threats
or violence as a method for promoting change.

Despite the prominence of speeches of advocacy, many conflicts in our society cannot be unilaterally solved by declaring one side winner and the other side loser. A position must be found for accommodating both sides, perhaps indefinitely. Consequently, speeches of conciliation are highly significant for their role in resolving conflicts. Spokesmen for business and labor disagree, often bitterly, over wage contracts, but they also recognize their interdependence and usually accept compromise proposals when settling their disputes. Disagreements between students and administrators frequently lead to speeches designed to ameliorate the friction. Impasses over legislation in state and national legislatures are traditionally broken by a senator's appeals for compromise to his colleagues and his constituency. In a more limited way, conciliatory speeches are used by government spokesmen to lessen international tensions. Unfortunately, speakers seem far more skilled in advocacy than conciliation. But with the increased research in conflict resolution may come better insight into how compromises may be promoted by public speeches.

There is another category of speeches that largely ignores the use of arguments or evidence to advocate a position. Its chief goal is to present the speaker in the most favorable light possible. This image-building speech concentrates on using strategies and situations that leave the listeners entranced by the spokesman or the organization he represents. Candidates for public office often make speeches calculated to advance their own charismatic power more than to propose solutions to problems. Large corporations send their officials to address community groups primarily to improve their image. The United States State Department provides a speakers bureau service, chiefly for campuses and large metropolitan groups, to promote its image as an alert, well-organized branch of government. Kenneth Boulding's *The Image: Knowledge in Life and Society* (Ann Arbor: University of Michigan Press, 1959) should be especially helpful in providing you with additional insights about this kind of speech.

The final category of speeches is the most intriguing because of its persistence in our culture. If we can accept the definition of a ritual as an occasion marked by a set form of actions and reactions and one in which obedience to the form carries meaning, then numerous rhetorical situations call for ritualistic speeches. Such speeches may be extraneous to the situation, but custom and audience expectations call for them. Commencement audiences have long perspired in cavernous gymnasiums while waiting for "the speaker" to finish with his clairvoyant views about the graduates. A parachute drop by a sky-diving team into the nearby football field would have just as much relevance and be more exciting, but tradition calls for a speech. Protestant ministers face serious problems with their congregations because the sermon is a regular feature of the Sunday morning ritual. If something else is offered in its place, some parishioners are likely to complain about irreverence, although congregations seldom retain much of what they hear—nor are they expected to. The meaning is in the act and not in the message. What concerns the rhetorical critic is not that such speeches exist but that more and more public speeches fit into this category. If these speeches carry no message of value to the society, what is their function? What does this portend for the role of speechmaking in our society?

Certainly it means that numerous service clubs and private organizations throughout the country are willing to pay, according to one estimate, as much as $100 million a year to hire speakers for get-togethers they would hold even if the speaker didn't appear. For the speaker it means that if he is trying to make money out of his profession, "the effect he wants to achieve on his audience," according to lecturer Dan Tyler Moore, "is the feeling that they would like some day to ask the speaker back to make another speech, possibly even at a higher fee." Under these circumstances speechmaking may become such a profitable business that we will need rhetorical critics to protect us from the fraudulent performer just as we already have art, music, drama, and movie critics. At least we need trained listeners, and high school is an excellent place to begin the training.

Whether you prefer this or some other approach to understanding the rhetorical situation, a warning concerning the hazards of studying a contemporary speech chiefly as a historical act seems appropriate. A critic can easily become fascinated with the social milieu, the psychological pressures upon the audience, the political issues surrounding the occasion, or a myriad of other details affecting the climate for the speech, and never adequately examine the speech itself. The critic's task is to focus on details and yet see everything at once. As he searches for clues for gaining deeper insights about the speech, he must not become preoccupied with the setting for the speech.

After helping your students select a rhetorical situation for analysis, you should guide them in identifying the major observable historical facts leading to its creation. Suppose, for instance, that you have selected President John F. Kennedy's speech, "The Strategy for Peace," delivered at American University on June 10, 1963. A brief examination of Kennedy biographies by Arthur M. Schlesinger, Jr., or Theodore Sorenson, would provide you with considerable background information. You would learn, for example, that this speech represents a major statement of the Kennedy administration's policy for reducing Cold War tensions. It is a continuation of the initiative the President took in 1961, when he spoke to the United Nations on behalf of general and complete disarmament under effective international control. It follows the crises in Berlin, Laos, and Cuba.

The timing of this speech was crucial. Pope John had just issued his famous *Pacem in Terris* message and further heightened the interest in international peace. With the attitude of the United States Senate softening toward adoption of a nuclear test-ban treaty, the President lost no time in asking his personal advisers to send their best thoughts on a "peace" address to his chief speech writer, Ted Sorenson. For maximum benefits abroad, the speech needed to be given before the Soviet Communist Party Central Committee met in mid-June and before President Kennedy left for his European trip later that month. Consequently, the American University commencement speech, which he was already scheduled to give, seemed the perfect time and place for a major policy address.

All this is just a way of saying that the critic studies both the general and the specific setting for the speech. In general, he wants to know the state of the world as it affects speakers and audiences. What are the major issues confronting those affected by the rhetorical situation? What restrictions are likely to control what is said? What symbols or sentiments can be used by the speaker? What specific items in the physical surroundings enhance or impede communication?

The point was made earlier that a rhetorical situation involves the action and reactions of people caught in exigencies. Accordingly, we can designate the speaker and his listeners as co-producers of the discourse and look critically at the makeup of each to see what effects they have upon the final shaping of the speech. The rhetorical critic, unlike his counterpart in art, drama, and music, must know a great deal about the nature of audiences, since their attitudes and behaviors are deliberately subjected to the speaker's influence. They are, in other words, a part of the action.

At the outset, the critic must determine how many audiences there are for each rhetorical situation. It is probably more important to think about primary and secondary audiences than to concentrate only upon the listeners physically present when the speech is first delivered. In the case of President Kennedy's American University address, the 10,000 people gathered at Reeves Athletic Center were probably the least important of his audiences, although this does not mean they can be ignored by the critic. The speech was also broadcast and televised for American audiences. Later, a Russian translation of the speech was broadcast by the Voice of America, and for the first time in many years the Soviet Union chose not to jam the transmission. Evening television and radio newscasts replayed segments of the speech. American and foreign presses, including the Soviet, printed the full text of the speech. Official government publications reprinted the speech, and numerous anthologies continue to reprint it. Obviously, the critic of this and similar speeches has to consider, not one, but multiple audiences.

Since many contemporary speeches are not centered around the audience that is physically present, the critic often must study disseminated discourse. Most listeners, perhaps the key ones, are isolated from the speaker. The role of the listeners' shaping what the speaker says through their overt responses is eliminated. A statement that is acceptable to a majority of the listeners may anger others. Under these circumstances the speaker may need to be more concerned with affecting the action of the few, not the many. Consider Senator Robert Kennedy's statement about military aid to Israel, during his debate with Senator Eugene McCarthy in California. The statement is allegedly responsible for triggering the tragic events leading to his assassination. Although Senator Kennedy did not expect all his listeners to share his belief on this issue, he may well have overlooked the possibility that some Arab sympathizers would hear his statements.

In at least one famous instance, the reporting by one listener of what he thought the speaker said had widespread consequences. In June, 1965, William McChesney Martin, Jr., chairman of the Federal Reserve Board, in an address to the Columbia University Alumni Federation, noted, "We find disquieting similarities between our present prosperity and the fabulous twenties." After his remarks were circulated, stock market prices dropped by thirty-four billion dollars within thirty days. Martin denied that his statement caused the slump, but he quickly returned to the speaking circuit to try to counteract the misinterpretation of his words.

Since identification of listeners becomes a major problem when investigating any mediated communication, you may wish to divide the audience into four classes: those who are present when the speech is delivered; those who watch a live telecast version of the speech event; those who see, hear, or read the speech at some date after its original presentation; and those who see, hear, or read only excerpts from the speech. Such a division, of course, assumes that immediate or delayed reception of the speech, and the medium by which it is transmitted, causes listeners' reactions to vary. These variables, despite all the recent probing by Marshall McLuhan, have not yet been determined by media scientists. Until they are, the critic must use his own ingenuity in discovering significant points about the speaker's audiences. For your high school students, you at least will have awakened a broader understanding of the audiences involved in the rhetorical situation.

To aid you in teaching the role of the audience in shaping a discourse, you will find Raymond Bauer's conclusions helpful. The major initiative in the communication process, he says, rests with the audience, not the communicator. This seems plausible because (1) images of audiences, both real and imaginary, external and internal, affect the way in which speakers organize and retain information and what they believe; (2) the audience sometimes commits the speaker to a public position to which he may later accommodate his private belief; and (3) a speaker has in mind a single audience, and secondary reference-group audiences may often exert the determining influence in the organization and retention of information, as well as in the flow of communication. In addition to noting these influences, critics find it helpful to generalize about the basic characteristics of the audience. You may use some of the following questions to guide you: What generalizations can be made about the background, experiences, interests, and values of the audience? Is there a sizeable minority of the audience that does not share the conventional beliefs and values of the majority? What symbols, taboos, and formal requirements for a speech are shared by members of the audience? Is the speaker discussing issues related to the major interests of the audience? Is the audience polarized in its basic attitude toward the competence of the speaker?

Finding answers to these questions is a major task for any critic and will, no doubt, be particularly troublesome in high schools. You may find it advisable to invite the social studies teacher to team-teach a few days with you. After selecting a major national address or an important local speech, you can work together to identify convenient sources of information or social characteristics of the rhetorical situation, discuss the reliability of polls and other sampling techniques, and direct the students in reaching some conclusions about the audience.

Before focusing directly upon the speech text, the critic needs to know the speaker well. While it is probably impossible to know too much about any speaker, your students can complete this step quite well without spending long hours in biographical study. They need information in four areas: (1) the quality of the speaker's thinking as revealed by past performances, (2) his attitudes toward the world in general, (3) his relationship to the listeners and his attitudes toward them, and (4) the dimensions of his involvement in the specific issues discussed in the speech. Once again, in assessing contemporary speeches the critic has some disadvantages. The record of the speaker's life is incomplete and, in some instances, highly controversial. On the other hand, the speaker is still accessible and can often clarify why he acted as he did. Perhaps the greatest problem for the high school critic is finding objective information about the speaker, since information about contemporary speakers is often highly colored by the writer's biases and by public opinion. In all the questions he raises, the critic strives to determine how the speaker perceives his world and how this perception influences him when talking to others.

The final element for scrutiny is the speech itself. This is the segment that is capable of being subjected to the widest possible methods of analysis. It represents the culmination of the forces acting to produce a rhetorical situation. It is a highly personalized response to an exigence. A detailed study of the speech text by high school students should give them (1) a better understanding of contemporary practices for composing speeches, (2) a clearer grasp of language devices designed to win response, (3) an introduction to rhetorical strategies and arguments, (4) a firsthand examination of patterns of organization, and (5) if a voice or video-tape recording is available, a vivid exposure to the factors contributing to effective delivery.

For this analysis to be meaningful, the critic must find an accurate text or recording of the speech and must know who is responsible for its composition. He cannot assume that every copy of the speech is a true record of what was said. In his study of textual accuracy, Richard Murphy reported that a plaque of President Kennedy's inaugural address as issued by the Government Printing Office contained thirteen deviations from tape recordings of the speech. A similar study of President Johnson's

March 31, 1969, retirement speech shows that the printed versions, as distributed by the White House and by *Vital Speeches of the Day*, vary considerably from an actual recording of the speech. The critic also faces the problem of finding a complete speech text. Editors frequently delete large portions without warning the reader. The copy of Sir Charles P. Snow's "The Moral Un-Neutrality of Science" as printed in the Appendix of the *Congressional Record* has no notes to the reader, yet it is only a segment of the speech delivered to the American Association for the Advancement of Science.

A third problem for the critic is determining who wrote the speech. Prominent public figures seldom write their own speeches, and the role each of them plays in the preparation of the speech varies widely. President Eisenhower used the services of Bryce N. Harlow, Kevin McCann, Sherman Adams, and I. Jack Martin. President Kennedy relied heavily upon Ted Sorensen and Arthur Schlesinger, Jr. President Johnson's speech to a joint meeting of Congress and to the nation following the assassination of President Kennedy featured the combined efforts of Ted Sorensen, John K. Galbraith, and Abe Fortas. President Nixon entrusts most of his speech writing to Jim Keogh, Patrick Buchanan, and Raymond K. Price, Jr.

Businessmen also turn to professional writers for help. An Austin, Texas, newspaper recently carried an advertisement offering an annual salary of $20,000 for a speech writer for a major corporation. Although members of the speech profession continue to debate the ethics of ghostwriting, the public seems quite willing to accept whatever a speaker says as his personal views of the situation. For the critic, the major question is not whether the practice is right or wrong, but what effect the work of several writers has had upon the finished discourse.

A fifth problem for the critic, if he investigates congressional speaking, lies in determining whether the speech was actually delivered. This is an important issue for anyone teaching rhetorical criticism in high school, since senators and representatives are good sources of speech texts. Nevertheless, you and your students should know that a member of Congress can have remarks entered into the *Congressional Record* and distributed to his constituents without actually delivering the speech. While such a pseudo-speech may certainly be worthy of analysis, a critic should know the history of the text he studies.

Each teacher will develop his own favorite method for analyzing the content of speeches. This is a perfectly acceptable procedure as long as he doesn't build a Procrustean bed for studying every speech. The classical speech concepts of invention, arrangement, style, memory, and delivery have lost most of their critical usefulness due to slavish application of them to all rhetorical situations. They have remained viable terms in criticism chiefly because rhetorical critics have been sluggish in their search for alternatives. For the high school student who wants to be a citizen-critic, a series of questions designed to help him gain insights about rhetorical strategies seems more appropriate.

From an examination of the speech text, the critic can determine (1) what the speaker intended to communicate, (2) what he communicated unintentionally, and (3) the quality of what he actually communicated. As he makes his judgments about the speaker, he simultaneously asks: Was this the best that could be done under the circumstances? Has the speaker been honest and fair? These issues are especially important when applied to speeches of advocacy, conciliation, and image-building.

In performing this rhetorical autopsy, the critic examines three aspects of the presentation. He studies the organizational schematic and the stated purpose of the speaker, the speaker's arguments and verbal strategies, and his use of physical support while delivering the speech. Listed below are questions to aid your students in investigating these three areas.

Organization and Purpose

1. Did the speaker plan his message for a primary or a secondary audience?
2. Did he state his purpose in language clearly meaningful to his listeners?

3. What was the relationship between his goals and the value system of the audience?
4. Did his pattern of organization reveal special strategies designed to make his ideas more acceptable to the audience?
5. What proportion of the speech was devoted to establishing an interest in the topic, developing each main point, and in summarizing the main arguments?
6. What novel techniques did he use for beginning, developing, or concluding the speech?

Arguments and Verbal Strategies

1. What method did the speaker use for establishing or reminding his listeners of a need for his proposals?
2. What were his major lines of argument?
3. What kinds of evidence did he use to support his position? Was it personal opinion, documented evidence, biased testimony, expert testimony, examples, or others?
4. What proportion of the speech was devoted to restating beliefs and attitudes already shared with the audience?
5. What techniques did he use for making the audience aware of the significance of the evidence?
6. How often did he use appeals to love, pity, fear, and anger?
7. How often and with what effect did he use the appeal of his own reputation, character, integrity, and special qualifications?
8. What strategies did he use for refuting opposing points of view?
9. What was the nature of his language? Sweet, tough, stuffy, obscene, labored?
10. How effective was his use of simile, metaphor, personification, metonymy, hyperbole, and other figurative devices?
11. Was the impact of his language hindered by ambiguous passages characterized by jargon, unanswered rhetorical questions, lack of development, and indirect statement?
12. What examples can you cite to show his ability to form memorable phrases and exciting sentences?

Physical Support

1. What effect did the speaker's physical appearance and platform behavior have upon the listeners' willingness to believe him?
2. What effect did his vocal qualities have upon the perception of his ideas?
3. Did the speaker appear poised and concerned with communicating a message, rather than with his own comfort?
4. Did he have any mannerisms that caused a breakdown in communication?
5. If he used visual or audio materials, were they imaginative, carefully planned, and easily seen by the audience?
6. What evidence is there that he responded to his listeners' reactions as he spoke?

These questions by no means exhaust the possibilities for analysis. You know your students' capacities for raising questions, and you should lead them in asking meaningful ones. The important point is that a beginner in rhetorical criticism needs a starting point and careful guidance when confronting his first speech for analysis. Your goal is to make him an intelligent consumer of public speeches, not a critic for *The New York Times*.

There are, of course, several levels at which your students can make judgments, just as the reactions of people attending an opera can reflect their reasons for liking it. Here, for example, are the comments of four people who attended an outdoor presentation of *Carmen* at Indiana University.

BUSINESSMAN:

It was dazzling. The music and dancing made me forget my troubles for a while and just enjoy a good show.

STUDENT:

I thought it was a great show. It was an excellent study in human relationships.

MUSICIAN:

> I thought the singer portraying Carmen gave an excellent performance. She was flat only twice. The attack of the orchestra was good; the conducting, brilliant for an outdoor performance.

MUSIC CRITIC:

> The performance thrilled the audience tonight. The cast brought to life the intrigues and foibles of human beings in a memorable and cathartic manner. The sets, orchestration, and musicians blended magnificently to show grand opera at its best.

Each of the people commenting on the opera liked it, but for different reasons. The businessman liked it for its effect; the student, for its ethical or philosophical value; the musician, for its artistic qualities; and the critic, for its total impact. A speech may evoke similar reactions.

A teacher of English or speech, of course, tries to train students to react to the combination of the effect, the ethical qualities, and the artistry of the speech when judging its worth. Accompanying any attempt to judge a speech by just considering one criterion are far too many hazards to make it a safe procedure. Suppose you decide to use only the effect of the speech upon the audience as the standard for judging its worth. Then do you label the Gettysburg Address, the Crittenden Compromise speech, the Adlai Stevenson or Hubert Humphrey campaign speeches poor speeches because they failed to produce the reactions desired by the speakers? Are the speeches of Hitler and Mussolini, on the other hand, great ones because they produced such vehement responses? Although a speaker always wishes to affect his listeners, he may face such overwhelming circumstances and such a short time span for addressing his audience that one speech will not produce any detectable changes.

The question of ethics and persuasion is discussed in another chapter by Richard Johannesen. Study it when assessing the ethical qualities of the speaker. For now, keep in mind that good men speaking for good causes have often been rejected because they lacked artistry and the ability to affect their listeners. Empty churches in England and America and bored students in high schools and colleges are eloquent testimony to the inadequacy of good intentions. Yet the ethics of the speaker must be considered by the citizen-critic if intelligent decisions are to be made in electing leaders and choosing ways to improve society.

Artistry, too, is important when judging the qualities of a speech. Like the French horn player who can blow the notes but isn't ready for a symphony, so most people can stand before an audience and talk but aren't trained to give a unified speech. You may recognize the horn player's tune or the speaker's message and still find little pleasure in either experience. Nevertheless, artistry alone is inadequate in speechmaking. The records of the second century A.D. with speeches on "The Fly," and the nineteenth-century elecutionary speeches, in which form and action won plaudits, reveal the dangers of praising artistry alone.

Despite all the difficulties confronting the citizen-critic, his decision about the value of any speech should be based upon its intrinsic merits, the ethical and moral intentions of the speaker, and his virtuosity in affecting the audience. We hope that high school students will learn, while exercising such criticism, that there are more psychological and rhetorical forces at work in any speaker-listener situation than they usually suppose. We assume that they will learn how to distinguish between the demagogue and the crusader or between the quack and the professional.

To aid students in learning this process, you may wish to assign exercises that focus upon only one segment of the critical act. You, for instance, could undertake a case study of Nixon's inaugural address by studying first the events surrounding it. Second, determine how he prepared his speech and who assisted him. Third, locate and establish the authenticity of various texts of the speech by comparing printed versions with each other and printed versions with disc or video-tape recordings of the address. Fourth, have your students determine the intrinsic quality of the speech by answering the questions listed on pages 211 to 213. Fifth, have your students find out which segments of the speech were most widely reported in local and national newspapers. After the preceding projects have been completed by either small groups or individuals in the class, have each student give his own evaluation of the speech orally or in writing.

The evaluation of a single speech could be carried out with greater ease by having each student hear, tape record, and evaluate a local speaker. In this instance encourage your students to have an interview with the speaker to determine how he prepared the speech and what his reactions were to his audience during and after the speech. This information will have to substitute for what observers usually report about a major national speech.

The natural tendency for a student making this kind of evaluation is one of over-praising the speaker for his speech, since the student-critic is easily impressed by professional speakers in his hometown. Moreover, unless the topic is one about which a teenager has personal feelings and opinions, he may feel overwhelmed by the erudition of the speaker and make only a superficial attempt to judge the quality of the discourse. Consequently, in the beginning you will find it helpful to assign speeches for study that deal only with the subjects of greatest interest to your students.

Encourage your students to examine speeches from as many of the six different categories discussed earlier as possible. It would be helpful to have them evaluate several speeches made under different circumstances by the same speaker. President Nixon's acceptance speech at Miami, a campaign speech, and a post-inaugural address would reveal significant variations. Or a similar study for Hubert Humphrey could concentrate on his acceptance speech at Chicago, a campaign speech, and a post-election speech.

Another exercise for your students involves analyzing the speeches given in support of a movement. Speeches on civil rights, black power, peace, and educational reform are readily available by tape recording and in print. The Department of Speech of the University of Texas at Austin, for example, has numerous contemporary speeches on tape. A list of its holdings can be acquired simply by writing the department. The Center for the Study of Democratic Institutions, Santa Barbara, California, and the Media Services Division of the United States State Department, Washington, D.C., have tape recordings of speeches available for a small fee. Investigation and study of speeches from these sources should stimulate some exciting discussions about speech in contemporary affairs.

For teaching a unit on rhetorical criticism, several kinds of material are indispensable. You need to have available in the school library copies of *The New York Times* and, if possible, other high quality national newspapers. An annual subscription to *Vital Speeches of the Day* will also provide valuable raw materials for analysis. A letter to your senators and congressmen will put you and the school on the mailing list for printed copies of congressional speeches.

Many schools are now equipped with video-tape recorders that you can also use to record major televised speeches. During election years you and a government teacher should be able to use the VTR for effectively teaching the evaluation of campaign speeches.

Among the published materials available to assist you in understanding and teaching rhetorical criticism, you should find the following most helpful. One of the best anthologies of speeches by public figures and college students is *Contemporary American Speeches*, edited by Wil A. Linkugel, R. R. Allen, and Richard L. Johannesen (Belmont, California: Wadsworth Publishing, 1969). The index of rhetorical terms found in the appendix of this collection makes it especially useful for high school teachers. Another work is my *In Pursuit of Peace* (New York: Random House, 1970), a collection of speeches by representative spokesmen of the peace movement.

The finest collection of examples of speech criticism by trained critics is J. Jeffery Auer's *The Rhetoric of Our Times* (New York: Appleton-Century-Crofts, 1969). This work is an indispensable aid to anyone who wants to understand contemporary public address. For further study of problems and approaches to speech criticism you will want to read Edwin Black's *Rhetorical Criticism* (New York: Macmillan, 1966), Robert Cathcart's *Post Communication: Criticism and Evaluation* (Indianapolis: Bobbs-Merrill, 1966), and *Essays on Rhetorical Criticism*, edited by Thomas R. Nilsen (New York: Random House, 1968).

The teaching of speech criticism is not an easy task, nor is it one traditionally associated with the high school speech class. The success you have in teaching it will depend primarily upon your creativity in planning exercises for your classes. The major purpose of all the exercises is to train citizen-critics in evaluating speeches directed at them. We may have said farewell to rational discourse, as some critics have argued, but we have not yet eliminated oral discourse from its role in shaping our society. A unit on speech criticism is one way of insuring that we continue to produce knowledgeable consumers of public speeches.

On Teaching the Social
Responsibilities of a Speaker

RICHARD L. JOHANNESEN
Associate Professor of Speech
Northern Illinois University

As speakers and audience members, we have the responsibility to uphold appropriate ethical standards in discourse, to encourage freedom of inquiry and expression, and to promote the health of public dialogue as the essence of democratic decision making. To achieve these goals, we must understand their complexity and recognize the difficulty of implementing them. We must also understand the central role of speech in American society, as underscored clearly by William N. Brigance: "Not only is history written with words. It is made with words. Most of the mighty movements affecting the destiny of the American nation have gathered strength in obscure places from the talk of nameless men, and gained final momentum from leaders who could state in common words the needs and hopes of common people."

In order for persuasion, debate, and public discussion to function effectively in our political system, at least four prerequisites must be fulfilled.[1] First, we must promote full and fair freedom of expression for all opposing points of view on an issue. Minority opinions must be heard. The system of public dialogue should provide sufficient time and opportunity for points of view to be fully presented.

Second, the varied views on an issue should be presented by advocates of approximately equal skill. Citizens must be trained in oral communication so that each, if called upon, can argue his opinion adequately. A good idea should not fail for want of an articulate advocate to present it.

Third, arguments should be tested in the crucible of public examination and modified if a contrary view proves valid. Each advocate should take into account sound evidence and argument of the opposition. Arguments must be able to withstand the public scrutiny of informed opponents.

Finally, on a controversial issue, advocates should agree to abide by the decision of a third party to which they appeal for support, whether that party be a voter, group member, commission, judge, or jury. Advocates should willingly abide by majority decision. Of course participants in a controversy need not uniformly endorse such a decision. They are free to mount a further campaign of public persuasion aimed ultimately at a subsequent majority decision for their cause.

Now let us turn our consideration to four complex areas that speech students should be encouraged to explore: (1) ethical problems in persuasion, (2) ghostwriting and speaker responsibility, (3) public confidence in public communication, and (4) freedom of speech.

Ethical Problems in Persuasion

Aristotle's observation that "rhetoric [persuasion] is an offshoot of dialectic and also of ethical studies" is often quoted. But an understanding of the nature of the rhetorical act, more than Aristotle's assurance, establishes the close relation between ethics and persuasion. The persuasive transaction inherently involves ethical considerations. One way to view persuasion is to see it as communication whose function it is to advise by presenting good reasons for a choice among probable alternatives. In *The Ethics of Rhetoric*, Richard M. Weaver noted that "rhetoric [persuasion] at its truest seeks to perfect men by showing them better versions of themselves, links in that chain extending upward toward the ideal. . . ."[2]

The process of persuasion necessitates choices by the persuader with regard to the method and content to be used in influencing the audience to accept the alternative which he advocates. These choices involve issues of desirability and of personal and societal good. What standards are to be utilized in making these choices among techniques, contents, purposes, and ideals? What should be the ethical responsibilities of a persuader in contemporary American society?

The answers to these questions have not been clearly or universally established. But the questions are ones that teachers of oral communication must assist their students to face squarely. Interest in the nature and effectiveness of persuasive techniques must not outstrip concern for the ethical use of such techniques. Ethical judgments concerning persuasive means employed to achieve ends, or judgments of the ethics of the ends, cannot be escaped. Speech teachers must discuss not only *how* to, but also *whether* to, employ persuasive techniques. Each student must be encouraged to formulate meaningful ethical guidelines for his own persuasive behavior and for use in evaluating the persuasion of others.

What follows is an explanation of one possible classroom approach to dealing with problems of ethics in persuasion. This approach encompasses two broad goals: to stimulate awareness of the fact that ethical issues are involved in persuasion, and to expose students to alternative ethical perspectives for viewing ethical problems in persuasion.

At least five major ethical perspectives can be identified and employed as vantage points for analyzing specific ethical issues in persuasion. As categories, these perspectives are neither mutually exclusive nor exhaustive.

First is the religious perspective. Various world religions emphasize moral and spiritual injunctions that can be employed as standards for evaluating the ethics of persuasion. The Old Testament clearly admonishes Jews and Christians against the use of lies and slander. The Lord commands Moses, "You shall not steal, nor deal falsely, nor lie to one another." And the Psalmist reports, "Let not the slanderer be established in the land." In the New Testament, Christians are told, ". . . Let everyone speak the truth with his neighbor. . . ." Jesus warns, "I tell you, on the day of judgment men will render account for every careless word they utter; for by your words you will be justified and by your words you will be condemned."

Several oriental religions also provide religious perspectives for accepting or shunning certain persuasive appeals.[3] The Confucian religion has, according to Robert Oliver, generally tended to shun emotional appeals and to stress fact and logic. But within the Confucian religious stream, various subdivisions and splits have occurred. A sixteenth century scholar named Yulgok developed a rhetorical view that sanctioned appeals to any or all of seven passions (joy, anger, sorrow, fear, love, hatred, and desire) as means of persuading listeners to the four principles of charity, duty to neighbors, propriety, and wisdom. The School of Rites, a sixteenth century variation of Confucianism, emphasized ritualistic patterns of behavior. Thus, the policy advocated, the facts of the matter, and the depth of understanding were less crucial than proper modes of procedure. Taoist religion stresses empathy and insight, rather than reason and logic, as roads to truth. Citing facts and demonstrating logical conclusions are minimized in favor of feeling and intuition.

Philosophical premises afford a second ethical perspective. Some writers isolate unique characteristics of man's nature which should be enhanced. These characteristics then can be used to judge the ethics of specific techniques. A determination can be made of the extent to which a technique either fosters or undermines a uniquely human attribute. According to Aristotle, a truly human act stems from a rational person who recognizes what he does and freely chooses to do it.[4] Thus a persuasive device should be judged by the interrelated criteria of intent of persuader, nature of the means, and accompanying circumstances as they combine to promote or defeat man's rationality and his choice-making ability. Because of man's capacity for reason and his need for mutual interdependence, Garrett believes that in persuasion man has the obligation to communicate as rationally as possible, to present truthful information, and to help others act rationally.[5] Advertising must not, then, seek to bypass or render inoperative man's reflective powers. Wieman and Walter identify man's symbol-using capacity and his need for mutual understanding as uniquely human characteristics.[6] Persuasive techniques which retard or pervert this symbol-using ability and which prevent mutual understanding are unethical.

Political systems provide a third perspective. Within the context of American representative democracy, for instance, analysts pinpoint specific values or processes that seem basic to the health and growth of our society. Such values and processes can function as criteria for assessing the ethics of persuasive means and ends. Haiman's belief is that development of man's capacity to reason is a goal to which our democratic society is inherently committed.[7] This view condemns as unethical a persuasive technique that aims at circumventing our mind and reason in order to gain non-reflective, semi-conscious, or unconscious responses. Kruger, too, presumes the democratic values that "people can think for themselves and govern themselves intelligently." Thus the standard to be promoted in persuasion is man's rational processes and any technique that "by-passes or demeans reason" is unethical.[8]

The essential values of democracy, Wallace contends, are belief in the dignity and worth of the individual, faith in equality of opportunity, belief in freedom, and belief in each person's ability to understand the nature of democracy.[9] Citizens should promote freedom of speech and assembly, general diffusion of information, and width and diversity of communication channels. To be ethical, communicators must recognize that during their presentations, they are the sole source of argument and information; they must select and render fact and opinion fairly, they must reveal the sources of their information and opinion; and they must respect diversity of argument and viewpoint. Thomas R. Nilsen discusses both values and procedures characteristic of American democracy, in "Free Speech, Persuasion, and the Democratic Process."[10] Crucial democratic values are belief in enhancement of the human personality, acceptance of reason as an instrument of personal and societal development, and self-determination through free, informed, rational, and critical choice Necessary democratic processes include unrestricted debate and discussion; varied forms of public address; parliamentary procedure and legal procedure;

freedom for inquiry, criticism and choice; and publicly defined rules of evidence and tests of reasoning. Nilsen suggests how, in light of these values and processes, persuasive techniques, whether in politics or other contexts, might be evaluated for their degree of ethics. In a somewhat similar manner, Day judges the ethics of debate by procedures essential to democracy, particularly the promotion of full confrontation of opposing opinions, arguments, and information relevant to decision.[11]

Because certain methods of persuasion poison, instead of refresh, the lifeblood of democracy, Hook lists ten "ground rules of controversy in a democracy" that encompass both basic values and procedures.[12] These "truisms" to be used in evaluating the ethics of persuasive means and ends include: Nothing and no one is immune from criticism; participants in a controversy must inform themselves; criticism should be directed first to policies and arguments, and against persons and motives only when relevant; the speaker should not hesitate to suspend judgment or admit lack of knowledge; and the speaker should avoid action that blocks discussion.

Weaver, from the stance of a political conservative, deems most modern advertising unethical because it consistently misconstrues reality.[13] Advertising, he claims, minimizes the worth of strenuous work, distorts history to the point of unreality, and promotes simplistic views of cause-effect processes. Based upon the democratic values of the intrinsic worth of the human personality and the process of self-determination as the means to individual fulfillment, Keller and Brown develop an interpersonal communication ethic. In their view, techniques employed and loyalty to rationality are less important considerations than the degree to which a communicator is sensitive to freedom of choice for his audience.[14] They would ask, for example, is the communicator willing to accept an audience response contrary to the one he sought?

Other political systems may present different frames of reference for assessing the ethics of persuasion. Russian Communism espouses values that give a special ethical slant to persuasive techniques and goals in the Soviet societal context.[15] Values propagated include supreme love of nation, trust in the Party, hatred toward defined enemies, and promotion of the class war. A persuader need not be impartial and display an objective concern for events. He may, for instance, define terms to suit his purposes, rather than the facts, and he may introduce spurious or irrelevant issues. In the Communist perspective, words are tools to achieve ends, not means to communicate in the search for truth. Communist ethical standards flow from, and are subordinated to, the interest of the class struggle as formulated by the Party.

In Germany under Hitler's Nazi influence, the ends of national survival and National Socialism justified any propaganda means.[16] The soundness of propaganda was measured, not by objective truth, but solely by effectiveness of results. Nazi persuasion frequently reflected black-white oversimplification, inconsistency, questionable premises, faulty analogies, innuendo, and appeals to power, fear, and hate. Goebbels felt lies were useful when they could not be disproved and that the source of propaganda should be concealed when revelation might risk failure. Hitler's own oratory, not bounded by logic, plausibility, or historic accuracy, reveals lies, slander, verbal smoke screens to conceal intent, and scapegoat counterattacks.

A fourth perspective is a utilitarian emphasis. Criteria of usefulness and expediency are used to analyze the ethics of persuasion. Brembeck and Howell developed a "social utility" approach, rooted in usefulness to the people affected and in the survival potential for groups involved.[17] This approach, involving identification of intermediate and long-term consequences and awareness of whether beliefs are based on fact or opinion, is employed to probe the ethical problems in persuasion, including the means-ends controversy. Another utilitarian view is presented by philosopher A. K. Rogers in "Prolegomena to a Political Ethics," in *Essays in Honor of John Dewey*.[18] Simplified application of moral truisms will not suffice for political persuasion. Rogers argues for the standard of reasoned debate in tune with enlightened self-interest.

A fifth, and final, ethical perspective can be labeled situational. A critic of persuasive ethics, contends Rogge, cannot employ a "timeless, universal set of standards. . . ."[19] The ethical criteria vary as factors in the speech situation vary, as the need for implementation of the persuader's proposal varies, and as the persuader's leadership role varies. Rogge suggests that hyperbole might be ethical in a political speech but unethical in a classroom lecture. A situation such as imperiled national survival might sanction otherwise unethical techniques. A leader in some situations has the responsibility to rally support and action and thus could employ emotional appeals that circumvent man's rational processes of choice.

Diggs believes that a persuader's role or position, as defined by the situation, audience, and society, determines what standards are useful in judging the ethics of his means and ends.[20] In trying to persuade us, a friend, lawyer, or salesman would be subject to somewhat different ethical standards. Even generally accepted universal ethical norms often depend for their interpretation on the position or role of the persuader. In the situational perspective, then, an estimation should be made of the goals and values held by the immediate audience, of the expectations of the audience, and of the role of the persuader. For example, is the persuader speaking solely for himself, for an organization but not for all the members, or for an organization with fixed policies?

In light of these five ethical perspectives, or according to their own code of persuasive ethics, students should be encouraged to confront and resolve a variety of questions relevant to ethical problems in persuasion. The following groups of questions merely are suggestive rather than exhaustive.[21]

1. What are some of the basic premises or value standards held by contemporary American society? Is enhancement of man's capacity to reason a societal goal? How does our educational system reflect this goal? Is public confidence in the truthfulness of public communication a societal goal? Is such confidence necessary for healthy public dialogue? Are acceptance of distortion in political campaigns and accusations of "managed" news indicative of weakening of such confidence?

2. To what degree should the ethics of persuasion be absolute or relative? Are there any unvarying and absolute ethical standards to which a persuader must always adhere? To what extent

are a persuader's ethics relative to the time, situation, audience, subject, and society? Are there any ethical standards for persuasion that cut across nations and cultures? Does the individual have a responsibility for forming his own code of ethics in addition to or apart from those dictated by the situation or society?

3. What functions do the nature of the persuader, his techniques and methods, his purposes and goals, and the consequences of his persuasion play in determining ethical standards for persuasion? Does persuasion by a "good" man mean that his persuasion necessarily is ethical? Are all emotional appeals unethical? Do all such appeals short-circuit man's reasoning processes? How easily can we distinguish between emotional and logical appeals? Is it unethical to fail to present both sides of an issue in the same speech? Are lawyers thus unethical? Are there some techniques of persuasion which should always be condemned? Does sincerity release a persuader from ethical responsibility relative to means and effects? When, if ever, do the ends act as sole determinants for the ethics of the means of persuasion? Why should persuasive techniques be judged by ethical criteria apart from and in addition to the ends sought? Should necessity, such as personal or national survival, ever override ethics?

4. To what extent can the ethics of persuasion be enforced by law? Who bears the prime responsibility for the level of persuasive ethics, the persuader or the audience? At what points do problems of the persuader's ethics and his right of free speech converge?

An intensive consideration of actual or hypothetical examples is another method of developing student understanding of the ethics of persuasion. What ethical considerations concerning means and ends can be extracted from the following proposed technique of persuasion?

> There is the head of one of the great educational institutions in the East (not Harvard, incidentally) whom at least some of us believe to be a Communist. Even with a hundred thousand dollars to hire sleuths to keep him and his present contacts under constant surveillance for awhile, and to retrace every detail of his past history, I doubt if we could prove it on him. But—with just five

thousand dollars to pay for the proper amount of careful research, which could be an entirely logical expenditure and undertaking of the magazine, I believe we could get all the material needed for quite a shock. Of course we would have to satisfy ourselves completely as to whether our guess had been correct, from the preliminary research, before going ahead with the project and spending that much money.

But if we are right, and with the research job done and the material assembled which I think would be available, we would run in the magazine an article consisting entirely of questions to this man, which would be devastating in their implications. The question technique, when skillfully used in this way, is mean and dirty. But the Communists we are after are meaner and dirtier, and too slippery for you to put your fingers on them in the ordinary way—no matter how much they look and act like prosperous members of the local Rotary Club.[22]

The seven "propaganda devices" popularized by the Institute for Propaganda Analysis can be examined in various contexts and assessed as to their degree of ethics. The seven are: name-calling, glittering generalities, transfer, testimonial, plain-folks, card-stacking, and band-wagon.[23] The plain-folks technique, for example, may not be uniformly unethical. In his whistle-stop speeches during the 1948 Presidential campaign, Harry Truman typically used the plain-folks appeal to establish common ground in introductions of his speeches. He used the device to accomplish one of the purposes of any speech introduction, establishment of rapport, and did not rely on it for proof in the body of his speeches. But if a politician relied primarily on the plain-folks appeal for pseudo-proof in *justifying* the policy he advocated, such usage probably would be condemned as unethical.

A careful analysis of the persuasive techniques and purposes of acknowledged demagogues and controversial speakers still further promote understanding of ethical problems in persuasion. With Reinhard Luthin's *American Demagogues* as a point of departure, students individually or in groups can carry on additional research to determine the ethical level of persuaders such as Mary E. Lease, Benjamin R. Tillman, William Jennings Bryan, James K. Vardaman, Theodore G. Bilbo, Vito Marcantonio, Huey

Long, Gerald L. K. Smith, and Joseph R. McCarthy. And persuasive techniques in specific speeches of less questionable figures, such as F. D. R., Adlai Stevenson, Dwight Eisenhower, Everett M. Dirksen, Hubert Humphrey, John or Robert Kennedy, and Lyndon Johnson, should be scrutinized.[24]

In sum, a student's recognition of the fact that ethical implications and problems do exist in any persuasive transaction can be promoted by exposure to the religious, philosophical, political, utilitarian, and situational ethical perspectives. By answering crucial questions concerning the ethics of persuasion and by examining techniques as applied in specific cases or by specific persuaders, students can understand Aristotle's view that ethics and persuasion inherently are interrelated.

Ghostwriting and Speaker Responsibility

Is a speaker violating social responsibility when he employs a ghostwriter? Should a speaker use a person, or staff, to write his speech, to write parts of his speech, to contribute ideas, or to do research? Nationally prominent figures, such as Franklin D. Roosevelt, Adlai Stevenson, and John F. Kennedy, relied on ghostwriters. But speech critics stress that each of these speakers played an intimate role in the creation of his own speeches. Were they, nevertheless, socially irresponsible in using speechwriters? Is speechwriting a "trivial task," properly assigned to some staff member? Students should explore a number of interrelated issues when analyzing the ethics of ghostwriting.[25]

First, what is the speaker's intent and what is the audience's degree of awareness? Clearly condemned by some critics is the speaker who deceives his audience by pretending to write his own speeches when in fact they are ghostwritten. However, if the audience is fully aware that ghostwriting is a normal circumstance, such as for Presidents and Congressmen, then no condemnation is warranted. Everyone seems aware that certain classes of speakers use ghostwriters and make no pretense of writing, in toto, each of their speeches.

Second, does the speaker use ghostwriters to make himself appear to possess personal characteristics he really does not have? Eloquent style, wit, coherence, and incisive ideas are possessions all speakers desire but which some speakers can obtain only with the aid of ghostwriters. Consideration must be given to the extent to which ghostwriters may be used to improve a speaker's image without unethically distorting his true character.

Third, what is the speaker's role and what are the surrounding circumstances? Pressures of time and duties are invoked to sanction the necessity of ghostwriting for some speakers. In a speech course, most people agree that the student is entirely responsible for creating his own speech. Training in analysis, research, and speech composition is subverted when a student relies on someone else to do all or part of his work. However, the President of the United States, a senator, a college president, or a corporation executive may be unable to avoid using ghostwriters. But what about a college professor, state senator, or local businessman? Are they ethical when they use a ghostwriter? And some critics would argue that when the President of the United States speaks, not as the head of the executive branch, such as in a State of the Union Message, but as an individual politician, such as in a presidential campaign, he should avoid using ghostwriters.

Fourth, to what degree does the speaker himself participate in the writing of his speeches? Adlai Stevenson and F. D. R. participated extensively in the writing of their major addresses, even though each used a staff of speechwriters. They are not often condemned for employing ghostwriters; their speeches reflected accurately their own style and intellect. But what of the speaker who lets his ghostwriter research and write the entire speech and then simply delivers it?

Finally, does the speaker accept responsibility for the speech he presents? Some argue that even if a speaker did not write his speech, or help write it, he still is ethical as long as he accepts responsibility for the accuracy and ethics of its content. When his address is criticized, he should not disclaim authorship and "pass the buck" to his ghostwriters.

By fully exploring these five issues, then, one should be able to assess perceptively the social responsibility of a speaker who uses ghostwriters. Depending upon the standards we employ, our judgment may not always be clear-cut. However, through such analysis we may avoid oversimplification inherent in most black-or-white evaluations.

Public Confidence in the Validity of Public Communication

Is public confidence in the validity of public communication a goal or value to which contemporary American society is commited? Should the populace generally assume that the public communication they receive is accurate until *they* have evaluated it as less than so? As a society, we probably are not committed to the assumption that public communications, even of certain types, are false, without our bothering to evaluate them. As with a defendant in a courtroom, a message should be presumed innocent until proven guilty.

If we are dedicated to the enhancement of such public confidence, this goal or value may be used as one standard for judging the ethics of public persuasion. When techniques of persuasion, whether in federal governmental communication, political campaigning, or advertising, weaken or undermine this public confidence in public communication they could be condemned as unethical. Weakening of this public trust is already evident. Citizens increasingly complain of "managed news" and a "credibility gap" in communication from the federal government. They tend to dismiss as untrue, without analysis, much governmental communication.[26] During national political campaigns, citizens also dismiss most speeches, often characterized by gross hyperbole, as "mere campaign oratory." They have so little confidence in campaign speaking that they believe a substantial portion of it is not even worthy of their thoughtful scrutiny.

What are the effects of weakened public confidence in validity of public communication? Repercussions are both political and economic. Wallace stresses that unethical persuasive techniques "undermine confidence in communication and, indeed, in all human relations; and with confidence gone, nothing is left but distrust and suspicion."[27] Marston argues that lies, half-truths, attacks on personality and integrity, and appeals to unworthy emotions are bad means because they destroy "the confidence between men, which is the basis of our freedom."[28]

The stability of our social structure is the concern of Merton.[29] "No single advertising or propaganda campaign may significantly affect the psychological stability of those subjected to it. But a society subjected ceaselessly to a flow of 'effective' half-truths and the exploitation of mass anxieties may all the sooner lose that mutuality of confidence and reciprocal trust so essential to a stable social structure." Felknor contends: "The real danger lies in warping the channels of political communication; in confusing the real differences between men; in twisting facts so that voters give up in dismay and vote blindly or stay at home. The danger, finally, is alienation of the electorate from the political system."[30] Ladd argues that citizen disbelief of government leaders weakens the process of representative democracy and increases the possibility of despotism.

> The credibility of a nation's government is absolutely crucial. To the extent that a government is believed, it will function effectively. To the extent that a government is doubted, it will inevitably fall short of its goals. The widening scope of government secrecy, lying, and news management, therefore, contributes to a trend that threatens the basis of democracy. When the government's credibility is impeached, democracy is diminished.[31]

Untruthfulness in some advertising breeds consumer distrust of all advertising. Sandage and Fryburger state the danger bluntly: "If advertising does not have the confidence of most consumers, it will lose its influence and surely die. If people grow to disbelieve a substantial percentage of the advertising messages that come to them, they will soon reject most or *all* advertising."[32]

In light of such possible repercussions on our political and economic system, public confidence in the validity of public communication should be a societal goal. Public communication must be presumed innocent until evaluated as guilty. Without initial trust between communicator and audience, the basis for meaningful communication is severely undermined.

Freedom of Speech

As stressed earlier in this essay, one of the prerequisites for effective public dialogue in our society is full and fair freedom of speech. To ensure the existence of this prerequisite, students must probe the basic issues of free speech and thus enhance their understanding of its necessity.

Various Supreme Court justices constantly have underscored the essential role of free public address in our democracy. In the case of *Whitney* v. *California,* Justice Louis Brandeis argued that the "path of safety lies in the opportunity to discuss freely supposed grievances and proposed remedies; and that the fitting remedy for evil counsels is good ones." Justice Hugo Black, in *Kovacs* v. *Cooper,* observed that the "transmission of ideas through public speaking is . . . essential to the sound thinking of a fully informed citizenry." And in *Terminiello* v. *City of Chicago,* Justice William O. Douglas contended: ". . . a function of free speech under our system of government is to invite dispute. It may indeed best serve its high purpose when it induces a condition of unrest, creates dissatisfaction with conditions as they are, or even stirs people to anger."

The First Amendment to our Constitution seems rather categorical in tone when it declares, in part, "Congress shall make no law . . . abridging the freedom of speech. . . ." Yet scholarly analysts disagree over its meaning. Some argue that it clearly indicates there shall be no restrictions on any kind of public speech. Others believe it refers only to certain types of speech, such as political discourse, and that restrictions on other types of speech are allowable. Still other critics feel that the First Amendment does allow some restrictions on all public speech.[33]

What are some of the major arguments in favor of complete freedom of speech and, on the other hand, in favor of some restrictions on public expression? The libertarian viewpoint upholding complete free speech rests on two general contentions. First, freedom of expression is a necessary condition for true fulfillment of each human's intellectual and psychological potential. Human self-actualization is promoted under conditions of free speech.

Restriction and censorship thwart personality growth. Second, the high quality public policy decisions necessary for a healthy representative democracy are best achieved in full and open presentation of varying arguments, ideas, values, and programs. Effective decision-making presupposes free access to all relevant information.

English philosopher John Stuart Mill, in his book *On Liberty,* elaborated incisively the arguments that sustain the libertarian position.[34] If a single person held an opinion contrary to that held by all other men, mankind would not be justified in silencing that one person. Censorship of free speech robs mankind by depriving it of the opportunity of exchanging error for truth or of gaining the clearer perception of truth produced by collision with error. Mill's prime arguments were three in number.

First, the suppressed opinion actually may be true and the accepted opinions in error. Censors generally assume their own infallibility. But there is a basic difference between assuming the truth of an opinion for the purpose of not permitting its refutation and presuming an opinion true because, after free debate, it remains unrefuted. Man is capable of rectifying his mistakes by experience and discussion.

Second, even though they are true, accepted beliefs become sterile prejudices unless challenged and tested. An accepted truth cut off from public scrutiny becomes not a living truth but a dead dogma. And listeners must evaluate opposing views presented not only in textbooks and by teachers but also, contends Mill, by "persons who actually believe them; who defend them in earnest, and do their very utmost for them."

Finally, varied opinions all may possess an element of the truth. Truth may be shared between two conflicting doctrines. On issues of public policy, disputes are decided in the realm of probability, rather than absolute certainty. Free public dialogue stimulates analysis of conflicting views so that a probably workable policy can be determined.

In contrast to the libertarian position, there are several arguments that support some restrictions on some types of public speech. Preservation of national security is the basis for some controls on free speech; attempts are made to control advocacy of violent overthrow of our federal government, especially in wartime. Preservation of civil order also is invoked; public speech is restricted which exhorts to riot or mob rule. Preservation of public morality affords another basis; pornography and obscenity are censored. In addition, some political processes, such as lobbying or political campaigning by those under civil service laws, are restricted. Finally, some critics argue that the First Amendment now is historically outmoded; its sanction of complete free speech is not wholly applicable or appropriate to complex and disaster-threatened modern America.

When interests in national security and freedom of speech collide, one major area of concern is pressed upon us. In his book, *Freedom of Speech: Issues and Cases*, Franklyn Haiman presents the four crucial issues in dispute: (1) Should a society permit the advocacy of its own destruction? (2) At what point is it permissible to interfere with speech that might ultimately culminate in acts of revolution? Is the advocacy of revolution as an abstract idea to be allowed? Is the advocacy of action, divorced from the probability of any action immediately ensuing, to be barred? Must a society, believing certain individuals to be dedicated to its overthrow, wait to move against them until guns are in their hands? (3) Is it possible or desirable to distinguish between advocacy and incitement? Between a "speech-act" and "mere speech"? (4) Shall the courts or our legislative bodies determine what limits are to be set on the freedom of political dissent?[35]

In *Schenck* v. *United States*, Justice Oliver Wendell Holmes enunciated the view that Congress has the right to restrict speech posing a "clear and present danger" to the security of the nation, particularly in wartime. But how does one define wartime? A war declared by Congress? The Vietnam war? Elaborations on the "clear and present danger" standard came in such cases as *Whitney* v. *California, Dennis* v. *United States,* and *Yates* v. *United States.* For example, the Supreme Court stressed that restriction is justified only if the danger resulting from free speech is imminent and serious and if there is no time to avert the danger through further free discussion exposing falsehood and fallacies.

A second area of concern is conflict between free speech and preservation of public order. The basic disputed questions again are posed by Haiman: (1) Does the majority, as represented by elected or appointed public officials, have the right to require individuals to obtain a permit or license in order to use public property to express their views? If so, under what, if any, circumstances can such permits be denied? (2) If no permit is required, may other methods, such as interference at the discretion of the police or a court injunction, be employed to prevent individuals, prior to the act, from expressing or disseminating their beliefs? (3) Does an individual or a group have the right to disobey a law that later may be regarded by the courts as an unconstitutional abridgment of free speech? (4) Is there a certain kind of speech which, because it offends the audience, arouses their anger, or provokes them to violence, may be stopped by the police, and may cause the speaker to be punished for his behavior?[36]

Two major concepts relevant to issues of public order are those of prior restraint and subsequent punishment. Prior restraint of free speech involves censorship before one is allowed to speak. An agitator, such as George Lincoln Rockwell or Stokely Carmichael, could be denied a city permit to speak in a public park. Subsequent punishment means that a speaker is legally punished after he speaks. If Carmichael spoke in the public park and ignored the denial of a city permit, he could be arrested and tried. Two Supreme Court decisions which provide fruitful cases for analysis are *Terminiello* v. *Chicago* and *Feiner* v. *New York*.[37] In the *Feiner* case, Justice Hugo Black dissented against restriction of Feiner's right to speak. Black condemned the heckler's veto concept implicit in the case; instead, a speaker's right to be heard should be protected, even to the extent of restraining the audience.

Conflict between free speech and control of obscenity represents a third area of concern. Haiman's questions demand thoughtful analysis of the issues: (1) May a majority, acting in the alleged interest of public morality, prohibit the expression or portrayal of ideas and feelings which it regards as immoral or in bad taste? (2) Should different treatment be accorded to communication depending upon whether it stimulates "normal" sexual desires, appeals to "abnormal" sexual interests, is scatological (dealing in images related to excrement), profane (dealing irreverently with religious concepts), or portrays violence? Is there a basis for assuming that any or all of these is conducive to antisocial or illegal behavior? (3) Can a valid distinction be made between pure entertainment and the communication of ideas? Are there certain kinds of communication which have no social importance or value whatsoever? (4) Is it possible, and desirable, to establish different standards for the permissibility of communication depending upon whether the audience consists of children or adults? (5) Are different standards justified on the basis of whether communication is written or oral, or on the basis of whether oral communication occurs via radio, TV, motion pictures, theatre, or night club? (6) At what point, if any, do extralegal pressures against disliked communication become sufficiently coercive to run afoul of the protections of the Constitution?[38]

Consistently the Supreme Court has held that obscenity and pornography are not types of communication protected by the First Amendment. However, the problem is that of defining "obscenity" in a clear and workable manner. What appears obscene to one person may not appear so to someone else. Do any or all of the following comprise characteristics of pornography? Cuss words? The four letter word for sexual intercourse? Explicit description of sexual intercourse? Descriptions of sexual perversions? Descriptions of an uninterrupted series of sexual episodes aiming solely at sexual arousal and progressing from simple to complex sexual activities?

In the case of *Roth* v. *United States*, the Supreme Court attempted to specify criteria to be used in judging pornography. Communication is obscene if it is "utterly without redeeming social importance" and if the "average person, applying contemporary community standards," judges that the "dominant theme of the material taken as a whole appeals to prurient interests." But even these criteria are open to interpretation and sometimes difficult to apply. What constitutes redeeming social importance? Who is the average person? Are contemporary community standards those of the national cross section or of the city involved? How does one determine the dominant theme? What is prurient interest? A more recent Supreme Court case, *Ginzburg* v. *United States,* evolved a different standard for judging obscenity: for example, although a book may have some redeeming social importance, it is not entitled to Constitutional protection if the manner in which it is advertised and promoted utilizes salacious appeals permeated with the leer of the sensualist.

Issues of obscenity and free speech have been joined in such examples as the supposedly obscene nightclub routine of a comedian, a radio discussion program exploring homosexuality, and presentation of a play titled "A Cat Called Jesus." Should there be different standards for books, television, and movies? Should obscenity standards differ for adults and children? If censorship is allowed, should it be censorship of production of the communication or of the consumption of the communication?

The high school or college campus increasingly serves as a focal point for free speech controversies.[39] Political disputes over the Vietnam war, social disputes over civil rights and the military draft, and educational disputes over extent of student control of educational policies have frequently served as stimuli for free speech controversies.

Freedom of speech issues in the educational setting can be discussed under three headings. First, what rights of academic freedom should the teacher have? Refusals to sign loyalty oaths, statements of frank positions on sexual morality, and advocacy of abhorrent political views have brought restrictions on the freedoms of some teachers. Second, what rights of free speech does the student have on campus? To be explored fully is the issue of whether an administration should place any restrictions on the political, social, or educational views espoused by students. In a similar vein, proper rules governing picketing and demonstrations should be discussed. Is picketing action, or "symbolic speech?" Finally, what rights do students and faculty have in inviting controversial off-campus speakers to appear on their campus? Consider what restrictions, if any, should be placed on speeches by Communists, fascists, racists, and civil agitators.

Some analysts contend that considerations for restriction differ depending upon whether the campus is that of a publicly supported or privately supported institution. A libertarian view of campus free speech is expressed by philosopher Sidney Hook: "If students and faculty cannot cope with the 'arguments' of the Lincoln Rockwells and Gus Halls, then the college is failing badly in its educational task."[40]

What, then, is a speaker's responsibility concerning freedom of speech? As a producer of public communication, he must utilize his free speech rights with great wisdom; to abuse his free speech rights is to weaken them. Social consequences must be carefully weighed. As a consumer of public communication, he must protect the rights of free speech for all others, particularly those espousing controversial or minority viewpoints.

If students are stimulated to explore ethical problems in persuasion and crucial issues of free speech, hopefully the quality of public discourse will be improved and the scope of public debate expanded. They may be led to share the sincere concern for free and ethical communication expressed by Dag Hammarskjold:

> Respect for the word—to employ it with scrupulous care and an incorruptible heartfelt love of truth—is essential if there is to be any growth in a society or in the human race.
>
> To misuse the word is to show contempt for man. It undermines the bridges and poisons the wells. It causes Man to regress down the long path of his evolution.[41]

NOTES

1. See Wayne Minnick, *The Art of Persuasion*, 2d ed., Boston: Houghton Mifflin, 1968, chapter 1; Douglas Ehninger and Wayne Brockriede, *Decision by Debate*, New York: Dodd, Mead, 1963, chapter 2.

2. Richard M. Weaver, *The Ethics of Rhetoric*, Chicago: H. Regnery, 1953.

3. Robert Oliver, *Culture and Communication*, Springfield, Illinois: Thomas, 1962, pp. 111–135.

4. Lawrence J. Flynn, "The Aristotelian Basis for the Ethics of Speaking," *Speech Teacher*, September, 1957.

5. Thomas M. Garrett, S.J., *An Introduction to Some Ethical Problems of Modern Advertising*, Rome: Gregorian University Press, 1961.

6. Henry Wieman and Otis Walter, "Toward an Analysis of Ethics for Rhetoric," *Quarterly Journal of Speech*, October, 1957.

7. Franklyn S. Haiman, "Democratic Ethics and the Hidden Persuaders," *Quarterly Journal of Speech*, December, 1958.

8. Arthur N. Kruger, "The Ethics of Persuasion: A Re-Examination," *Speech Teacher*, November, 1967.

9. Karl R. Wallace, "An Ethical Basis of Communication," *Speech Teacher*, January, 1955.

10. Thomas R. Nilsen, "Free Speech, Persuasion, and the Democratic Process," *Quarterly Journal of Speech*, October, 1958.

11. Dennis G. Day, "The Ethics of Democratic Debate," *Central States Speech Journal*, February, 1966.

12. Sidney Hook. "The Ethics of Controversy," *The New Leader*, February 1, 1954.

13. Richard M. Weaver, *Life Without Prejudice and Other Essays*, Chicago: H. Regnery, 1965, pp. 121–128.

14. Paul Keller and Charles T. Brown, "An Interpersonal Ethic for Communication," *Journal of Communication*, March, 1968.

15. See Jack Butler, "Russian Rhetoric: A Discipline Manipulated by Communism," *Quarterly Journal of Speech*, October, 1964; Alex Inkeles, *Public Opinion in Soviet Russia: A Study in Mass Persuasion*, Cambridge: Harvard University Press, 1962; Stefan Possony, *Wordsmanship: Semantics as a Communist Weapon;* United States Government Printing Office, 1961.

16. See Adolf Hitler, *Mein Kampf*, available in paperback from Houghton Mifflin; Z. A. B. Zeman, *Nazi Propaganda*, London: Oxford University Press, 1964; Ernest K. Bramstead, *Goebbels and National Socialist Propaganda*, East Lansing: Michigan State University Press, 1965; Leonard Doob, "Goebbels' Principles of Propaganda," *Public Opinion Quarterly*, 14 [1950], pp. 419–442.

17. Winston L. Brembeck and William S. Howell, *Persuasion*, Englewood Cliffs, New Jersey: Prentice-Hall, 1952.

18. A. K. Rogers, "Prolegomena to a Political Ethics," in *Essays in Honor of John Dewey*, New York: H. Holt, 1929.

19. Edward Rogge, "Evaluating the Ethics of a Speaker in a Democracy," *Quarterly Journal of Speech*, December, 1959.

20. B. J. Diggs, "Persuasion and Ethics," *Quarterly Journal of Speech*, December, 1964.

21. Adapted from Richard L. Johannesen, *Ethics and Persuasion: Selected Readings,* New York: Random House, 1967, p. xii.

22. *The Blue Book of the John Birch Society,* 9th printing, 1961, pp. 95–96.

23. See W. H. Werkmeister, *An Introduction to Critical Thinking,* Revised Edition, Lincoln, Nebraska: Johnsen, 1957, chapter 4.

24. For speeches to analyze, see Charles W. Lomas, *The Agitator in American Society,* Englewood Cliffs, New Jersey: Prentice-Hall, 1968; Floyd W. Matson, *Voices of Crisis,* New York: Odyssey Press, 1967; Wil A. Linkugel *et. al., Contemporary American Speeches,* 2d ed., Belmont, California: Wadsworth Publishing, 1969; Arthur L. Smith, *Rhetoric of Black Revolution,* Boston: Allyn and Bacon, 1969.

25. See Ernest Bormann, "The Ethics of Ghostwritten Speeches," *Quarterly Journal of Speech,* December, 1961.

26. See, for example, Bruce Ladd, *Crisis in Credibility,* New York: The American Library, 1968.

27. Karl Wallace, "An Ethical Basis of Communication," *Speech Teacher,* 4 (January 1955), p. 3.

28. John Marston, *The Nature of Public Relations.* New York: McGraw-Hill, 1963, p. 358.

29. Robert K. Merton, *Mass Persuasion.* New York: Harper & Brothers, 1946, p. 189.

30. Bruce L. Felknor, *Dirty Politics,* 1st ed., New York: Norton, 1966, p. 129.

31. Ladd, *Crisis in Credibility,* p. 9.

32. C. H. Sandage and Vernon Fryburger, *Advertising Theory and Practice.* 6th ed., Homewood, Illinois: R. D. Irwin, p. 84.

33. The following books will provide representative analyses of the various viewpoints: C. Herman Pritchett, *The American Constitution,* New York: McGraw-Hill, 1959, chapters 22, 24, and 25; Alexander Meiklejohn, *Political Freedom,* New York: Oxford University Press, 1965; Zechariah Chaffee, Jr., *Free Speech in the United States,* Cambridge, Massachusetts: Harvard University Press, 1954; Thomas I. Emerson, *Toward a General Theory of the First Amendment,* New York: Random House, 1966; Harold C. Gardiner, *Catholic Viewpoint on Censorship,* New York: Doubleday, 1958; Walter Berns, *Freedom, Virtue, and the First Amendment,* Baton Rouge: Louisiana State University Press, 1957; Alan Barth, *The Loyalty of Free Men,* New York: Viking Press, 1951; Sidney Hook, *The Paradoxes of Freedom,* Berkeley: University of California Press, 1962; Ralph Ross and Ernest Van Den

Haag, *The Fabric of Society,* New York: Harcourt, Brace, & World, 1957, pp. 631–634, 645–655; E. G. Williamson and J. L. Cowan, *The American Student's Freedom of Expression,* Minneapolis: University of Minnesota Press, 1966; Abe Fortas, *Concerning Dissent and Civil Disobedience,* New York: New American Library, 1968; Howard Zinn, *Disobedience and Democracy,* New York: Random House, 1968.

34. John Stuart Mill, *On Liberty,* Chicago: H. Regnery, 1955, chapter 2.

35. Franklyn Haiman, *Freedom of Speech: Issues and Cases,* New York: Random House, 1965, pp. 49–50.

36. Haiman, *Freedom of Speech,* pp. 4–5.

37. Both reprinted in Haig Bosmajian, ed., *Readings in Speech,* 2d ed., New York: Harper & Row, 1971.

38. Haiman, *Freedom of Speech,* pp. 95–96.

39. See Robert M. O'Neil, *Free Speech: Responsible Communication Under Law,* Indianapolis: Bobbs-Merrill, 1966, chapter 1; Williamson and Cowan, *The American Student's Freedom of Expression.*

40. Quoted in O'Neil, *Free Speech,* p. 20.

41. Dag Hammarskjold, *Markings,* New York: Knopf, 1964, p. 112.

SELECTED REFERENCES

Bosmajian, Haig A., ed. *Principles and Practice of Freedom of Speech.* New York: Houghton Mifflin, 1971. A collection of major court cases concerning freedom of speech and of essays analyzing free speech issues.

————. ed. *Readings in Speech,* 2d ed. New York: Harper & Row, 1971. Among the 29 selections in this anthology are ones which explore the ethics of oral communication, the nature of propaganda, the characteristics of demagogues, and issues of free speech.

Clor, Harry M. *Obscenity and Public Morality.* Chicago: University of Chicago Press, 1969. An analysis of Supreme Court decisions on obscenity and pornography and a presentation of the author's own conception of obscenity.

Felknor, Bruce L. *Dirty Politics.* New York: Norton, 1966. As former director of the Fair Campaign Practices Committee, Mr. Felknor is uniquely qualified to assess the ethics of political campaigning. A fascinating sourcebook of examples and cases.

Haiman, Franklyn S. *Freedom of Speech: Issues and Cases.* New York: Random House, 1965. An original synthesis and interpretation of basic free speech issues and cases in the areas of national security, preservation of public order, and obscenity.

Johannesen, Richard L., ed. *Ethics and Persuasion: Selected Readings.* New York: Random House, 1967. A collection of 13 essays by experts who probe ethical problems in persuasion within the contexts of public address, political campaigning, public relations, and advertising. Included in the anthology are many of the essays on ethics mentioned in this chapter.

Lomas, Charles W., ed. *The Agitator in American Society.* Englewood Cliffs, New Jersey: Prentice-Hall, 1968. Three introductory chapters explore the nature and evaluation of agitation. Then speeches of selected agitators are presented for four categories: violence, socialism and social reform, civil rights, and anti-communism.

Luthin, Reinhard H. *American Demagogues.* Boston: Beacon Press, 1954; reprinted by Russell and Russell, 1959. Analyzes in depth ten American demagogues of the Twentieth Century, including Huey Long and Joseph R. McCarthy. Chapter 12 discusses the characteristics which mark demagogues.

Nilsen, Thomas R. *Ethics of Speech Communication.* Indianapolis: Bobbs-Merrill, 1966. An original treatise which provocatively explores the ethics of oral communication within the context of values and goals necessary to the American political system.

O'Neil, Robert M. *Free Speech: Responsible Communication Under Law.* Indianapolis: Bobbs-Merrill, 1966. An insightful analysis of cases and philosophical and legal issues. Of special value are chapter 1 on the college campus, chapter 2 on dangerous speech and the hostile audience, and chapter 4 on radio, television and politics.

Qualter, Terence H. *Propaganda and Psychological Warfare.* New York: Random House, 1962. After exploring definitions of propaganda, the author discusses the development, techniques, and wartime use of propaganda. Differences between propaganda in a dictatorship and a democracy are examined.

Summers, Marvin, ed. *Free Speech and Political Protest.* Boston: D. C. Heath, 1967. An excellent anthology of excerpts from court cases and analytic essays concerning the dimensions of free speech.